STORY

OF THE

CONFEDERATE STATES

Joseph T. Derry

ARNO PRESS
A New York Times Company
New York • 1979

Reprint edition 1979 by Arno Press Inc.

Library of Congress Catalog in Publication Data

Derry, Joseph Tyrone, 1841-
    Story of the Confederate States.
    Reprint of the ed. published by B.F. Johnson,
Richmond, Va.
    Includes index.
    1.   United States—History—Civil War, 1861-1865.
2.   Confederate States of America—History. I. Title.
E468.D43   1979   973.7'13   79-13239
ISBN 0-405-12295-0

Manufactured in the United States of America

Story of the Confederate States;

OR,

History of the War for Southern Independence,

*EMBRACING

A BRIEF BUT COMPREHENSIVE SKETCH OF THE EARLY SETTLEMENT OF THE
COUNTRY, TROUBLE WITH THE INDIANS, THE FRENCH, REVOLUTIONARY
AND MEXICAN WARS, AND A FULL, COMPLETE AND GRAPHIC
ACCOUNT OF THE GREAT FOUR YEARS' WAR BETWEEN THE
NORTH AND THE SOUTH, ITS CAUSES, EFFECTS, ETC.

BY

JOSEPH T. DERRY,

OF GEORGIA.

WITH AN INTRODUCTION BY GEN. CLEMENT A. EVANS,

OF GEORGIA.

———————

SUITED TO ALL OF THOSE WHO WISH AN INTERESTING, INSTRUCTIVE AND
TRUE ACCOUNT OF THE WAR FOR SOUTHERN INDEPENDENCE,
BUT DESIGNED ESPECIALLY FOR THE BOYS AND
GIRLS OF THE SOUTH.

———————

Beautifully Illustrated.   Over 130 Fine Engravings.

———————

RICHMOND, VA.:
B. F. JOHNSON PUBLISHING COMPANY.
1895.

JOSEPH T. DERRY.

INTRODUCTION.

THE history contained within this book traces rapidly the early progress of these United States, and marking those national events which led up to the crisis of 1860, describes the remarkable epoch of that Confederate War which will be studied hereafter with growing interest. Lee and Johnston, Grant and Sherman have furnished descriptions of great military movements as directed by chieftains, but this Work, while succinctly noting these movements, has put a living interest into them by glowing details of individual heroism and suffering. The "Constitutional View of the late War between the States" came long since from the pen of the great statesman, Alexander H. Stephens, designed "to embrace a consideration of the causes, character, conduct, and results of the War in relation to the nature and character of the joint government of these States"; and it is the merit of this work that it outlines these ponderous questions with lucid statements, which are as granite in the graceful structure of the whole story, which it tells. The general field has been entered by many, and will be explored by more, who will essay to inform the present and the future generations concerning that most romantic era of our country's history; but none will probably excel the author, who has intelligently, fairly and ardently portrayed the great struggle in the following chapters.

If here and there his enthusiasm is made apparent, it will be found guarded with such fairness and intelligence in narration as to win the confidence of the public. It will be well considered, too, that he treats of a great national enterprise which had no lack of justice in its design or execution; which was maintained with high intelligence by statesmen who had no superiors; which was made pathetic by the sufferings of a great people and the bravery of an unsurpassed soldiery; and which lacked only the element of success to win the laudation of the world. Its failure was due to inferiority of resources—money, numbers and international sympathy. The strong confronting adversary possessed all these.

Certainly will there be a substantial result obtained, when this book shall have the close perusal of the young men and women of our country. These readers will gain a clear view of the *casus belli* and a comprehensive understanding of the merits of the Southern resort to separate independence. Satisfied, as all are, with the termination of the struggle, there still remains that just defence of the South which true history makes before all the world. But, besides this acquaintance with the argument of statesmen, they will read herein with glowing enthusiasm the story of their people's domestic trials, and the thrilling account of the marches and battles in which their fathers won a worthy martial fame. They will rise from the reading inspired with proper pride in their Southern land; with reverence for their gallant ancestors, and with the wise purpose of head to make the Union worthy of such a South, and their beloved South worthy of the Federal Union.

The author deserves the praises of his countrymen. His noble work will bring to him the pleasing reflection that he has contributed greatly to the truth of history and to the patriotism of his country.

CLEMENT A. EVANS.

PREFACE

THE design of this work is to give the thrilling story of the great War for Southern Independence, its causes and results, in such form as to place it within the reach of the mass of readers, and in such style as to attract the attention of young people to the noble record of Confederate heroism.

Great pains have been taken to give the facts accurately and impartially. The statements of the numbers engaged and the losses sustained in the various battles are taken from the revised official returns published by the United States Government. Where only approximate estimates could be given, it is so stated.

All the standard authorities on both sides have been carefully consulted. The author desires to make special acknowledgment of the great help obtained in the collection of important facts from that very valuable publication of the Century Company, "Battles and Leaders of the Civil War."

Every effort has been made to avoid mistakes; but, if in spite of the most careful pains they do occur, correction will be cheerfully made on *proof* of error furnished to the author.

JOSEPH T. DERRY.

TABLE OF CONTENTS.

PART I.

A Short Sketch of United States History from the Colonial Times to the Establishment of the Government under the Constitution.

CHAPTER FIRST.

A Brief Sketch of Colonial History.

CHAPTER SECOND.

The War for American Independence and the Establishment of the Government of the United States.

CHAPTER THIRD.

The Formation and Adoption of the Constitution and the Establishment of the Government thereunder.

PART II.

The Growth of the United States and the Causes which led to the Formation of the Government of the Confederate States.

CHAPTER FIRST.

Politics in the United States from Washington to Monroe.

CHAPTER SECOND.

Disputes between the Federal Government and Some of the States. Georgia and the Indians. South Carolina and Nullification.

CHAPTER THIRD.

The Slavery Quarrel.

TABLE OF CONTENTS.

PART III.

The Formation of the Confederate Government. The War between the States and its Results.

SECTION I.

EVENTS OF 1861.

CHAPTER FIRST.

Secession of Seven Southern States. Formation of the Confederate Government. Efforts at Reconciliation.

CHAPTER SECOND.

The Beginning of the War. Secession of Four Other States. The Campaign in West Virginia.

CHAPTER THIRD.

The Campaign of the First Manassas (Bull Run). Other Events in Virginia and West Virginia.

CHAPTER FOURTH.

The War in the West and on the Coast during 1861.

SECTION II.

EVENTS OF 1862.

CHAPTER FIRST.

Some Minor Events both in the East and West in the Beginning of 1862. The Western Campaign of the Spring and Early Summer.

CHAPTER SECOND.

From the Beginning of the Campaign of 1862 in Virginia to the Close of the Campaign of the Second Manassas.

CHAPTER THIRD.

The Maryland and Kentucky Campaign.

CHAPTER FOURTH.

Fredericksburg. Second Attempt upon Vicksburg. Murfreesboro (Stone River).

TABLE OF CONTENTS.

SECTION III.

EVENTS OF 1863.

CHAPTER FIRST.

The Emancipation Proclamation. The Admission of West Virginia. Early Military Operations of 1863.

CHAPTER SECOND.

Chancellorsville and Gettysburg.

CHAPTER THIRD.

Fall of Vicksburg. Chickamauga. Chattanooga and Missionary Ridge.

CHAPTER FOURTH.

Other Important Events of 1863.

SECTION IV.

EVENTS OF 1864.

CHAPTER FIRST.

Events in tne East and West in the First Months of 1864.

CHAPTER SECOND.

From the Opening of the Virginia Campaign to the end of July, 1864.

CHAPTER THIRD.

From the Opening of the Georgia Campaign to the first part of August, 1864. Events in Mississ'ppi. Discouragement at the North.

CHAPTER FOURTH.

The Tide Turns. Mobile Bay. Fall of Atlanta. Sheridan and Early in the Shenandoah. Hood's Tennessee Campaign. Sherman's March Through Georgia. Confederate Successes Around Petersburg and Richmond.

SECTION V.

THE FINAL CAMPAIGNS—RECONSTRUCTION.

CHAPTER FIRST.

Prisoners of War. The Final Campaign.

CHAPTER SECOND.

Reconstruction. The Union Restored. Closing remarks.

PART I.

A Short Sketch of United States History from the Colonial Times to the Establishment of the Government under the Constitution.

STORY OF THE CONFEDERATE STATES.

CHAPTER I.

A BRIEF SKETCH OF COLONIAL HISTORY.

SOON after the discovery of America by Columbus, Spain began to plant colonies in various parts of the New World. For more than one hundred years the civilization of America was Spanish, and Spain regarded the whole continent as rightfully her own.

2. But England claimed North America because John Cabot, sailing under her flag, had discovered its mainland at least fourteen months before Columbus sighted the coasts of South America. It was long, however, before she began seriously to make good her claim, and not until the beginning of the seventeenth century was her first colony established at Jamestown (1607). Having once secured a firm foothold, she rapidly extended her power until, by the middle of the eighteenth century, her possessions reached from Maine to the southern border of Georgia and contained a million and a half inhabitants.

3. The settled portions were near the coasts and reached some distance into the interior. Each English colony claimed the whole country from the settlements on the coast all the way to the Pacific ocean.

4. In the Southern colonies the wealthy people lived on large plantations which were worked by negro slaves. The poorer people lived on small farms. The

RUINS OF JAMESTOWN.
First English Settlement in America.

chief employment was agriculture. The people of New England were much more closely settled than those of the South. There was also much greater diversity of industry in New England. More manufactured goods were made there and more people engaged in trade.

5. There were negro slaves in all the colonies; but a great many more of them were needed on the large plantations of the South than on the small farms of New England.

6. According to some authorities in 1620, according to others in 1619, some Dutch traders had brought twenty negroes to Jamestown, Va., and sold them to the settlers. This was the beginning of negro slavery in the English settlements in North America. The merchants and seamen of New England engaged actively in the African slave trade, bringing great numbers of negroes from Africa and selling them to the Southern planters. They had gone into the business as early as 1636 when the "Desire," the first American slave ship, was built at Marblehead, Massachusetts.

7. The people of Virginia became alarmed at the great number of ignorant barbarians that were thus being brought into the colony; and the legislature passed laws to stop the traffic. But the king of England compelled them to repeal these laws. The founders of Georgia prohibited slavery and rum in that colony; but after several years these restrictions were removed.

8. Each colony had its own legislature, but only the New England colonies elected their own governors. In the other colonies the governors were appointed by

the king or by the proprietors, who like William Penn and Lord Baltimore held their power from the king.

9. Education was more general in the New England and Middle States, because the people lived nearer to each other and dwelt more in towns. Harvard University was founded in the early days of the colony of Massachusetts (1638). William and Mary College in Virginia was founded during the reign of William and Mary.[1] Princeton College, in New Jersey, was founded in 1746. In South Carolina the wealthy planters sent their sons to Charleston and sometimes to England to be educated. In Georgia, for the purpose of promoting education, the rents of certain lands were set apart by the crown in every parish, as the counties were then called, and good schools were established at Savannah and Augusta.

10. The people of all the colonies were very industrious. The various grains were raised and in the South tobacco and rice were also cultivated. Some attention was given to the raising of indigo, and in Georgia some silk was made. As the colonies grew in population they increased in wealth and power.

11. England wished to keep all the trade of the colonies for her own advantage. Hence the government in England passed laws restricting trade and manufactures in the colonies. These laws were not well enforced, and, whenever attempts were made to carry them out, the people showed a disposition to be rebellious.

[1] About the year 1619, a college had been opened for both sexes at Henrico. Under an order from the king, large contributions had been made for its support. At the time of the Indian massacre in 1622 this College was destroyed, as was also a free preparatory school which had been established at Charles City in 1621.

WILLIAM AND MARY COLLEGE.

12. The peace of the English colonies was often disturbed by Indian wars, which always ended in the triumph of the whites and the acquisition of additional lands for settlement. The English colonies were also disturbed by frequent hostilities on the part of the Spaniards and French. Spain had extensive possessions on the south and asserted her right to all the country south of South Carolina. Hence Spain resented the founding of Georgia and gave the settlers of that colony much trouble. On the north and west France claimed immense possessions, and often harrassed the New England colonies and New York with bloody wars.

13. The question of dominion in North America was settled at last by the great French and Indian war which lasted about eight years. In this mighty struggle France and Spain assisted by numerous Indian allies fought against Great Britain and her American colonies. The decisive battle on the Plains of Abraham, near Quebec, established the supremacy of England in North America.

14. By the treaty of 1763 France gave up to England all her possessions in North America east of the Mississippi River except the city of New Orleans. At the same time she ceded to her ally Spain the city of New Orleans and all her possessions west of the Mississippi. Spain ceded to England her possessions of East and West Florida.

15. At this time England extended the limits of the colony of Georgia to the Mississippi river on the west, and to latitude 31° and the St. Mary's river on the south.

CHAPTER II.

THE WAR FOR AMERICAN INDEPENDENCE AND THE ES-
TABLISHMENT OF THE GOVERNMENT OF THE UNITED
STATES.

AT the close of the French and Indian War
Great Britain came to the front as the most
powerful nation in the world. She now
occupied the proud place held by Spain at the beginning of the seventeenth century and had also humbled
the pride of her haughty rival, France.

2. The people of the English colonies in America
had borne their full share in these great achievements
and gloried in being a part of the British Empire.
At the same time they had learned something of the
value of united action, and knew enough of their own
power to be unwilling to submit to any law, which
they considered unjust.

3. Yet such was their love for the Mother country
and such their pride in the noble empire of which
they formed a part, that they were prepared to endure
much, before coming to an open rupture with the
British government.

4. The laws restricting American trade and commerce gave great dissatisfaction; but when the British
Parliament prepared to go still farther and impose a
direct tax, the patience of the American people was
tried to the utmost.

5. The French and Indian War had added largely
to the debt of Great Britain, and, as it had been carried on for the benefit of the colonies, the British Par-

liament thought that the Americans ought to pay a share of the debt.

6. The colonies declared their willingness to pay their share, but insisted on the right to lay their own taxes. As they had no representation in Parliament they claimed that Parliament had no right to tax them.

7. It was in 1765 that the British government adopted the scheme of taxation by the passage of the Stamp Act. The Americans were thoroughly aroused against this measure and the act was repealed the next year. But other schemes of taxation were adopted, and when the Americans resisted, the government of Great Britain resorted to force. Troops were sent to Boston and other places to overawe the inhabitants, and the Americans were treated, not as equal members of the British Empire, but like people of a conquered nation.

8. In 1765 when the dispute began, the people of the colonies were proud of their connection with the British Empire and loved the flag of England as the banner under which they had fought against a common foe. By 1775, though they were still unwilling to dissolve their union with Great Britain, their old love had vanished, and the red-coated soldiers, instead of being regarded as friends, were now detested as oppressors. Such was the change of feeling produced by ten years of tyranny and wrong.

9. The king and Parliament spoke of the Americans as rebels, and called their leading men traitors. They claimed that Parliament had the right to bind the colonies in all cases whatsoever, and demanded of the Americans absolute submission to their will.

10. But the Americans claimed that in coming to the wilds of the New World to build up for Britian a

BATTLE OF LEXINGTON.

great empire they had lost none of their rights as free-born Englishmen. They acknowledged allegiance to the King, but claimed that only their colonial assemblies had the right to tax them. Their cry was, "No taxation without representation." They felt that they were contending for a great principle, and cared nothing for the hard names given them by their oppressors.

11. At length the war of words and contending opinions led to a conflict of arms at Lexington and Concord, and the great struggle for American liberty began.

12. At first the Americans were fighting only for their rights as British subjects. They did not at first desire separation from the British government, but after several months of fighting, the great majority began to desire absolute freedom from British rule.

13. One colony after another instructed its delegates to vote for independence. When the unanimous consent of the thirteen colonies in rebellion had been secured, the Continental Congress declared the united colonies to be "free and independent States," (July 4th, 1776).

14. At the time of the Declaration there was no British army on the soil of the United States. By the fight at Lexington the whole country had been aroused. Bunker Hill, though an American defeat, had the moral effect of a victory. Washington by his skillful management had compelled the British to evacuate Boston; a British fleet had been repulsed at Charleston; at Savannah the Americans had gained an important success, and in North Carolina at More's Creek a band of American adherents of the king—

called by the British, Loyalists, but by the Americans, Tories—had been completely defeated.

15. It was not long, however, before a powerful British army and fleet appeared before New York. They defeated the Americans on Long Island, captured

BUNKER HILL AND WARREN.

New York city and compelled Washington's army to retreat across New Jersey. But when the American cause seemed almost ruined, Washington most skillfully turned the tide by his brilliant victories at **Trenton** and **Princeton.**

16. The year 1777 was productive of great results. Notwithstanding the disaster to the Americans at the Brandywine, the fall of Philadelphia, their capital, and their repulse at Germantown, the capture of Burgoyne and a British army at Saratoga in New York made almost certain their final success. For the victory of Saratoga secured to the Americans the alliance with France, the powerful rival of Great Britain. The British were obliged to retire from Philadelphia and to abandon every important conquest in the United States except the city of New York.

17. The British government now offered to give the Americans all that they had ever asked if they would only renew their allegiance to the British Crown. But the offer came too late The Americans were now determined to accept nothing short of independence. Great Britain, though ready to yield everything else, was unwilling to consent to the dissolution of the great British Empire. So the war went on.

18. The most important event of 1778 was the conquest of the Northwest. General George Rogers Clarke, of Virginia, at the head of a force of bold riflemen crossed the Ohio river and marched against the Indians and their British allies. He defeated them in several engagements, conquered the country between the Ohio and the Great Lakes and the Mississippi river, and annexed it to Virginia as the county of Illinois.

19. Sir Henry Clinton, the British commander in America, now concluded that the chance for success would be much better in the thinly settled South than in the more thickly settled States of New England and the Middle section. In the New England

States alone at that time there were nearly 800,000 white inhabitants, while in South Carolina and Georgia there were less than 200,000 white people, and these were widely scattered. Hence it was always much easier to concentrate a large force against the invaders in New England than in the two Southern States, so sparsely settled and so far removed from the centres of population.

20. At the end of December, 1778, a British force captured Savannah and soon afterwards advanced northward and occupied Augusta. But the South Carolina and Georgia militia by their brilliant victory at Kettle Creek recovered Augusta and the up country of Georgia to within fifty miles of Savannah. Though the Americans soon after this suffered a severe defeat at Brier Creek, and though a combined French and American army met a disastrous repulse before Savannah in October, 1779, yet Augusta and all the up country of Georgia remained in their possession until the summer of 1780.

21. About the middle of March, 1780, Sir Henry Clinton, with a fleet and army, attacked Charleston, which was defended by an American army under General Lincoln. After a siege of seven weeks Clinton captured the city and with it all the regular soldiers and most of the organized militia of South Carolina and Georgia. These two States were thus by one disastrous blow laid prostrate at the feet of the conqueror. The most important points were occupied by the British, and many of the people feeling that they had been left to their fate by their sister States, accepted British protection.

22. But scattered throughout the rural districts were patriot bands who, under their favorite leaders, made

the open country unsafe for the British. The most noted of these leaders were Marion, Sumter, and Pickens in South Carolina, and Elijah Clarke in Georgia. By their daring and successful exploits they kept alive the spirit of freedom. Notwithstanding the defeat of a succoring army under Gates, near Camden, and the seeming hopelessness of farther resistance, they kept up the struggle. To their rescue came the rifle militia of North Carolina and Virginia, many of them from what we now know as Tennessee and Kentucky, and at King's Mountain captured nearly one-third of the British army.[1]

23. The battle of King's Mountain turned the tide in the South, and when General Nathaniel Greene entered South Carolina with troops from Delaware, Maryland, Virginia and North Carolina, all the patriot leaders of South Carolina and Georgia began an active warfare upon the various posts of the enemy. Morgan's brilliant victory at Cowpens was a good beginning of the new campaign in the South. General Greene, though sometimes repulsed upon the field, managed so skillfully that even defeats were turned to the advantage of the Americans. With the main army he ever kept the British too busy to go to the rescue of their detatched posts, which were one after another captured by the patriot militia of South Carolina and Georgia. Colonel Henry Lee, familiarly known as "Light Horse Harry," leading some of Greene's best troops, assisted Marion to capture forts

---

[1] These mountain riflemen led by Campbell Cleveland, Sevier and Shelby had started to help Colonel Elijah Clarke capture Augusta, but hearing of that officer's defeat and Ferguson's attempt to intercept him, had marched against Ferguson

Watson, Granby, Motte and Orangeburg, and then rendered valuable help to Pickens and Clarke in the recapture of Augusta from the enemy. At Eutaw Springs Greene gave the finishing blow to the British power in the South.

SURRENDER OF CORNWALLIS.

24. During the latter years of the war the conflict had been confined mostly to the South. The American army, under Washington, had kept close watch upon the British in New York and had thwarted all their plans in that quarter. The timely discovery of Arnold's treason had saved the American cause from great disaster, and the British forces were unable to take the offensive. At length Washington, securing

the co-operation of a French fleet and army, left a sufficient force to keep the enemy from marching out of the city of New York into the open country, and at Yorktown, in Virginia, struck the finishing blow to British power in the United States by the capture of the veteran army of Cornwallis (October 19, 1781).

25. Negotiations for peace were now entered into. Nearly two years after the decisive American victory at Yorktown the treaty of peace was signed (September 3, 1783). The first article of the treaty began as follows: " His Britanic majesty acknowledges the said United States, viz., New Hampshire, Massachusetts Bay, Rhode Island and Providence Plantations, Connecticut, New York, New Jersey, Pennsylvania, Delaware, Maryland, Virginia, North Carolina, South Carolina, and Georgia, to be free, sovereign and independent States. He treats with them as such."

26. The Mississippi was fixed as the boundary of the United States on the west and the Great Lakes on the north. At the same time Great Britain made peace with France, Spain, and Holland, which had all been allied against her, and ceded back to Spain her former possessions of East and West Florida.

27. The struggle which had been commenced by the Americans in defense of their chartered rights, and which had been converted into a war for independence, had ended in the establishment of a new republic among the nations of the earth.

CHAPTER III.

THE FORMATION AND ADOPTION OF THE CONSTITUTION, AND THE ESTABLISHMENT OF THE GOVERNMENT THEREUNDER.

THE new republic was not a consolidated government, but a Confederacy of thirteen independent States. On the 12th of July, 1776, eight days after the Declaration of Independence, a plan of union, which had been drawn up by a committee appointed by the advice of Richard Henry Lee of Virginia, had been laid before Congress. According to this plan, known as the Articles of Confederation, the States conferred upon the United States in Congress assembled, certain powers that were deemed necessary for the common security and defense, but reserved to themselves many other powers, naming among them sovereignty, freedom, and independence. The States were very careful not to centralize too much power in Congress.

2. Most of the States agreed to these "Articles of Confederation and Perpetual Union in 1777," and by 1779 all had adopted them except Maryland. The hesitation of Maryland was owing to a dispute over lands west of the Ohio river. Virginia claimed these lands, both because they had been embraced in her charter and because of their conquest by George Rogers Clarke in 1778. New York also claimed a large part of them by right of cession from the Indians. Connecticut and Massachusetts claimed that part of them were covered by their charters. Maryland insisted that

these lands should become the common property of
the United States, and refused to enter the confederation unless this should be done.

3. Virginia felt that her claim was a just one; for
the claims of the other States were only on paper,
while she had actually conquered and occupied the
country; but for the sake of union she generously
offered to cede to the United States the whole of her
just claim to the country northwest of the Ohio
(January 2, 1781). The other States followed her
example except that Connecticut reserved certain
parts of her claim to create a school fund and to pay
her citizens for losses by Tory raids. Maryland then
agreed to the Articles of Confederation (March 1,
1781), and the Union was made complete.

4. The cession of all this northwest territory was
completed fully in 1786. Virginia coupled the surrender of her claims with the condition that there should
be in the said territory neither slavery nor involuntary
servitude, except as a punishment for crime, and when
Congress organized the northwest territory in 1787
this condition was made a part of the act of organization.

5. Soon after the establishment of independence it
became evident that the government under the Articles of Confederation was not strong enough to hold
the States together in peace. It was very plain that,
unless some remedy could be found, the Union would
go to pieces, and that instead of one republic there
would be thirteen.

6. All felt the need of union, but the States were so
jealous of their own rights that it was doubtful whether
they could be induced to give any additional powers

to the Federal Government. At that time the enforcement of any law passed by Congress was left entirely to the States. Hence the authority of the Federal Government was very limited.

7. An effort to get the States to send delegates to a convention in 1786 failed, only five States responding to the call. But a second effort was more successful. All the States except Rhode Island sent delegates to the convention which met in Philadelphia on the 14th of May, 1787. George Washington, of Virginia, was chosen president of the convention.

8. The assembling of the convention to revise the Articles of Confederation was due to the earnest efforts of three men—James Madison and George Washington, of Virginia, and Alexander Hamilton, of New York. The formation and adoption of the Constitution was due to James Madison more than to any other one man. He was the author of many of its chief features, and has been called the " Father of the Constitution."

9. Some of the delegates to the convention wished to establish a strong national government. But the majority would not even allow the word " national " to appear in the new constitution. They were willing to greatly enlarge the powers of the Federal Government, but they were determined to adhere to the idea of a confederation.

10. After four months of careful labor the new plan of union, called the Constitution of the United States, was ready to be offered to the people of the several States. Under this plan the States gave to the Federal Government much larger powers than it had possessed before; but each State reserved to itself the

right to manage its domestic affairs and to pass any law which did not interfere with the rights of other States or of the Federal Government.

11. Under the first union Congress exercised all the powers given to the government. Under the new plan the government was to consist of three departments—one, styled the Legislative, was to make the laws; another, called the Judicial, was to explain the laws; and the third, named the Executive, was to see that the laws were carried out

12. **The Legislative Department.**—The law-making power was vested in Congress, which consists of two houses—a Senate and House of Representatives. The number of representatives allowed to each State depends upon the population of the State. These representatives are elected by the people and hold office for two years. Two senators are allowed to each State, and these are chosen by the State legislatures, and hold office for six years. Congress is allowed to control in all matters that pertain to the general interest of all the States.

13. **The Judicial Department.**—This consists of one Supreme Court and of such inferior courts as may be established by Congress. If the judges of the Supreme Court declare that any law of Congress or of any of the States does not agree with the Constitution, then such law becomes at once null and void.

14. **The Executive Department**—This consists of a President and a Vice-President. It is the duty of the President to execute the laws passed by Congress. If he vetoes any measure of Congress, it cannot become a law, unless two-thirds of both Houses vote for it again. The Vice-President presides over the Senate, and in

case of the death or disability of the President, takes his place.

15. **The President's Cabinet.**—The President is allowed to name certain officers styled the Cabinet, with whom he can consult. These officers must be confirmed by the Senate. Congress establishes these offices, which at first were those of Secretary of State, Secretary of the Treasury, Secretary of War, and Attorney-General. Congress afterwards created the Cabinet offices of Secretary of the Navy, Secretary of the Interior, and the Postmaster-General.

16. **Amendments.**—The Constitution can be amended by the consent of three-fourths of the States. But no amendment can be made which shall deprive any State without its own consent of its equal vote in Senate.

17. **Ratification of the Constitution.**—Under the Articles of Confederation no change could be made without the consent of all the States. Now the preamble to the Constitution, as at first adopted by the convention, mentioned each State by name; but it became so evident that there would be great difficulty in getting all the States to accept the new Constitution, that it was determined by the convention that the consent of nine States should suffice for its establishment between the States so ratifying the same. As it was uncertain which of the States would ratify the Constitution and thus constitute the new Union, the preamble was altered so as to read: "We the people of the United States," etc. The seventh and last article of the Constitution as submitted by the convention reads: "The ratification of the conventions of nine States shall be sufficient for the establishment of this Constitution

between the States so ratifying the same." Thus no State would be without its own consent bound by the new Constitution.

18. Mr. Madison, often styled "the Father of the Constitution," in number xxxix of the Federalist, while urging upon the States the ratification of the Constitution says: "That it will be a Federal and not a national act, as these terms are understood by objectors,—the act of the people as forming so many independent States, not as forming one aggregate nation,—is obvious from the single consideration that it is to result neither from the decision of a majority of the people of the Union nor from that of a majority of the States. It must result from the unanimous consent of the several States that are parties to it. Each State in ratifying the Constitution is considered as a sovereign body, independent of all others, and only to be bound by its own voluntary act."

19. Patrick Henry and others urged against the new Constitution that "we the people" meant a consolidated government instead of a Confederation, and on this ground earnestly opposed its ratification by Virginia. But in answer to his objection Mr. Madison said: "Who are parties to it (the Constitution)? The people, but not the people as composing one great body, but the people as composing thirteen sovereignties. Were it a consolidated government, the assent of a majority of the people would be sufficient for its establishment, and as a majority have adopted it already, the remaining States would be bound by the act of the majority, even if they reprobated it; but, sir, no State is bound by it, as it is, without its own consent."

20. After much opposition, eleven States ratified the Constitution. The method was the same in each State. Delegates were chosen to meet in convention and decide the question according to the wish of the people who had elected them. The seventy thousand people of the little State of Delaware had precisely the same weight—one vote—in the ratification of the Constitution, as the more than seven hundred thousand of Virginia, or the four hundred thousand of Pennsylvania.

21. It is quite certain that the Constitution would never have received the ratification of Massachusetts, New Hampshire, New York, and perhaps other of the eleven ratifying States, but for the well-grounded assurance that certain amendments securing more carefully the rights of the States would be adopted, as soon as the requisite formalities could be complied with. Chief among these amendments was the safeguard to State sovereignty, afterwards embodied in the tenth amendment. It reads as follows: "The powers not delegated to the United States by the Constitution, nor prohibited to it by the States, are reserved to the States respectively, or to the people."

22. Mr. Samuel Adams, of Massachusetts, said of the tenth amendment: "It is consonant with the second article in the present Confederation,[1] that each State retains its sovereignty, freedom, and independence, and every power, jurisdiction, and right, which is not by this Confederation expressly delegated to the United States in Congress assembled."

23. Thus we see, our fathers, while anxious to form a more perfect union, guarded carefully the sovereignty

[1] That existing under the Articles of Confederation.

of the States.   They were determined to make it plain that nothing was surrendered by implication.

24. By the 26th of July, 1788, the conventions of eleven States had ratified the Constitution.   The following table gives the names of the eleven States so ratifying it, and the dates of their ratification :

Delaware, December 7, 1787.
Pennsylvania, December 12, 1787.
New Jersey, December 18, 1787.
Georgia, January 2, 1788.
Connecticut, January 9, 1788.
Massachusetts, February 6, 1788.
Maryland, April 28, 1788.
South Carolina, May 23, 1788.
New Hampshire, June 21, 1788.
Virginia, June 26, 1788.
New York, June 26, 1788.

25. Virginia accompanied her ratification with the assertion of the right of the people to resume the powers granted under the Constitution, whenever the same should be used for their injury or oppression.   As each State ratified the Constitution separately, the word people here meant the people of Virginia, who were then ratifying the Constitution in behalf of that State.   The natural inference would be, that, if the people of Virginia had that right, the people of each of the other ratifying States had the same right.   New York's convention made a declaration similar to that of Virginia.

26. North Carolina and Rhode Island had not ratified.   Steps were immediately taken for the establishment of the new government by the eleven ratifying

GEORGE WASHINGTON.

States. In all of these eleven States except New York
the necessary elections were held. George Washington of Virginia received every electoral vote cast for
the office of President, and John Adams of Massachusetts was elected Vice-President by a majority of
the votes cast. On the 30th of April, 1789, in the city
of New York, the inauguration took place amid imposing ceremonies. Under the guidance of the beloved
Washington, whom all Americans of every section
have ever delighted to honor as the "Father of his
Country," the United States entered upon a brilliant
career.

27. The new Union formed the most perfect model of
a Confederated Republic, as both Washington and
Hamilton styled it, that the wisdom of man ever
devised. There were, as we have seen, only eleven
States in the new republic; for North Carolina and
Rhode Island had thus far refused to adopt the Constitution. But there was no claim on the part of the
eleven States that had formed the more perfect union
to control the action of the other two. Their accession
to the Union was desired, but their right to do as they
pleased in this matter was never questioned. There
was no inclination to violate the very principle for
which they had contended in the war for independence
by attempting to coerce any State which did not see
fit to unite with them.

28. In September, 1789, while Rhode Island was
still holding aloof from the new Union, President
Washington received and sent in to the Senate of the
United States a letter from the General Assembly of
Rhode Island, addressed to " the President, the Senate,
and the House of Representatives of the eleven United

States of America in Congress assembled."[1] This letter is interesting, as showing the relation then existing between Rhode Island and the United States. It was a request that trade and commerce might be free and open between that State and the United States.

29. On November 21, 1789, North Carolina, after becoming satisfied that the most important of the amendments and " Declaration of Rights " proposed by her and other States would be adopted, agreed in her convention to " adopt and ratify " the Constitution. On May 29th, 1790, Rhode Island gave her long-withheld assent to the Constitution, after being fully convinced that certain proposed amendments would be adopted.

30. When Washington announced to Congress that North Carolina had ratified the Constitution of 1787, he expressed his gratification at the accession of that State. On June 1st, 1790, he announced by special message the like accession of the State of Rhode Island, and congratulated Congress on the happy event which " united under the General Government all the States which were originally confederated."

31. It is well to close this chapter with the statement that, though the Federal Government, under the Constitution, had larger powers than under the Articles of Confederation, the Union was still a confederacy and not a consolidated nation. Hamilton, whose inclination was for a strong government, repeatedly, in the *Federalist* (Nos. ix. and lxxxv.), speaks of the

[1] For the letter, see "American State Papers, Vol. I., Miscellaneous," or " The Rise and Fall of the Confederate Government," by Jefferson Davis, page 112.

new government as a "Confederate Republic" and a "Confederacy," and calls the Constitution "a *Compact*." Washington, also, on different occasions referred to the Constitution as a "*Compact*," and spoke of the Union as a "Confederated Republic."

PART II.

The Growth of the United States, and the Causes which led to the Formation of the Government of the Confederate States.

CHAPTER I.

POLITICS IN THE UNITED STATES FROM WASHINGTON TO MONROE.

EDERALISTS and Anti-Federalists.—During the discussions and debates in the several States about the Constitution previous to its ratification, those who favored the adoption of that instrument were known as Federalists, while their opponents were styled Anti-Federalists. Some of the most earnest patriots were found in the ranks of both these parties. After the ratification of the Constitution by the several States and the formation of the government thereunder, the Anti-Federalist party ceased to exist, and at the beginning of Washington's administration party lines seemed to be extinct.

2. **The Democratic or Republican Party.**—But it was not a very long while before there arose divisions as to the proper construction of the constitution. Those who favored a free or loose construction of the constitution, desiring a stronger Federal Government than that instrument had provided for, continued to be called Federalists, while those who favored a strict construction of the constitution, and opposed loose methods of interpretation were known as Republicans or Democrats.

3. The Republican, or Democratic party, of which Jefferson has been called the father, was, however, something quite different in its attitude from the Anti-Federalist party of 1787. Mr. Madison and others who like him had been zealous Federalists, became

leaders in the Democratic party, and within twenty-five years by far the larger part of the original Federalist party had become absorbed in the Democratic or (as it was then also called) Republican party. They had abandoned the Federalist party because of the loose construction views of those who had become its leaders.

JOHN ADAMS.

4. It was while John Adams of Massachusetts the second President of the United States, was in office, that measures were enacted by the Federalist majority in Congress and approved by the President, which

made the administration and the Federalist party exceedingly unpopular.

5. Difficulties between France and the United States that had been commenced during Washington's administration, reached such a point during the administra- of John Adams, that the two countries were on the very verge of war. Congress passed acts for the protection of navigation, for the defense of the sea-coast, for increasing the land and naval forces, and also what were known as the Alien and Sedition Acts.

6. The Alien Act authorized the President to order any foreigner, whom he might believe to be dangerous to the United States, to depart from the country, under heavy penalty for refusing to obey the order. The Sedition Act made it a crime, with a heavy penalty to write, print or utter anything scandalous against the Congress or President of the United States.

THE VIRGINIA AND KENTUCKY RESOLUTIONS.

7. These acts and the arbitrary manner in which they were enforced created great discontent and indignation. The legislature of Virginia, at that time the largest and most influential State in the Union, passed resolutions drawn up by Mr. Madison, in which it was declared that on entering the Union the States had surrendered only a portion of their powers and that, whenever the Federal Government transcended its powers, the States should interfere and pronounce such acts unconstitutional. The legislature of Kentucky,[1] one of the States admitted during Washington's administration, also passed a series of resolu-

---

[1] Three States were admitted during Washington's administration, Vermont, Kentucky, and Tennessee.

THOMAS JEFFERSON.

tions drawn up by Mr. Jefferson. The Kentucky resolutions went even farther than those of Virginia, and mentioned nullification as a remedy.

8. So great hostility was excited against the Federalist party that in the election of 1800 the Democratic (also called Republican) party came into power with Jefferson at its head. One of the first acts of Mr. Jefferson was to release all persons imprisoned under the Sedition Act. He treated this act as a complete nullity, declaring that no one was any more bound by it than if Congress had set up a golden image and ordered the people to bow down to it. He showed his disapproval of the Alien Act in a similar manner.

9. **Purchase of Louisiana.**—One of the most popular acts of Mr. Jefferson's administration was the purchase of Louisiana Until this event the Mississippi river was the western boundary of the United States. Ever since the close of the French and Indian war, Spain had possession of the country west of the Mississippi until 1800, when that part known as Louisiana was ceded to France. Napoleon Bonaparte, by a treaty consummated on the 30th of April, 1803, ceded to the United States for $15,000,000 the whole of Louisiana, which at that time embraced the vast region lying between the Mississippi river and the Rocky mountains. It was also claimed that the northern portion extended to the Pacific ocean,

10. Although this acquisition more than doubled the original limits of the United States and added greatly to the power and importance of the young republic, there were found people who earnestly opposed the purchase of Louisiana.

11. This opposition came from New England. Mr. George Cabot, who had been United States senator from Massachusetts, declared that "the influence of our (the northeastern) part of the Union must be diminished by the acquisition of more weight at the other extremity."[1] Colonel Timothy Pickering, who had been an officer of the Revolution, afterwards a member of Washington's Cabinet, and still later senator from Massachusetts, and who may well be called the leading secessionist of his day, was so opposed to the purchase of Louisiana that he advocated the formation of a northern confederacy.[2]

12. This extreme sectional jealousy was again shown in 1811, when the bill for the admission of Louisiana into the Union as a State was under discussion. On this occasion Hon. Josiah Quincy, a member of Congress from Massachusetts, said: "If this bill passes, it is my deliberate opinion that it is virtually a dissolution of the Union; that it will free the States from their moral obligations; and as it will be the right of all, so it will be the duty of some, definitely to prepare for a separation—amicably if they can, violently if they must."

13. Let it be remembered that these men, whose opinions are here quoted, were not Southern men nor Democrats, but New England men and advocates of the highest type of Federalism and of a strong central goverment.

14. The general sentiment of the Union, however, heartily endorsed the purchase of Louisiana. For a while the Federalist party almost disappeared from

[1] See "Life of Cabot" by Lodge, page 334.
[2] See "Life of Cabot," page 491; also pages 338-340, 445, 446.

politics, and Mr. Jefferson was elected to a second term by a very large majority over the Federalist candidate, Charles Cotesworth Pinkney of South Carolina. George Clinton of New York, was at the same time chosen Vice-President over the Federalist candidate, Rufus King also of New York.

15. The Embargo Act.—In 1807, on account of depredations upon American commerce by both Great Britain and France, an embargo act was passed by Congress forbidding American trading vessels to leave their ports. This was done in hope that those two nations, who were at war with each other, would so suffer from the loss of American trade that they would cease from their acts of hostility. But the embargo hurt the Americans more than it did England and France, and caused great dissatisfaction in the New England States. Mr. Jefferson received information which he deemed reliable, that there was even danger that some of the New England States would withdraw from the Union unless the act was repealed. This was accordingly done by Congress at Mr. Jefferson's suggestion.

War of 1812 and 1815.

16. James Madison of Virginia, another Democrat, succeeded Mr. Jefferson as President. His term is especially noted for the second war with Great Britain. The main cause of this war was the conduct of the British government in claiming and enforcing the right to search American ships on the high seas. We will not attempt a history of this war. It is enough to say that, although the Americans suffered some disastrous defeats in the beginning of the war, yet by many brilliant victories, both on land and sea,

JAMES MADISON.

the prestige of the United States as a warlike power was greatly increased. The most noted of these American victories were General William Henry Harrison's overthrow of the British and Indians at the Thames in Canada, Perry's great naval victory on Lake Erie, McDonough's equally brilliant success on Lake Champlain, and the crowning triumph of the

BATTLE OF NEW ORLEANS.

war at New Orleans, where General Andrew Jackson gained imperishable renown. It would be difficult to decide, whether during this war the brave seamen of New England or the gallant soldiers of other sections of the Union shed the greater lustre on American arms.

HARTFORD CONVENTION.

17. During the summer and fall of 1814 many of the people of New England became greatly dissatisfied

with the management of the war. The result was that in December, 1814, a convention was held at Hartford, Connecticut, consisting of delegates from Massachusetts, Rhode Island, New Hampshire, Vermont and Connecticut. This convention sat with closed doors, and the real designs of its leaders have never been clearly ascertained. It has been generally understood, however, that they did discuss the question of the withdrawal of their States from the Union.

18. Though the decision of the convention, as published, was adverse to such a measure at that time, yet they did declare the circumstances under which they thought it might be expedient to dissolve the Union, and the method by which it should be effected.

19. The indignation which was felt throughout the Union against the members of this convention was due chiefly to the fact that this meeting at such a time tended to paralyze the arm of the Federal Government while engaged in a war undertaken to defend the rights of American seamen, most of whom were from the very States represented in the Hartford Convention.

20. The Federalist party was considered by most people as responsible for the Hartford Convention, and was held to account for its opposition to the policy of the government during the war of 1812–1815. Accordingly in the autumn of 1816 the Federalist candidates for the office of President and Vice-President—Rufus King of New York, and John Howard of Maryland—were overwhelmingly defeated by their Democratic opponents—James Monroe of Virginia, and Daniel D. Tompkins of New York.

JAMES MONROE.

CHAPTER II.

DISPUTES BETWEEN THE FEDERAL GOVERNMENT AND SOME OF THE STATES—GEORGIA AND THE INDIANS—SOUTH CAROLINA AND NULLIFICATION—CONTROVERSY WITH GEORGIA ABOUT THE INDIAN LANDS.

IN 1802, when Georgia ceded to the Union her western lands, embracing nearly all of what we now know as the States of Alabama and Mississippi, the United States agreed to extinguish the Indian title to lands within the limits of Georgia.

2. Many efforts had been made to get the Creek Indians to cede their lands within the limits of Georgia, but without success. At last, at Indian Springs, on the 12th of February, 1825, McIntosh and other Creek chiefs met commissioners appointed by the United States and made such a treaty as the authorities of Georgia desired. The treaty was sent to Washington and ratified by the United States Senate on the 3d of March, 1825. The treaty also received the signature of James Monroe, the President. The Georgia authorities now began to take measures for the survey of the lands thus ceded.

3. Some of the Creeks were very much provoked at the treaty which McIntosh had made, and on the 1st of May murdered him and two others of their chiefs who had signed the treaty with him. The dissatisfied party of the Creeks then requested the United States Government to make a new treaty in place of the one made at Indian Springs.

4. The President acceded to their request, and on the 24th of January, 1826, a new treaty was made. It was ratified by the Senate, and received the signature of the President, John Quincy Adams. George M. Troup, the Governor of Georgia, claimed that the new treaty deprived Georgia of rights already vested. He therefore paid no attention to it, but proceeded with the survey of the lands ceded by the first treaty. The President ordered the arrest of the surveyors.

5. But Governor Troup ordered the arrest of any one who should interfere with the surveyors, and called out the militia to repel any hostile invasion of the State. Happily for the whole country the President did not attempt to carry out his threats of force. The surveys were completed, and the entire territory covered by the treaty of Indian Springs was occupied by the Georgians in 1827.

6. While Andrew Jackson was President Georgia had trouble with the Cherokees also, but Mr. Jackson's sympathies were with the Georgians, and everything was settled to their satisfaction.

South Carolina and Nullification.

7. Another serious trouble was that which arose between South Carolina and the Federal Government about the tariff. In 1816 a law had been passed by Congress imposing a duty (or tariff) on goods manufactured in foreign countries. This was done for the double purpose of enabling American manufacturers to compete with those of Europe, and of raising a revenue for the support of the government.

8. The tariff proved so useful to the Northern manufacturers that they wanted it increased. This was

done by the tariff act of 1828; but it gave great dissatisfaction to the Southern people, who preferred to buy cheap goods in Europe. In the election of that year the party in favor of a lower tariff triumphed, and Andrew Jackson of Tennessee, and John C. Calhoun of South Carolina, were elected President and Vice-President over John Quincy Adams and Richard Rush, the candidates of the high tariff men.

9. But the tariff of 1832 also failed to please the low tariff men. During the excitement over this question occurred another presidential election. The original Democratic or Republican party had split into two parties. The party which favored the high tariff and internal improvements by the general government at first called itself National Republican, but afterwards adopted the name of Whig. Henry Clay of Kentucky, was nominated by this party for President and John Sargent of Pennsylvania, for Vice-President. The Democratic party, which opposed the measures advocated by the Whigs, nominated Andrew Jackson of Tennessee, for President and Martin Van Buren of New York, for Vice-President. The Democrats elected their candidates by a very large majority.

10. In the meantime a convention of the people of South Carolina had assembled and declared that the tariff of 1832 was contrary to the Constitution of the United States, and therefore null and void. The convention also stated that the courts of the State would decide on the matter, and that, if the government of the United States interfered, the State of South Carolina would withdraw from the Union. This measure was to take effect on the 12th of February,

ANDREW JACKSON.

1833, if the high protective policy should not be abandoned by Congress by that time.

11. In December the President in his message to Congress recommended a reduction of the tariff. A few days afterwards he issued a proclamation against nullification, in which he advised the people of South Carolina not to persist in the enforcement of their nullification policy, as it would bring on a conflict between the Federal Government and the State of South Carolina.

12. Soon after Jackson's proclamation Mr. Verplanck of New York introduced a bill for the further reduction of the tariff. The Legislature of Virginia also sent Benjamin Watkins Leigh as a peace commissioner to South Carolina to urge a suspension of the execution of the ordinance of nullification, at least until after the 4th of March. South Carolina acceded to this request.

13. Meanwhile Henry Clay of Kentucky introduced a compromise which was satisfactory to all parties. It passed both houses of Congress, and was signed by the President on the 2d of March, 1833. The South Carolina convention then re-assembled and repealed the ordinance of nullification. Both the President and South Carolina had been determined, but Mr. Clay's influence had secured a peaceful termination of the dispute. When told by the high tariff men that his conduct on this occasion would ruin his chances of ever being elected President, Mr. Clay's noble reply was, "I would rather be right than President."

HENRY CLAY

CHAPTER III.

THE SLAVERY QUARREL.

NOTWITHSTANDING sectional jealousies and occasional jars between States and the Federal Government the United States grew in power, population and wealth in a manner unequalled by any other country of ancient or modern times. The Union was the pride of every American, and the people of our country were the freest and most prosperous on earth. But over all the bright scene of prosperity hovered a dark cloud which was destined to finally burst in fury on the land. This was the slavery quarrel.

2. My readers have already seen how slavery was introduced into our country during the colonial period; how Dutch, English and New England sailors went to the coast of Africa to get negro slaves, and then brought them to America and sold them to the colonists. In many parts of the country there was strong opposition to this bringing of slaves from Africa. Virginia opposed it earnestly. In Georgia some opposed it, while others favored it.

3. **Slavery During the Confederation.**—After the establishment of independence the more Northern States, where there had never been any profit in slavery, began to free their slaves. In the Southern States, where the negroes were very numerous, slavery was retained, partly because the people found their slave property valuable and partly because they feared the

result if so many people of the African race should
be set free in their midst.   But many Southern people
at that time looked upon slavery as an institution, of
which they would like to be rid if they only knew
how.   Virginia in the ceding of her northwest territory stipulated that slavery should be kept out of it.

4. **The Constitution and Slavery.**—The Constitution
recognized property in slaves, and provided for the
return of runaway slaves to their masters.[1] As a compromise between the New England merchants and the
planters of South Carolina and Georgia, in return for
certain commercial favors allowed the former, the
African slave trade was not to be interfered with by
the government of the United States until 1808.

5. **Abolition of the African Slave Trade.**—But long
before the end of the time allowed for the continuance
of this trade most of the States had passed laws against
it.   Virginia was the first of all the States to forbid it.
Georgia followed, and put a clause into her State constitution forbidding the bringing of slaves into Georgia from Africa or any other foreign country.   This
was in 1798—ten years before the expiration of the
time allowed by the Constitution of the United States
for the continuance of the African slave trade.   When
the year 1808 came Congress abolished this trade.
New England seamen engaged in it to the very last.

6. **First Attempt at Slavery Agitation.**—The first attempt to bring the question of slavery into national
politics was in February, 1790, when Benjamin Franklin, of Pennsylvania, headed a petition to Congress
urging the Federal authorities to adopt measures look-

[1] Constitution of the United States—Article IV., section 2.

ing to the final abolition of African slavery throughout the Union.   But Congress passed a resolution declaring that it had no authority to interfere in the emancipation of slaves, and that settled the question for the time.

THE MISSOURI COMPROMISE.

7. The slavery question did not enter much into national politics until 1819.   Up to that time several new States had been admitted into the Union—some with slavery, others without.[1]   The States whose laws allowed slavery were agricultural; the people of the Northern States were chiefly engaged in commerce and manufactures.   Hence arose a conflict of interests. When Missouri, whose laws allowed slavery, applied for admission a strong effort was made on the part of the Northern members of Congress to refuse admission except on the condition that there should be no slavery in Missouri.   This was the first time that any such condition had ever been demanded of a territory applying for admission into the Union.

8. The Southern members felt that it was a direct attack upon the South, prompted more by a desire for power than by opposition to slavery on moral grounds.[2] They saw in the conduct of the Northern members the same sectional spirit that had prompted New

---

[1] The following table gives a list of the States admitted up to the time of the application of Missouri: States with slavery—Kentucky, June 2, 1792; Tennessee, June 1, 1796; Louisiana, April 8, 1812; Mississippi, December 10, 1817. States without slavery—Vermont, March 4, 1791; Ohio, November 20, 1802; Indiana, December 11, 1816; Illinois, December 3, 1818.

[2] James D'Wolf, a citizen of Rhode Island, who had been largely connected with the African slave trade, was sent from that State to the United States Senate as late as the year 1821.

England representatives to threaten secession at the time of the purchase of the Louisiana territory, and again upon the admission of Louisiana as a State.

9. The dispute over the admission of Missouri grew so serious that fears were entertained for the safety of the Union. But both sides loved the Union, and were willing to make sacrifices for its preservation. So the dispute was settled in 1820 by an agreement known as the Missouri Compromise, according to which it was decided that Missouri should be admitted with slavery, but that slavery should not be allowed in any other part of the northwestern country north of the southern boundary of Missouri.[1]

10. This compromise kept the slavery question out of Congress for many years. Look at the map of the United States for 1820 and you will see what each side yielded for the sake of the Union.

ATTEMPTS AT SLAVERY AGITATION.

11. The pioneer of the anti-slavery movement in America, Benjamin Lundy, did not propose to do anything contrary to the laws. A great part of his time was spent in the States where slavery existed. At Jonesborough, Tennessee, he published a paper called the *Emancipator* (1821). Lundy traveled thoughout North Carolina, speaking in many places. One of his meetings was held at Raleigh, the capital. Before he had left the State he had organized more than a dozen Abolition societies.

---

[1] Missouri, however, was not admitted until August 10, 1821. Meanwhile Alabama and Maine had been admitted—the former on December 14, 1819, and the latter on March 15 1820.

12. Lundy also lectured in Virginia and organized societies. The members of these various societies in North Carolina and Virginia were neither very numerous nor very influential. They were not molested, however, nor persecuted.

13. Up to 1830 there were frequent manumissions. In parts of the South the people were gradually freeing their slaves. The American Colonization Society, which had been organized in 1816, with Henry Clay as president, had members in almost every Southern State. In 1821 they organized on the coast of Africa the colony of Liberia, with Monrovia[1] as its capital. Liberia was founded as a home for negroes who should be set free by their masters. The plan was to form a free negro republic in Africa, with the hope that the negroes who had been Christianized as slaves would as freemen spread throughout that benighted region the truths of the Christian religion. Even as far south as Georgia there were men of influence who liberated their slaves and sent them to Liberia.

14. But William Lloyd Garrison of Massachusetts about 1829 began his work of agitation. Lundy did not go far enough to suit him. Lundy, before he finished his career, had become so aggressive as to give great offense and drew down upon himself persecution. He had been forced to cease from publishing any papers in any part of the South. But Garrison and his followers were so violent that they soon made the name Abolitionist hated not only in the South, but also in most parts of the North. He condemned colonization and gradual emancipation, and insisted that

[1] Named after President James Monroe, a Virginian and a slaveholder.

immediate and unconditional emancipation was the right of the slave and the duty of the master.

15. Garrison and his followers declared that there ought to be no Union with slaveholders, and proclaimed the Federal Constitution to be "A covenant with death and an agreement with hell." These men scattered throughout the country tracts filled with abuse of slaveholders. Some of these tracts fell into the hands of the negroes, and roused them to deeds of violence. At Southampton, Virginia, under the lead of Nat. Turner, the negroes started an insurrection, in which men, women and children were murdered in their beds.

16. The South was thoroughly aroused. Conservative men in the North denounced the Abolitionists and broke up their meetings. Those in the Southern States who had favored a gradual emancipation of the slaves changed their views. Up to 1835 free negroes with property were allowed to vote in North Carolina; but in that year North Carolina changed her State constitution and took from these free negroes the right to vote. Virginia passed laws forbidding free negroes to enter her borders. Even Ohio, a State which did not allow slavery, passed similar laws.

17. There were many men in the North opposed to slavery who did not sympathize with extreme men of the Garrison sort. But the conduct of the fanatics caused the people of the South to regard all anti-slavery men as belonging to the same class. In 1837 many efforts were made by Northern men to procure the abolition of slavery in the District of Columbia. Mr. Calhoun of South Carolina introduced into the Senate a series of resolutions to the effect that the

JOHN C. CALHOUN.

Federal Government was created by the States with a view to their increased security against all dangers, domestic as well as foreign; that the citizens of one State had no right to interfere with the domestic institutions of another State; and that the Federal Government had no right to interfere with slavery in either the States or the Territories of the Union. The Senate by a large majority adopted these resolutions.

18. In 1838 an attempt was made in the House of Representatives to renew the slavery agitation. But Mr. Atherton of New Hampshire introduced a series of resolutions, whose purport was that, under the Constitution of the United States, Congress had no right to interfere with slavery in the several States of the Confederacy; that Congress had no right to do indirectly what it could not do directly, and therefore should not interfere with slavery either in the District of Columbia or in the Territories. These resolutions were adopted by an overwhelming majority of the House of Representatives Henry Clay, who had warmly favored the resolutions, and most of the other public men of the country, hoped that this exciting agitation would now be abandoned.

19. But the Abolitionists cared nothing for the restraints of the Constitution. Neither of the great parties of the country was at this time connected with the anti-slavery agitators. The mass of the American people regarded the Abolitionists as men disloyal to the Constitution and as the foes of the Federal Union.

20. A Slaveholders' Convention met at Annapolis in Maryland in 1842 to consider what measures must

be taken to secure the safety of the Southern people. Considering the fact that the terrible massacres that had occurred in Hayti (one of the West Indies) were the work of free negroes, and that free negroes had been the fomenters of discord in many places, they concluded that the only security for the South lay in restricting the privileges of free negroes and in throwing greater restrictions around the slaves.

21. Thus the utter disregard of the restraints of the Constitution shown by the ultra Abolitionists of the Garrison type in their attack upon slaveholders, and their determination to effect their purpose regardless of consequences, alarmed the Southern people and put a complete stop to the idea of gradual emancipation, which, previous to their work, had begun to make considerable progress in the border Southern States.   The violent abuse of all slaveholders indulged in by the Abolitionists made it impossible for those Southern men, who really disliked the institution of slavery, to speak a word for even gradual emancipation, for fear that they should be regarded as the enemies of the South and the allies of the Abolitionists.   Without the work of the agitators the abolition of slavery would have been gradual and in some places long delayed, but it would have been free from that bitterness which estranged two great sections of our country and brought about the most dreadful war of the nineteenth century.

THE ANNEXATION OF TEXAS.

22. The acquisition of Texas was an event which had a very great influence on the slavery question and on the destinies of our country.   The great State of Texas, larger than the whole kingdom of France, had

JOHN TYLER.

been a possession of Spain,[1] and when Mexico gained her independence became a part of that country.   Before Mexico gained her independence Spain had encouraged immigration into Texas from the United States, and many Americans had settled there.   The Mexican Congress, in 1824, declared that, as soon as Texas had a sufficient population, it should be admitted as a State into the Mexican Union.

23. But soon after Santa Anna became President of Mexico he overthrew the Constitution of his country and made himself dictator.   He treated the American residents of Texas so badly that they rebelled and declared Texas an independent republic.   After a short but fierce struggle, in which victory inclined sometimes to one side and sometimes to the other, the Texans, under General Sam Houston, totally defeated the much larger Mexican army, led by Santa Anna, who, with nearly half his men, was captured.   A treaty was now made between Houston and Santa Anna, by which all the Mexican forces were withdrawn from the soil of Texas.   The independence of Texas was soon after acknowledged by France, Great Britain, and the United States.

24. In 1837 the Texans asked to be admitted into the American Union as a State.   But their application was not at this time granted, because Mexico still claimed the country.   But after seven years of waiting, during all which time Texas had maintained

[1] There was for some time a dispute between the United States and Spain about Texas, the former claiming it as a part of the Louisiana territory, but the latter insisting that the river Sabine formed the boundary between the possessions of Spain and the United States. When Spain ceded Florida to the United States and gave up all claim to any part of Oregon, the United States gave up all claim to Texas.

ZACHARY TAYLOR.

her independence and Mexico had made no attempt at conquest, another application was made by the Texans to the Government of the United States. John Tyler, then President of the United States, favored this application, but the Senate would not agree to it. So the annexation of Texas became the main issue in the presidential election of 1844.

25. It is frequently stated that the North opposed the annexation of Texas, and that the South favored it. But such a statement is not correct. The truth is that the great mass of the American people would have favored the acquisition of Texas, if they had thought that such acquisition would not involve the United States in a war with Mexico. The Democrats who favored immediate annexation asked what claim the Mexicans had to a country which had driven them out and had maintained its independence for nearly nine years without any effort on the part of the Mexican government to reconquer it. The Whigs, on the other hand, said that the boundary between Mexico and Texas was in dispute, and that if Texas were admitted into the Union before the question had been settled, her quarrel would become that of the United States also.

26. Many Northern men of both parties were opposed to the admission of Texas, on the ground that it would bring in another "slave State." But they were not in the majority. On the other hand, most Southern men desired the admission of Texas in order to preserve the balance of power between the "free" and "slave" States. But thousands of these were opposed to the admission of Texas, on the ground that it would cause a war with Mexico, the probable result of which

would be the acquisition of additional territory for the North and South to quarrel over.

27. Accordingly the Whig party opposed annexation and nominated Henry Clay of Kentucky for President, and Theodore Frelinghuysen of New Jersey, for Vice-President. This ticket was just as warmly supported in the South as in the North. Robert Toombs, of Georgia, at that time an ardent Whig, declared that he wished nothing done that would re-open the slavery quarrel, and said that he "would rather have the Union without Texas than Texas without the Union."

ROBERT TOOMBS.

28. The Democrats favored territorial expansion and were equally earnest in desiring the admission of Texas and in insisting upon the enforcement of the claims of the United States to every foot of Oregon.[1] They nominated James K. Polk

[1] The United States had long claimed Oregon on account of, 1st, the navigation of the Columbia River in 1789, by Captain Grey, of Boston. 2nd, as part of the Louisiana purchase of 1803. 3rd, the exploration of Lewis and Clarke in 1805, and 4th, the settlements of John Jacob Astor at Astoria, from 1809 to 1813. The United States claimed this country almost to Alaska; Great Britain claimed it to California. The dispute was settled in 1846 by adopting the 49th parallel as the boundary between the possessions of Great Britain and the United States.

of Tennessee, for President and George M. Dallas of Pennsylvania, for Vice-President.

29. In the election the Democrats triumphed, carrying the following states; Maine, New Hampshire, New York, Pennsylvania, Virginia, South Carolina, Georgia, Louisiana, Mississippi, Indiana, Illinois, Alabama, Missouri, Arkansas and Michigan. The following States voted for the Whig candidates; Massachusetts, Rhode Island, Connecticut, Vermont, New Jersey, Delaware, Maryland, North Carolina, Kentucky, Tennessee and Ohio. Thus we see seven Northern and eight Southern States voted for the Democrats who favored the annexation of Texas, while six Northern and five Southern States voted with the Whigs who opposed such annexation.

JAMES K. POLK.

30. Congress seeing that the people had decided in favor of annexation now passed a law providing for the admission of Texas. This was approved by President Tyler a few days before the expiration of his term of office (March 1st, 1845).[1]

---

[1] Texas was not fully admitted until during the first year of Polk's administration.

31. The Mexican government was greatly displeased because Texas had been admitted into the Union. The Mexicans claimed that Texas still belonged to them and declared their intention to drive the Americans beyond the Sabine. Mexico also asserted that the river Nueces was the western boundary of Texas, while Texas claimed to the Rio Grande. Both the United States and Mexico sent troops into the disputed territory. The result was the Mexican War, by which the United States acquired a vast additional territory.

DISPUTES OVER THE MEXICAN CESSION.

32. As the Whigs had feared, the gain of new territory reopened the dispute about slavery that had been settled by the Missouri Compromise of 1820. Before the close of the war with Mexico, Mr. Wilmot, of Pennsylvania, tried to get a law passed by Congress to the effect that slavery should not be allowed in any part of the territory to be acquired from Mexico. As a large part of this territory lay south of the line established by the Missouri Compromise, the Southern people claimed that the passage of any such law would be a refusal on the part of the North to stand by the obligations of that compromise. Each section of the Union had always shown a disposition to preserve a balance of power for the protection of its own interests, and it was perfectly natural that the Southern people should resist what they considered an exclusion of the South from all share in territory won by the common blood and treasure. They also urged that the carrying of slaves to new States was not an extension of slavery, because it did not make a single new slave. Southern Whigs and Democrats were united in these views.

33. Mr. Wilmot's proposed law (known as the Wilmot Proviso) did not pass; but the slavery question was made prominent in the debates on the admission of California and the formation of territorial governments for Utah and New Mexico. All the Southern members of Congress were willing to settle the question by a division of the public lands between the North and South according to the ideas of the Missouri Compromise. When the Northern members would not agree to this, the Southerners insisted that Congress should not interfere with the question of slavery, either in the territories or on the admission of new States.

THE COMPROMISE OF 1850.

34. The dangerous dispute was settled in September, 1850, by a compromise introduced by Mr. Clay of Kentucky. Its main provisions were that California should be admitted without slavery; that territorial governments should be organized for Utah and New Mexico without slavery restriction and with the declaration that, when either of them, or any part of them, should be admitted to the Union, their people should decide the question of slavery for themselves; and that a law should be passed making it a duty of the Federal Government to see that runaway slaves were arrested and returned to their masters. Daniel Webster of Massachusetts cordially assisted Mr. Clay in bringing about this settlement, known as the compromise of 1850.[1]

[1] Honorable Jefferson Davis of Mississippi, and some others opposed this compromise as a virtual repeal of the Missouri Compromise, of which Mr. Davis says: " Pacification had been the fruit borne by the tree, and it should not have been recklessly hewed down and cast into the fire."

DANIEL WEBSTER.

35. There was strong opposition to this compromise by some in the North and by some in the South, for different reasons; but the great majority of the people in both sections of the Union heartily endorsed it. So popular was the compromise of 1850, that in the presidential election of 1852 both political parties pledged themselves to stand by it. The Whig party, which had been successful in 1848, nominated Gen. Winfield Scott of Virginia, for President, and William A. Graham of North Carolina, for Vice-President. The Democrats nominated Franklin Pierce of New Hampshire, for President, and William R. King of Alabama, for Vice-President. In 1848 a new party had been formed, who called themselves Free Soilers. Their purpose was to refuse admission into the Union to any territory which might apply, having laws allowing slavery. This party would have nothing to do with the compromise of 1850, and nominated for the Presidency John P. Hale of New Hampshire, and for the Vice-Presidency George W. Julian of Indiana.

36. In the election which followed the Democrats gained an overwhelming victory, carrying every State but four. The Free Soil party did not carry a single State, and their vote was less than it had been in 1848.[1]

THE KANSAS AND NEBRASKA BILL.

37. In January, 1854, Mr. Douglas of Illinois, introduced a bill organizing territorial governments for Kansas and Nebraska. This bill provided that the people of these territories should decide the question

[1] The candidates of the Free Soil party in 1848 were Martin Van Buren of New York for President, and Charles Francis Adams of Massachusetts, for Vice-President.

of slavery for themselves. In framing it Mr. Douglas employed the exact language that had been used in forming Utah and New Mexico in 1850. Now, since Kansas and Nebraska were a part of the country embraced in the Louisiana purchase, lying north of 36° and 30', those who opposed the bill offered by Mr. Douglas declared that it was a repeal of the Missouri Compromise of 1820. The Democrats replied that their opponents had long since disregarded that compromise, and had persistently refused in 1850 to accept the extension of that line to the Pacific as a settlement of the slavery quarrel. They claimed that the compromise of 1850 had taken the place of that of 1820, and that the Kansas and Nebraska Bill only sought to carry out in good faith the policy established by the new compromise, which had been ratified by both the great political parties. The Southern Whigs and some of the Northern agreed with the Democrats. After much warm discussion the bill was passed by large majorities in both houses of Congress.[1]

38. The struggle for Kansas, which now began, greatly increased sectional bitterness. Settlers from North and South flocked into the Territory. In the North "Emigrant Aid Societies" were formed, whose business it was to see that what they called the "right kind of settlers" should control Kansas. They supplied the emigrants sent out by them with arms. Large numbers of armed Southerners, mostly from Missouri, also went into Kansas. Before long difficulties arose between these armed settlers from the North

[1] The Kansas and Nebraska Bill was afterwards called the Squatter Sovereignty Law.

and the South, and a state of anarchy, knows as the "Kansas War," continued for several years.

NEW PARTIES.

39. The Whig party was now completely broken up. Most of its Southern members joined the Democrats. Many of the Northern Whigs and a few Anti-Slavery Democrats united with the Free Soilers in forming a new party, under the name of National Republicans. In their convention, which met in Philadelphia (June 17th, 1856), they declared it to be the duty of Congress to prohibit in the Territories what they called "those twin relics of barbarism—polygamy and slavery." Thus Southern slaveholders were classed by them with the polygamists of Utah.[1] The Republicans nominated John C. Fremont of California for President and William L. Dayton of New Jersey for Vice-President. Many of the Abolitionists, who had for years been trying to carry out their plans regardless of what might be the effect upon the interests of the South, also allied themselves with the new Republican party.

40. American was the name adopted by another new party, consisting of some of the former Whigs of the North and the South. The main features of this party were opposition to alien suffrage and to the election to office of Roman Catholics and men of foreign birth. They abandoned, however, their opposition to Roman Catholics, but insisted that the laws should be so changed as to require foreigners to remain in this

---

[1] Utah had been settled by large numbers of Mormons, followers of a man named Joseph Smith. The Mormons held as part of their religious belief, that a man should marry as many wives as he could support. Joseph Smith, the founder of the Mormon sect, was born in Sharon, Vermont, December 23d, 1805.

country a much longer time than was then required before being allowed to vote. The American party pledged itself to stand by the Compromise of 1850, and nominated Millard Fillmore of New York for President, and Andrew J. Donelson of Tennessee for Vice-President.[1]

41. The Democratic party pledged itself to stand by the Compromise of 1850, and the interpretation put upon it by them in the Kansas and Nebraska act of 1854. They nominated James Buchanan of Pennsylvania for President and John C. Breckinridge of Kentucky for Vice-President. In the election which followed the Democrats were triumphant carrying nineteen States. The Republicans carried eleven States, and the Americans one. Thus the people of the United States had again endorsed the Compromise of 1850 and the Democratic interpretation of it.

42. But the evil day had only been deferred for a while. A purely Northern party, though it styled itself "National," had developed unlooked-for strength in the recent election. Though the new "Republican" party declared that it did not intend to interfere with African slavery where it already existed, its leaders proclaimed an irrepressible conflict between "freedom and slavery," and were as abusive of all slave-holders as the most violent Abolitionists had ever been.

45. Clay and Webster, who had so long stood as peace-makers between the sections were dead. John C. Calhoun, who, though an ardent Southerner and de-

---

[1] The Old Line Whigs, who desired that the old line 36° 30′ be made the dividing line between the free and slave states, held a convention, but made no nomination except to endorse the candidates of the American party.

JAMES BUCHANAN.

fender of State sovereignty, loved the Union, and had heartily seconded the efforts of Clay and Webster in behalf of peace, was also dead.

44. The Fugitive Slave Law, which was one of the features of the compromise of 1850, greatly increased sectional animosity. Though it only sought to carry out a plain provision of the Constitution, it met with bitter opposition. The legislatures of several Northern States passed acts which nullified the law. Thus the attempt to enforce by Federal authority the provision contained in the second section of the fourth article of the Constitution produced "evils greater than those it was intended to correct."[1]

45. The plan of leaving the question of slavery to the white inhabitants of a territory as adopted by the compromise of 1850 and the Kansas and Nebraska Act of 1854, had only produced discord, and a state of war in Kansas. A decision of the Supreme Court of the United States (seven of the nine judges who composed it concurring) was rendered in 1857 to the effect, that Congress had no power to prohibit slavery in any of the Territories of the Union. But the anti-slavery agitators denounced the decision and utterly disregarded it.

46. **The John Brown Raid,** which occurred in October, 1859, greatly increased the bitter feeling between the North and South. A man by the name of John Brown had become notorious in the "Kansas War," where outrages of all sorts had been committed by both parties. He was so bitter against slavery that he determined to stir up the slaves to rebel against their

[1] See ' Rise and Fall of the Confederate Government," by Jefferson Davis, Volume I., page 17.

masters.   So with a few followers he seized upon the arsenal at Harper's Ferry, hoping to arm the slaves and lead them to war.   But none of them came to his help.   He and his associates were captured by the United States Marines, led By Colonel Robert E. Lee. They were tried and condemned by the laws of Virginia, and on the gallows paid the penalty of their crime.

47. Though the great majority of the Northern people condemned the conduct of Brown, some of the officials in States under the control of the Republican party publicly applauded that conduct.   The authorities of Iowa and Ohio refused to surrender fugitives from justice charged with murder and with participating in this raid.

The Election of 1860.

48. As the election of 1860 drew near, there was a serious split in the Democratic party.   One wing of the party declared that Congress had no right to interfere with slavery in any territory, but that the question should be left entirely to the white inhabitants of each territory.   The candidates of this wing were Stephen A. Douglas of Illinois, for President, and Herschel V. Johnson of Georgia, for Vice-President. The other wing of the Democratic party declared that Congress was bound to protect the right of every citizen of the United States to go into any territory with any species of property including slaves, and that when the territory formed a constitution for admission into the Union, then the white inhabitants of said territory could decide whether they would allow slavery or not.   The candidates of this wing were John C.

ABRAHAM LINCOLN.

HARPER'S FERRY.

Breckinridge of Kentucky for President, and Joseph Lane of Oregon, for Vice-President.

49. The American party nominated John Bell of Tennessee for President and Edward Everett of Massachusetts, for Vice-President. This party declared that it stood for the Constitution of the Country, the Union of the States, and the enforcement of the laws. The American party exerted but little influence in the election, because it did not touch the question at issue.

50. The Republican party, which embraced in its ranks not only Free Soilers, but also Abolitionists, declared that it was the duty of Congress to prohibit slavery in every territory. The candidates of this party were Abraham Lincoln of Illinois for President, and Hannibal Hamlin of Maine for Vice-President.

51. The conservative elements of the country were hopelessly divided, and accordingly the Republicans elected their ticket. Of the popular vote Mr. Lincoln received 1,857,610; Mr. Douglass, 1,365,976; Mr. Breckinridge, 847,953, and Mr. Bell, 590,631. The total conservative vote was 2,804,560. Had all the conservatives of the country stood together Mr. Lincoln would have been defeated. He was the first President of the United States elected exclusively by a single section of the Union.

52. The success of the party which had ever since its organization made slavery the chief issue in national politics thoroughly alarmed the South. In Part III. we will show how the success of this party caused the secession of eleven Southern States, and will give an account of the tremendous conflict between the States of the American Union.

PART III.

The Formation of the Confederate Government. The War between the States and its Results.

Section I.—Events of 1861.

CHAPTER I.

SECESSION OF SEVEN SOUTHERN STATES—FORMATION OF
THE CONFEDERATE GOVERNMENT—EFFORTS AT RECON-
CILIATION.

HE alarm in the South at the success of the
Republican party was perfectly natural.   In
1848 the Free Soil party had for the first time
entered into a presidential contest.   They polled at
that time a total vote of 291,342.   In 1852 the Free
Soilers polled only 155,825, or a little more than half
their vote of 1848.   In 1856, by constant agitation of
the slavery question, they had so aroused the people
of the North against what they called the aggressions
of the slave power that they succeeded in forming a
new party, which embraced a majority of the former
Whigs of the North, the Free Soilers and the Abolitionists.   To this new party they gave the name
"National Republicans."   It was a purely sectional
party, having no following outside of the North.   In
the presidential election of 1856 it had carried eleven
Northern States and had polled 1,341,264 votes.   And
now, in 1860, it had become strong enough to elect a
President by the vote of Northern States alone.[1]

2. As soon as the result of the election was known,
South Carolina called a convention of the people,
which on the 20th of December, 1860, passed an ordi-

[1] The Republicans were in a minority in the new Congress.   But such
had been the wonderful growth of that party that the majority of the
Southern people felt that, unless some new guarantees could be given
them, there was no safety for the South in the Union.

nance of secession, declaring that the union existing between South Carolina and the other States was dissolved. Congress had met seventeen days before this action was taken by South Carolina (December 3d). On the opening day of Congress every State was represented in the House, and all were represented in the

SECESSION HALL, CHARLESTON, SOUTH CAROLINA.

Senate except South Carolina, whose senators had resigned as soon as the result of the presidential election was known. Hopes were still cherished that something might be done to restore fraternal feeling and save the Union.

3. Mr. Crittenden of Kentucky proposed an amendment to the Constitution restoring the old line of the
Missouri Compromise, but his proposition failed. A
committee of thirteen, appointed in the Senate to find
some plan of agreement, failed. A like committee of
thirty-three in the House also failed to accomplish
anything.

4. Mr. Douglas of Illinois, who had been a member
of the Senate committee, stated in the Senate that Mr.
Davis of Mississippi and Mr. Toombs of Georgia had
shown their willingness to resume the Missouri Compromise as a measure of conciliation, and urged upon
the Republicans, as they had rejected every proposition, to make a positive declaration of their purposes.
Mr. Seward, a prominent Republican of New York,
was present in the Senate. He had in 1858 announced
the "irrepressible conflict," and in the same year,
speaking of Abolitionism, had said: "It has driven
you back in California and Kansas; it will invade
your soil." Mr. Seward made no response to the
appeal of Mr. Douglas. The trouble was that the two
great sections of the Union had become hostile to each
other, and neither side could look at the question from
the standpoint of the other.

5. On the 9th of January, 1861, Mississippi passed
an ordinance of secession. In the fall of 1860, after
the presidential election, Governor Pettus of Mississippi invited the senators and representatives of that
State in Congress to meet him at Jackson, the State
capital, so that he might consult with them about
the character of the message that he should send
to the legislature which he had summoned to meet
in extra session. In the conference with the gov-

ernor Mr. Davis opposed immediate and separate State action, declaring himself opposed to secession as long as the hope of a peaceful remedy remained. He said, however, that he would feel himself bound by the action of his State. On receipt of official information of the action of his State (January 21st), Mr. Davis, in a speech which, while justifying the action of Mississippi, was full of expressions of kindly feeling, bade farewell to the Senate of the United States.

ALEXANDER H. STEPHENS.

6. On January 10th, 1861, Florida seceded. The same step was taken by Alabama on the 11th, by Georgia on the 19th, by Louisiana on the 26th, and by Texas on the 1st of February. Mr. Stephens of Georgia, while believing in the right of secession, had

exerted all his influence against it.   He felt himself bound to abide by the action of his State.

7. The Southern people could never have been induced to go into secession, had they not believed that there was neither safety nor peace for the South in the Union.   The majority of them had come to the conclusion that peace with two governments was better than a Union of discordant States.

8. The doctrine of secession was no new doctrine. The Honorable Timothy Pickering of Massachusetts, in 1803, while opposing the purchase of Louisiana, had advised the formation of a Northern Confederacy. Again, in 1812, Honorable Josiah Quincy, while opposing the admission of Louisiana, had declared the right of a State to secede, and had threatened that the New England States would exercise that right.   Again, in 1844, the legislature of Massachusetts adopted a resolution declaring in behalf of that State, "that it is determined, as it doubts not the other States are, to submit to undelegated powers in no body of men on earth," and that "the project of the annexation of Texas, unless arrested on the threshold, may tend to drive these States[1] into a dissolution of the Union."

9. Peaceable secession was hoped for by many in the South.   The ground of this hope was their implicit belief in the right of a State to secede.   Many prominent men in the North, even some of the Abolitionists, ackowledged it.   In the early days of the Republic the majority of the American people believed in it.

10. In the convention which framed the Constitution of the United States a proposition was made to

___

[1] The New England States are meant.

allow the use of force against a State which might violate its obligations.   On this proposition Mr. Madison said that "the use of force against a State would look more like a declaration of war than an infliction of punishment, and would probably be considered by the party attacked as a dissolution of all previous compacts, by which it might have been bound."   The convention refused to confer the power to coerce a State, and so that proposition was lost

11. In 1860 and 1861 there were many in the North who did not believe in the right of the government to coerce a State.   Even the New York *Tribune*, a leading organ of the Abolitionists, declared that "if the cotton States wished to withdraw from the Union, they should be allowed to do so;" that "any attempt to compel them to remain by force would be contrary to the principles of the Declaration of Independence and to the fundamental ideas upon which human liberty is based;" and that "if the Declaration of Independence justified the secession from the British Empire of three millions of subjects in 1776, it was not seen why it would not justify the secession of five millions of Southerners from the Union in 1861."   Again, the same journal declared that it would "let the Union slide" rather than to "compromise with the South and abandon the Chicago platform."   Many prominent Northern men in public speeches expressed themselves as opposed to coercion.   Is it any wonder, then, that many in the South hoped for peaceable secession?

12. The organization of the government of the Confederate States took place at Montgomery, Alabama, in February.   The convention of delegates from the

INAUGURATION OF PRESIDENT DAVIS.

seceding States met in that city on the 4th of February, 1861. The delegates from Texas did not arrive until after the opening of the convention. A new Constitution, modelled after that of the United States, was formed by this convention, and a new Union was organized under the name of the Confederate States of America. Jefferson Davis of Mississippi, was elected President, and Alexander H. Stephens of Georgia, Vice-President.

13. **Slavery in the Confederate Constitution.**—Of course the Confederate Constitution recognized property in slaves. It at the same time forbade the African Slave Trade, or the bringing of negroes into the Confederacy from any foreign country other than the slave-holding States or territories of the United States of America.

14. A great deal has been said by the enemies of the South about the aggressions of the slave power. The Southern people always felt that the aggression was entirely on the other side. The most extreme Southerner had never asked for more than protection to himself in the right to carry with him into the common territories of the Union any property that he might possess including slaves, with the understanding, however, that when the territory adopted a constitution and applied for admission into the Union as a State, it could exclude slavery if it chose. All that he asked was that his Northern brethren should not interfere either directly or indirectly with the institutions of the South.

15 **The Peace Congress.**—Virginia made still another special effort to bring about a reconciliation between the North and the South by calling for a Peace Con-

gress of all the States to meet at Washington. Twenty
States responded to this call, thirteen Northern and
seven Southern. Ex-President John Tyler was chosen

JEFFERSON DAVIS.

presiding officer. But every offer of compromise
was voted down by the Northern delegates. So the
Peace Congress adjourned without accomplishing
anything.

16. Seizure of Forts and Arsenals.—The Confederate
authorities proceeded to occupy such forts and
arsenals as were peaceably surrendered to them, but

made no attack upon those held by United States troops.[1]

17. Confederate Peace Commissioners.—The Confederate Government sent commissioners to Washington to try and make a peaceful settlement of all questions at issue. Mr. Buchanan received them as private gentlemen, but not as embassadors from the Confederate government. He held that a State could not secede, but that at the same time the government had no power to coerce a State.

[1] Fort Sumter in Charleston Harbor, Fort Pickens at Pensacola, and the forts near Key West, Florida, were held by garrisons of Federal troops. The desire to settle everything peaceably prevented the Southern people from making any attack upon these forts.

CHAPTER II.

THE BEGINNING OF THE WAR—SECESSION OF FOUR OTHER
STATES—THE CAMPAIGN IN WEST VIRGINIA.

THE inauguration of Abraham Lincoln took place on the 4th of March, 1861. In his inaugural he declared his intention to collect the public revenues at the ports of the seceding States, and to recover the forts, arsenals and all other public property before held by the Federal authorities.

2. The Confederate commissioners[1] now addressed a note to Mr. Seward, the new Secretary of State (March 12th, 1861), saying that the Confederate States wished a peaceful settlement of all questions. They declared that it was neither the interest nor the wish of the seceding States to injure in any way the States lately united with them, or to demand anything that was not just. Mr. Seward replied that he was in favor of peace, and that Fort Sumter, in Charleston Harbor, would be evacuated in less than ten days. He assured the commissioners that notice would be given of any change either at Fort Sumter or at Fort Pickens in Florida.[2]

3. A fleet of seven vessels was meanwhile being fitted out at New York, and at Norfolk, Virginia. When the commissioners heard of this and inquired about it, Mr. Seward's answer in writing was, "Faith

[1] The Confederate Commissioners were John Forsyth of Alabama, Martin J. Crawford of Georgia, and Andrew B. Roman of Louisiana.

[2] Mr. Seward did not receive the commissioners officially, but communicated with them verbally and informally through Justice John A. Campbell of the Supreme Court of the United States.

as to Sumter fully kept, wait and see." At this very time the fleet was on its way to reinforce the fort. Mr. Seward did not notify the commissioners; but a written notice was sent by the government without date or signature, which was read to Governor Pickens of South Carolina (April 8th) by Mr. Chew of the

ATTACK ON FORT SUMTER FROM MORRIS ISLAND.

State Department, to the effect that the garrison in Fort Sumter would be supplied with provisions, peaceably, if permitted, forcibly, if necessary.

4. It was now evident that nothing was left to the Confederates but to attack the fort or back squarely down.[1] When the Confederate authorities heard of

[1] Horace Greeley, in his "American Conflict," admits the same when he says "whether the bombardment of Fort Sumter shall or shall not be justified by posterity, it is clear that the Confederacy had no alternative but its own dissolution." Yet after that statement he condemned the Confederates.

the approach of the fleet they ordered General Beauregard, their commander at Charleston, to demand of Major Anderson the surrender of the fort. Major Anderson refused to comply. Other fruitless efforts were made to secure the evacuation of the fort.

5. **The bombardmemt of Fort Sumter** began on April 12th, 1861. The Confederate authorities had in their desire for peace waited until the last possible moment before ordering the bombardment. At the very moment when General Beauregard gave Major Anderson the final notice of his intention to open fire, the fleet sent by the United States Government was lying off the mouth of the harbor and prevented from entering only by a gale. After a furious bombardment, during which the fort was set on fire by bursting shells, Major Anderson surrendered. The Confederates allowed the garrison to salute their flag and take it with them, departing with all the honors of war.

6. **A striking incident** occurred just before the surrender. Louis T. Wigfall, an ex-senator of Texas, seeing the fort on fire, and believing that the brave garrison was still struggling merely for the honor of its flag, went under fire in an open boat to the fort, and climbing through one of its embrasures asked for Major Anderson and begged him to desist from the hopeless fight, offering to him the same terms that had been proposed before his position had been rendered so desperate. Though Wigfall had acted without authority, upon Major Anderson's acceptance of the terms they were promptly ratified by General Beauregard.[1]

[1] Strange to say no life was lost during this fierce bombardment. The only casualty occurred when the garrison saluted the flag, as it was hauled down the day after the surrender. At that time one man was killed and several wounded by the bursting of a gun.

7. **The news of the battle of Fort Sumter** produced great excitement everywhere. On April 15th President Lincoln issued a proclamation calling for seventy-five thousand troops, and convening Congress to meet in extra session on the 4th of July. The Confederate President met this call of Mr. Lincoln's by a call for volunteers to repel aggressions. The North claimed that the South had begun the war by firing on Fort Sumter. The Confederates claimed that the government had commenced the war by sending a hostile fleet with the avowed intention of reinforcing the fort, thus leaving to the South no alternative but the reduction of Sumter, or the surrender of the city of Charleston.

8. **Four other States Secede.**—The border slave States had not seceded, preferring to remain in the Union. But when Mr. Lincoln called on them for their ratio of troops to coerce the seceding States, Virginia passed an ordinance of secession (April 17th). Her example was followed by Arkansas (May 6th), North Carolina (May 20th), and Tennessee (June 8th). These States seceded rather than countenance the policy of coercion, which they believed to be contrary to the principles of the Declaration of Independence and unwarranted by the Constitution of the United States. In Delaware, Kentucky, Maryland and Missouri secession encountered such strong opposition, that those States remained in the Union. The accession of Virginia, Arkansas, North Carolina and Tennessee greatly strengthened the new Confederacy.

9. **Sincerity of the Opposing Parties.**—Each party to the dreadful conflict thus begun believed firmly in the justice of its cause. The United States Govern-

ment declared that it did not wage the war for conquest or for the purpose of interfering with the established institutions of the Southern States, but merely to preserve the Union. The Confederates declared that they only wished to exercise the right claimed in the Declaration of Independence for any people to change their government whenever in their judgment their interests demanded it. They certainly did not fight, as has been wrongly said, to destroy the government. They earnestly desired peace, and fought only to maintain what they believed to be their right to secede and form a new confederacy. They did not appeal to arms, and did not fight until they were forced to do so in self-defense. They no more sought to destroy the government than did the American colonies in the War of the Revolution seek to destroy the British Empire.

10. The people of the seceding States would never have withdrawn from the Union, if they had not come to the conclusion that there was neither peace nor safety for the South in the Union. They believed that only in this way could they maintain

CONFEDERATE FLAG.

constitutional liberty. They showed their love for the old Constitution by taking it as the model for the new one, and their love for the old flag by adopting one as near like it as possible.

11. **Comparative Strength of the Combatants.**—The population of the States that remained in the Union, including West Virginia, which separated from Virginia, was in round numbers 23,000,000. Within the limits of the Confederate States were about 8,500,000, of whom 5,000,000 were whites and the rest negro slaves. Though the States of Kentucky, Missouri, and Maryland remained in the Union, many of their people sympathized with the Confederates, and each of these States furnished some soldiers to the Confederate armies, as did West Virginia also. These, however, were nearly, if not entirely, balanced by those who went into the Union army from some parts of the seceding States, as from East Tennessee, Northern Arkansas, and some other places.

12. **In the matter of arms** the North had an immense advantage over the South. All the foundries for the manufacture of arms, except one cannon foundry at Richmond, were in the Northern States, and in their armories were stored all the new and improved weapons of war. The Southern States had arsenals, but in them were only arms of the old and rejected models. The South had no powder factories, no navy to protect her ports, and no merchant ships for foreign commerce. One hundred and fifty thousand small arms were all that could be found in the Southern Confederacy, including both sides of the Mississippi. Nearly all the muskets were the old flint-lock altered to percussion. If soldiers enough were called into the field to handle these arms there would not be ten rounds of ammunition to the man. During the first year of the war there were not arms enough in the Confederate States to supply the men who desired to enter the army.

SERGEANT COLLIER'S BRAVE ACT.

"While the fuse was still smoking, and the men were flying from the danger of the apprehended explosion, Sergeant Isaac P. Collier, of Company K, Fifth Regiment, Georgia Volunteers, seized the projectile and threw it out of the ditch."

13. **The Slaves During the War.**—The conduct of the slaves during the war gives strong proof of the kind feeling that existed between them and their masters. The great majority of them remained on the plantations and by their labor supplied the armies in the field. Many negro men went with their young masters to war, faithfully waited on them, nursed them when sick, and, if they died in camp or in battle, returned with the lifeless bodies to lay them beside their kindred dead in the family burying-ground.

14. The fidelity of the slaves was due to the fact that most masters treated them kindly. Their toil was not unrequited, for they were supplied with whatever they needed and were cared for in sickness and in old age. Many of them were allowed opportunities for making money for themselves. Much attention had always been given to their religious instruction. Southern ladies labored for the conversion of their slaves. Missionaries sent by the Southern churches preached to them on the plantations. In malarial districts, where negroes only could live with safety, some of these devoted missionaries laid down their lives. The negroes had churches of their own in the towns and on many of the plantations. In the churches of the whites there were always galleries set apart for them, and in the city churches it was often difficult to say which were the better dressed, the masters or the slaves.

15. The activity of the Abolitionists in scattering their tracts caused the Southern States to enact very strict laws against teaching the negroes to read and write. Yet many of them were taught by their young masters and mistresses, and in the churches on the

Sabbath could be seen many slaves who had hymn books and knew how to use them. Your author has seen in the Sunday school room of Trinity Methodist Church in Charleston, South Carolina, and of St. Paul's Episcopal Church in Augusta, Georgia,[1] negro Sabbath Schools taught by the best ladies and gentlemen of those cities. At Lexington, in Virginia, Major Thomas J. Jackson, afterwards the noted "Stonewall" Jackson, was the superintendent of a negro Sunday School. One of the largest churches of Charleston was a negro Presbyterian Church, whose pastor, Dr. Girardeau, a celebrated preacher, and learned gentleman, could never be induced to leave it for any other charge.

16. Thus there were many ties of affection between the races. There were ills connected with slavery which the good people of the South tried faithfully to remedy. The best and kindest of masters firmly believed that the freedom of the large number of negroes who lived in the South would bring ruin to master and slave alike, and many of the slaves themselves shared in this feeling. It was the kindly sentiment that prevailed between the ruling and the servile class that prevented the latter from being a menace to the South, when the vast armies of the North were thundering at the gates of her cities, or ravaging her fields.

THE COUNTRY HURRYING INTO WAR.

17. As soon as Virginia joined the Southern Confederacy the capital of the Confederate States was moved from Montgomery, Alabama, to Richmond,

[1] Both of these were churches for white people.

CAPITOL OF THE CONFEDERACY AT RICHMOND.

Virginia. Eager volunteers from all over the South were sent to Virginia to defend that State from threatened invasion. Soldiers from the North were likewise hurried forward to the Virginia border.

18. Though Maryland did not secede, a strong effort was made by those in sympathy with the South to prevent Union troops from going through that State to invade Virginia. On the 19th of April a Massachusetts regiment, passing through Baltimore, was attacked by the citizens and several lives were lost on both sides. This was on the 86th anniversary of the battle of Lexington.[1]

19. The first conflict of arms in Eastern Virginia occurred near[2] Big Bethel Church, not far from Fortress Monroe. In this affair the Union troops, who formed a part of the force of General Benjamin F. Butler, were defeated by the Confederates, led by Colonel D. H. Hill (June 10th, 1861).

THE LAUREL HILL CAMPAIGN (WEST VIRGINIA).

20. When the ordinance of secession passed by the Virginia Convention was submitted to the people, it was ratified by a very large majority of the voters of the whole State; but the majority of the people of that part of Virginia lying west of the Alleghanies refused to abide by the decision of their State, and gladly welcomed the Union soldiers, who, under the command of General George B. McClellan, crossed the

---

[1] On the 24th of May a New York regiment, led by Colonel Ellsworth, took possession of Alexandria, Va. On entering the place Ellsworth was shot by a Mr. J. W. Jackson, who was also immediately slain.

[2] In this battle was killed Henry Wyatt, of Edgecombe County, N. C., the first Southern soldier slain in the war.

Ohio into Western Virginia. The whole force under McClellan, including reinforcements of West Virginians, amounted to 20,000 men.

21. A small Confederate force advanced to the Baltimore and Ohio railroad, a little west of Grafton, and destroyed some railroad bridges, thus cutting off communication between the West and Washington City. On the 29th of May two West Virginia Union regiments under Colonel (afterwards General) B. F. Kelley, approached Grafton, whereupon the Confederates withdrew southward to Philippi. Here the Confederate force, less than a thousand strong, under Colonel G. A. Porterfield was surprised on a dark and stormy night (June 3d) by three thousand Union troops, under General Kelley. Porterfield, by his coolness and courage, succeeded in getting his routed force safely off, and retreated to Beverly, some thirty miles farther to the southeast.

22. General Robert E. Lee, at that time Major-General of Virginia volunteers, had sent Brigadier-General Robert S. Garnett to Beverly, and Brigadier-General Henry A. Wise into the Valley of the Kanawha. General Garnett, with some Virginia regiments, moved out from Beverly and took post on Laurel Hill, a spur of the ridge known as Laurel Mountain. Here he was soon joined by the First Georgia regiment. The Staunton and Parkersburg turnpike divides at Beverly, one branch of it following the Tygart river to Philippi, and passing over Laurel Hill, the other branch of the road passing over a saddle in Rich Mountain and leading to Parkersburg. Garnett regarded the two positions at Rich Mountain and Laurel Hill as the gates to all the region beyond.

23. Garnett's whole force numbered 4,500 men. Thinking the position at Rich Mountain the stronger, he entrenched there 1,300 of his men and four cannon under Lieutenant-Colonel Pegram. The balance of his force, under his immediate command, he placed in a fortified position at Laurel Hill, where he also had four cannon, one of which was rifled.

24. Early in July McClellan ordered General Morris to march to a position one and a half miles in front of Laurel Hill, while he with the rest of his force advanced to Roaring Creek, about two miles from Colonel Pegram's position on Rich Mountain. The Union troops were resisted by skirmishers only. The Confederates were aware of McClellan's great superiority in numbers, and preferred to await his attack in their fortified position. The discomfort of the soldiers on both sides was greatly increased by frequent rains.[1]

25. At daybreak on the 11th of July General Rosecrans, guided by a West Virginia Unionist named Hart, started to lead a strong column of infantry from McClellan's army around Pegram's left flank and about two miles in rear of his position. Rosecrans reached the desired point early in the afternoon, and after a three hours' combat broke through the small force guarding that place; but reinforcements from Pegram's front line enabled the Confederates to hold out until night. At daybreak of the 12th Rose-

---

[1] While Garnett's command was at Laurel Hill a Georgia soldier meeting a Virginia mountaineer said: " Don't you think we are going to have a drouth? " " Why so? " asked the countryman. " Because," said the Georgian, " we haven't had any rain for about three hours."

crans found the position on Rich Mountain abandoned, but did not pursue until he could communicate with McClellan. Part of Pegram's force escaped and fled southward through Beverly. Pegram himself, with nearly six hundred men, was cut off from escape and surrendered to McClellan on the 13th.

26. Let us now see what had been going on at Laurel Hill. While Rosecrans was making his attack at

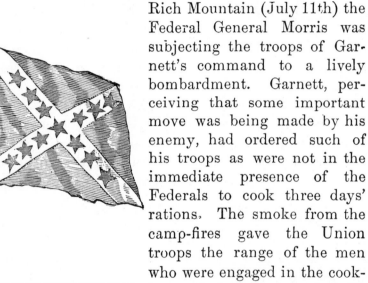

Rich Mountain (July 11th) the Federal General Morris was subjecting the troops of Garnett's command to a lively bombardment. Garnett, perceiving that some important move was being made by his enemy, had ordered such of his troops as were not in the immediate presence of the Federals to cook three days' rations. The smoke from the camp-fires gave the Union troops the range of the men who were engaged in the cook-

CONFEDERATE BATTLE FLAG.

ing, and the bursting of shells made their work quite hazardous. But with the coolness of veterans the men went on with their work. A man would place on the fire a frying-pan containing bacon or flap-jacks. At the sound of a whistling shell he would run behind some large rock for protection; then after the shell had burst, hurrying to the pan he would gather its contents, replenish it, and again take refuge from an approaching bomb. All the while the men were laughing and joking, as if no danger were nigh. About sundown Garnett was seated in front of his tent eating his supper. A bursting bomb threw a clod of dirt into his cup of coffee Emptying his cup he called to his servant to refill it and then went on with his supper, as if nothing had happened.

27. Late in the evening Garnett was notified that Rich Mountain could no longer be held. Accordingly he gave orders for the immediate evacuation of Laurel Hill. In a pouring rain, which had continued almost without intermission since the previous morning, the Confederates began their retreat to Beverly, sixteen miles distant from Laurel Hill, and only five miles from Rich Mountain. If they could reach Beverly ahead of McClellan they could march on and seize Cheat Mountain Pass, which they could hold against a force many times larger than their own. When within five miles of Beverly, Garnett was falsely informed that the Union troops had occupied that place. If Garnett had known the true state of affairs he might have continued southward through Beverly almost at leisure for McClellan's troops did not enter the town until past noon of the 12th.

28. Believing his information correct Garnett retraced his steps almost to his abandoned camp, and leaving the turnpike at Leadsville turned off upon an almost impassable road over Cheat Mountain into the valley of the Cheat river, following the stream northward towards St. George, in the forlorn hope of turning the mountains at the north end of the ridges and thus regaining his communications.

29. The Federal pursuit was not vigorous on the 12th. On the morning of the 13th, the column of

General Morris began the pursuit in earnest and over-took Garnett's army about noon. At Carrick's Ford quite a sharp combat occurred. A mile or two farther on, while the skirmishing was light, Garnett was killed, while withdrawing his skirmishers from a pile of driftwood which he had used as a barricade. One of his cannon which had stuck in the mud and about forty wagons fell into Morris's hands.

30. The direct pursuit was now abandoned, but McClellan dispatched to the Union General, C. W. Hill, to collect the forces along the Baltimore and Ohio railroad and prevent the Confederates from passing around the northern spurs of the mountains. The Confederates, now led by Colonels Ramsey and Talia-ferro, marched all night, and at daylight passed Red House.[1] By the time that Hill's advance reached this point the Southerners had turned the mountains and were moving southward on fairly good roads. Hill seeing that it was useless to try to overtake them, stopped the pursuit. Garnett's half-famished force, moving now through a friendly country, found no farther difficulty in getting all necessary supplies. When they reached Monterey they found reinforce-ments under General Henry R. Jackson of Georgia. At Monterey they rested for several weeks before

Red House was a road-side inn. Here some of the hungry Confeder-ates succeeded in getting one or two battercakes apiece. Just after passing Red House four or five West Virginia Unionists, who had cap-tured three straggling Confederates, mistaking Garnett's men for Feder-al troops, came up to the Southerners with the announcement that they had some "rebel" prisoners, and that they had some good news besides. They then proceeded to tell how McClellan had cut Garnett's army to pieces (a great exaggeration) and had cap ured 600 "rebels." What was their chagrin when their arms were taken from them and they them-selves put under the guardianship of their late captives?

breaking camp to begin a new campaign in West Virginia.

31. On the day of the combat at Carrick's Ford the larger portion of six companies of the First Georgia regiment became separated from the main body of the army. Concealed behind the thick mountain undergrowth, they watched the army of General Morris march by, and then started over the pathless mountains to escape to the southeast, if possible. After wandering about for three days without food, trying to appease their hunger by chewing the inner bark of the laurel trees, they were rescued by a Virginia mountaineer named Parsons. He took them to his own farm, where, with the assistance of his neighbors, he slew several beeves and gave food to the starving Georgians. After resting and filling their haversacks, they resumed their march under the guidance of Parsons, who led them safe to the Confederate camp at Monterey.

32. The Laurel Hill campaign, though productive of no great battles, with long lists of killed and wounded, had sorely tried the courage and fortitude of raw troops. Well had they stood the test. The unlucky termination of the campaign might have caused discouragement to the Confederates but for their brilliant triumph in another quarter.

CHAPTER III.

THE CAMPAIGN OF THE FIRST MANASSAS (BULL RUN)—
OTHER EVENTS IN VIRGINIA AND WEST VIRGINIA.

THROUGHOUT all of Virginia east of the Alleghanies the people espoused heartily the cause of the South.   Before the close of May General Robert E. Lee, at that time Major-General of Virginia forces, had organized, equipped and sent into the field more than 30,000 men.   During the month of June the Federal plan of operations became evident, and the Confederate line of defense was developed.   In addition to the advance by McClellan into West Virginia the authorities at Washington determined upon the capture of Richmond as the most speedy way to subdue the South.

2. The Confederate authorities were very diligent and active in preparations to defend Virginia at every point.   Soon after the secession of Virginia the State authorities had seized Harper's Ferry in the northeast, and in the southeast had occupied Portsmouth and Norfolk, with the navy-yard.   The Confederate Government hurried troops to Virginia from every part of the Confederacy.   By the last of June the total Confederate effective strength in Virginia was about 65,000 men.   Of these 5,000 were in West Virginia under Garnett, 15,000 were in the Shenandoah Valley under General Joseph E. Johnston, 20,000 were near and about Manassas under General Beauregard, 8,000 were at Aquia Creek and on the lower Potomac under General T. H. Holmes, while the rest

were under Magruder at Yorktown and Huger at Norfolk. At the same time the Union or Federal troops aggregated at least 100,000—part under Butler at Fortress Monroe, part under McDowell at Washington, some under Patterson at Williamsport on the

COLONEL R. E. LEE.

upper Potomac, and the rest under McClellan in West Virginia.

3. McClellan began his campaign, as we have seen, early in July. Patterson began his campaign about the same time. As he advanced towards Martinsburg, Johnston abandoned Harper's Ferry and retired

toward Winchester. By the middle of July McDowell
was ready to advance against Beauregard's position at
Manassas. On the 16th of July, at the head of the
best equipped army that had ever been seen in America, McDowell entered Virginia, confident of a triumphant march to Richmond.

FIRST BATTLE OF MANASSAS (BULL RUN).

4. If Beauregard could be attacked before reinforcements reached him, McDowell felt sure of victory.
General Scott,[1] the Federal commander-in-chief,
assured McDowell that Johnston should not join
Beauregard without having " Patterson on his heels."
Yet Johnston by his skillful management eluded Patterson and led 8,000 men to Manassas. Johnston
himself, with Bee's brigade, joined Beauregard on the
morning of July 20th. The brigade of T. J. (Stonewall) Jackson also came up and was placed in position. The rest of Johnston's 8,000 men reached the
field during the battle of the 21st. McDowell had at
first intended to attack the right of the Confederates,
but he concluded that their position was too strong
on that wing. Some of his troops under General
Tyler had advanced against the troops of Longstreet
at Blackburn's Ford (July 18th) and been repulsed.
McDowell determined to assail the Confederate left.

5. The Confederate commanders had issued orders
for an attack upon the Union centre and left, but
before these orders could be carried into effect Mc-

---

[1] General Winfield Scott, a native Virginian, who sided with the
government, was at this time commander-in-chief of the Union armies.
He was too old for active work in the field, but was a skillful strategist,
and hence his advice was highly prized.

GENERAL P. G. T. BEAUREGARD.

Dowell, leading a flanking force of 18,000 men, was crossing Bull Run with the purpose of passing around the Confederate left and .assailing them in the rear. General Nathan G. Evans, who was on this part of the Confederate line, had been ordered to prevent the passage of the Federals over Bull Run at the Stone Bridge. Perceiving that the movement of the Federal troops was to his left and rear, he ordered four companies to guard the bridge, and marching to the threatened point placed his brigade at right angles to his original position, thus covering the Warrenton turnpike and presenting a determined front to the Federal advance.[1]

6. Here Evans made a gallant fight, repulsing for a while many times his numbers. Bee and Bartow led their brigades to his support. After a two hours' desperate fight these troops were forced back to the plateau on which stood the Henry and Robinson houses. By this time Johnston and Beauregard found out that they must abandon their attack upon the Union left and hurry reinforcements to their own hard-pressed left. Johnston took charge of the movements of the troops, while Beauregard took immediate direction of the battle on the endangered wing. He found the troops of Evans, Bee and Bartow mingled together in great confusion. It was at this time that Bee rode up to Jackson and exclaimed, "General, they are beating us back." Jackson cooly replied, "Sir, we will give them the bayonet." Riding back to his men Bee shouted, "Look! there stands Jackson

---

[1] General B. F. Fry, of the Union army, says that Evans's action was one of the best pieces of soldiership on either side during the campaign.

FIRST BATTLE OF MANASSAS (BULL RUN).

like a stone wall!   Let us determine to die here and
we will conquer."   From that day Thomas Jonathan
Jackson was known as Stonewall Jackson.

7. When Beauregard came up, it looked as though
it would be impossible to restore order in the three
routed brigades.   But with fortunate presence of mind,
he ordered the colors of the various regiments to be
carried forward forty yards.   Beauregard and Johnston rode forward themselves with the colors of the
Fourth Alabama by their side.   At once the men who
had fought all the morning, and had finally been driven
back routed and disordered, rallied upon the colors,
and with the steadiness of veterans advanced again
into position.

8. Beauregard himself took command of the new
line, which consisted of Evans's South Carolinians
and Louisianians, Bartow's Georgians,[1] Bee's Alabamians, Mississippians, and North Carolinians,
and Jackson's Virginians, besides Hampton's Legion
and the batteries of Imboden, Stanard, and Pendleton.

9. Soon the Federals were seen advancing.   With
overpowering numbers, and exultant from the success
of the morning, they came eagerly onward.   After
holding the enemy at bay for some time, Beauregard
ordered a charge, and the Confederate line rushed forward, sweeping the whole plateau clear of the Federals.
But Union reinforcements arriving, the Federals regained their lost ground.   But as Fisher's Sixth North
Carolina and Withers's Eighteenth Virginia arrived
upon the field, Beauregard led a new charge, which
swept the enemy from the plateau and down the

---

[1] The Seventh and Eighth Georgia.

slope, securing to the Confederates final possession of the Henry and Robinson Houses, with most of Rickett's and Griffin's Union batteries. In this impetuous charge fell Bee and Bartow, two as gallant spirits as ever laid their lives upon the altar of their country.

10. The Federals on the opposite height, not yet sharing in the defeat of their comrades, presented a formidable front, as "stretching in crescent outline," with flanks advanced and a cloud of skirmishers in front, they started forward to renew the assault. But just about this time the balance of Johnston's Shenandoah army arrived upon the field. As they crossed the Sudley road their leader, Kirby Smith, fell severely wounded; but Colonel Elzey led them forward, and Early's brigade, which, by Johnston's orders, had swept around by the rear of the woods through which Elzey had passed, appeared on the field. All the Confederate commands upon the field now raising a loud cheer, went forward in a common charge. Before this full advance the whole Federal line broke and fled across Bull Run in every direction. Sykes's regulars, aided by Sherman's brigade, made a steady withdrawal, protecting the rear of the routed troops and enabling many to escape by the Stone Bridge.

11. About this time Captain Lindsay Walker, who had arrived from Fredericksburg with his six-Parrot-gun battery, took position on a high hill between the Lewis House and the Stone Bridge, and began to shell the retreating Federals on the road east of Bull Run. Then began an indescribable panic. The bridge over Cub Run being rendered impassable for vehicles by an overturned wagon, utter confusion set in. Am-

munition wagons, caissons, and pleasure carriages[1]
blocked the way; men threw aside their muskets and
everything else that could impede their flight, and
those who could do so cut horses from their harness
and rode off with them. The dismay of the fugitives
was increased by the cavalry of Colonel (afterwards
General) J. E. B. Stuart, who, with drawn sabres,
charging among them, captured many prisoners.

STONEWALL JACKSON AT BULL RUN.

12. Twenty-eight cannon, ten battle-flags, 5,000 muskets, 500,000 cartridges, and 1,300 prisoners were the
rich spoil that fell into the hands of the victorious
Confederates. Several surgeons were also captured,
who (the first time in war) were treated not as prison-

[1] Congressmen and citizens had gone out from Washington in carriages
with lunch-baskets and bottles of champagne in regular pic-nic style,
expecting to see the rout of the " Rebels " and the triumphant advance
cf the Union army upon Richmond.

ers, but as guests. General Beauregard recommended that they be sent home without exchange, together with some other prisoners who had shown personal kindness to Colonel Jones of the Fourth Alabama, who had been mortally wounded early in the day.

13. **Effect of the Battle.**—Manassas was the first great battle of the war. It was by far the greatest that up to that time had ever been fought on the American continent. The opposing forces were nearer equal than in any battle afterwards fought in Virginia. The total force on and near the battle-field amounted on the Confederate side to 32,000, and on the Union side to 35,000. In the beginning of the fight the Confederates actually engaged were outnumbered three to one—by noon two to one. They were nearly, if not quite, equal in strength to their opponents when the Federal rout occurred. The fact, however, that they had successfully resisted such great odds and had gained final possession of the hard-fought field just before the arrival of their last reinforcements, gave to the soldiers of the Confederate army in Virginia the confidence of their ability to fight superior numbers, which never forsook them, even down to the closing scene at Appomattox. The chief effect of this great battle was to completely break up the Union offensive in Virginia for the balance of the year 1861.[1]

OTHER EVENTS IN VIRGINIA AND WEST VIRGINIA.

14. The first great campaign of the war had ended in the triumph of the South. The North was at first

[1] The losses of the opposing armies in this battle were as follows: Union army—Killed, 460; wounded, 1,124; captured or missing, 1,312—total, 2,896. Confederate army—Killed, 387; wounded, 1,582; captured or missing, 13—total, 1,982.

overwhelmed with disappointment and chagrin.   But
this feeling was soon succeeded by a determination to
put fourth greater efforts.   General George B. McClellan, who had been successful in West Virginia, was
now called to the command of the defeated Union
army.   He at once went to work to organize, drill and
discipline a great army; but he did not feel ready to
advance until the next spring.

15. The Southern people were so elated by their
great victory that many of them imagined that the
war was about ended.   Their leaders, however, did not
share in this opinion, but prepared carefully for the
great struggle which they saw was before them.   The
Confederate Generals at Manassas, especially Beauregard, were very anxious for an offensive campaign,
and in October asked that additional troops might be
sent to them from various points along the seaboard,
at that time not even threatened; but Mr. Davis would
not venture to strip those points of the troops required.
Why it could not have been done then, as well as in
the next spring, is hard to understand.   There has
been much difference of opinion on this point, but it
does seem that it would have been much easier to
vanquish McClellan's army while still discouraged
by defeat and before its organization could be completed.[1]

[1] General Johnston in explaining why an immediate advance was not
made after the victory at Manassas says, that the Southern army "was
more disorganized by victory than that of the United States by defeat."
But Beauregard says "we had more than 15,000 troops who had not been
at all or but little in the battle, and were perfectly organized, while the
remaining commands in the high spirits of victory, could have been re-
organized at the tap of the drum, and many with improved captured arms
and equipments."   Considering all the circumstances Beauregard's opinion is more likely to be the correct one.

PRESIDENT DAVIS AND GENERAL JACKSON AT MANASSAS.

16. In October the Confederates did advance to
Fairfax Courthouse, with outposts flaunting their flags
in sight of Washington, hoping to provoke McClellan
to attack. The Federal troops, however, remained
idle on the opposite side of the Potomac. But on the
21st of October about 2,000 Federals under Colonel
E. D. Baker were thrown across the Potomac at Ball's
Bluff, near Leesburg. General Nathan G. Evans, who
had so distinguished himself at the battle of Manassas,
attacked this force with equal numbers, and utterly
defeated the Federals. Baker, their leader, was among
the slain. The total Union loss was over 1,000 men,
of whom 500 were prisoners. The only other affair
of this year in Eastern Virginia was at Dranesville, where General J. E. B. Stuart was repulsed,
but drew off his men in order, and retired unpur-
sued.

17. In West Virginia active operations continued
throughout the year. When McClellan was summoned to the command of the Union Army of the
Potomac, General Rosecrans was left in command of
the department of West Virginia. A large part of
the Federal army of West Virginia followed McClellan to Washington. It was a favorable time for the
Confederates to recover what they had lost in West
Virginia. General Loring, an officer of considerable
reputation, was sent to take charge of the Confederate
forces in that quarter. The forces of Floyd and Wise
in the Kanawha Valley were not under Loring's command. In August General Robert E. Lee was sent by
the Confederate authorities to command all the troops
of that department. Lee planned an expedition
against the Federal garrison at Cheat Mountain Pass.

18. About the middle of August it began to rain and continued to do so, without much intermission, for six weeks. The troops, unaccustomed to camp life, suffered from all camp diseases, such as measles, intermittent and typhoid fevers. At least one-third of the soldiers were rendered unfit for service by sickness.

MARCHES AND COUNTERMARCHES.

19. Lee determined to attack the Federals on the morning of the 12th of September. Colonel Rust, of the Third Arkansas regiment,[1] had discovered a mountain pass by which he could lead infantry into the rear of the Federal position. He was ordered to lead his regiment to this point, and General Anderson, with two Tennessee regiments from Loring's command, was to support him. Henry R. Jackson was to advance with his brigade from the camp at Greenbrier river, and Loring was to advance from Huntersville by the main road upon the Federal position. The troops reached the places assigned them with remarkable promptness and at the time appointed. Colonel Rust's attack was to be the signal for the advance of all the troops. Rust, hearing nothing of Anderson though he was in supporting distance, failed to attack. As the only hope of success was in a surprise, and as that expectation had been disappointed, the troops were withdrawn to their original position.

20. In these movements the Confederates killed twenty-five or thirty of the Federals and took seventy

[1] Of Henry R. Jackson's command.

prisoners. Their own loss was very small.[1] It is sometimes stated that Robert E. Lee was defeated at Cheat Mountain. A statement of this sort is misleading; for one not acquainted with the facts might suppose that Lee had fought a battle and been defeated.

GENERAL JOHN B. FLOYD.

Such is not the case. He had intended to fight a battle from which he expected good results; but on account of the failure of one of his subordinates to perform the part assigned him, the battle did not occur at all.

21. Meanwhile in the Valley of the Kanawha Wise and Floyd with divided commands and without unity of action were not accomplishing much against the Federal

[1] Colonel J. A. Washington of Lee's staff while making a reconnoissance fell into an ambuscade and was killed. Jackson's advance from the Greenbrier had been preceded by one hundred men from the First and Twelfth Georgia regiments, led by Lieutenant Dawson of the Twelfth whose duty it was to clear the way of the enemy's pickets. After performing this task, and while on their way to rejoin the main body they were mistaken for Federals and fired upon. Several shots were fired by both sides before the mistake was discovered, and two men were killed and one wounded.

Generals Cox and Rosecrans. On August 26th, at Cross Lanes General Floyd surprised and routed a Federal force under Colonel Tyler, inflicting a loss of about 200 men and losing none himself. General Rosecrans immediately marched against Floyd with a greatly superior force. He found him entrenched at Carnifax Ferry and assaulted his position, but was repulsed with a loss of 160 men. Floyd knowing that he was greatly outnumbered, retreated during the night, with difficulty carrying his artillery down the cliffs by a wretched road in the darkness. His infantry crossed on a slight foot bridge built over a little bit of smooth water known as the Ferry, on both sides of which the stream is an impassable mountain torrent. Floyd's total loss in the affair at Carnifax Ferry was twenty men of whom only one was killed.

22. General Lee now hastened to this quarter. He united the forces of Floyd and Wise and took up a strong defensive position along the eastern crest of Sewel Mountain. Rosecrans and Cox appeared before this position, but did not attack. Lee brought Loring to his assistance and was preparing to assail the Federals, when Rosecrans retreated.

23. General J. J. Reynolds had been left in command of the Union forces at Cheat Mountain. On October 3rd, Reynolds attacked Henry R. Jackson's camp at Greenbrier river, but after quite a sharp combat was repulsed. He then retreated to his mountain stronghold.

24. Toward the close of the year most of the troops on both sides were taken from West Virginia and sent to where they could be used to better advantage. The Confederate Government concluded to make no

farther effort to hold an unfriendly country, and for the rest of the war the line of the Alleghanies was the northern frontier of the Confederacy in Virginia

25. When Loring's forces were withdrawn from West Virginia they were sent to "Stonewall" Jackson, then commanding in the Shenandoah Valley A small force was left at Alleghany Summit under Colonel Edward Johnson. Here the Confederates were assailed on the 13th of December by General R. H. Milroy. The Federals were defeated, and Milroy retreated to his old camp.

CHAPTER IV.

THE WAR IN THE WEST AND ON THE COAST DURING 1861.

WHEN South Carolina seceded the legislature of Missouri, at the suggestion of Governor Claiborne F. Jackson, began to take measures for ranging Missouri with the South in the event of war. A State convention was called and provision was made to organize, arm and equip the militia.

2. An election was held for delegates to a State convention. The States Rights men of Missouri were disappointed at the result. Not a single delegate was elected who would say that he was in favor of secession.[1]

3. But when, after the bombardment of Fort Sumter, President Lincoln called upon Missouri for her quota of troops to support the government, Gov'nor Jackson replied that Missouri would not furnish a man. He then called together the legislature to adopt measures for the defense of the State. In accordance with an existing law of the State all the militia were ordered into camp for drill and discipline

4. General D. M. Frost, commanding a small brigade of volunteer militia, arranged with the governor to seize the arsenal at St. Louis. This plan was thwarted, however, by Captain Nathaniel Lyon, the commander of the arsenal. He distributed some of the arms to the Home Guards, a body of Missouri Unionists, who had been organized by Francis P. Blair immediately

---

[1] In Missouri there were three classes—the unconditional Union men, the Conservatives, and the Secessionists.

after the secession of South Carolina. The rest of the arms Lyon removed from the arsenal and sent to Illinois. Then with his own troops he occupied the hills around the arsenal. Frost then established Camp Jackson in a grove in the western part of the city, in all this acting under the militia laws of the State.

5. On May 8th Frost received some arms that had been sent him from Louisiana. Blair and Lyon heard of this and determined to break up Camp Jackson· To this point Lyon marched with nearly 7,000 men and

demanded the surrender of the camp.

Frost, who had only 635 men, was obliged to comply. While the surrender was taking place, a great crowd of people hurried to the scene. Most of the crowd sympathized with the prisoners, and some gave expression to their in-

GENERAL STERLING PRICE.

dignation, but did nothing to warrant what followed. One of Lyon's German regiments opened fire upon them, killing twenty-eight persons, among them women and children. A similar massacre occurred the next day.

6. Thus civil war was inaugurated in Missouri. The legislature, which was then in extra session, immediately took more effective measures for arming the

militia, and conferred almost absolute power upon the governor. Sterling Price, who had once been governor of the State, and up to that time a Union man, now offered his services to the governor. Price was presi- of the Missouri Convention, and had been opposed under all circumstances to the secession of his State. At the same time he was earnestly opposed to the invasion of the South by the Federal government. But considering the killing of peaceable citizens an unbearable outrage, he believed it the duty of Missouri to resent such wrongs.

7. Many of the conservative Union men followed Price's example and joined the secessionists in taking up arms. Volunteers began to crowd the streets of Jefferson City. Blair and Lyon wished to march against the militia at once; but General William S. Harney, commander of the Department of the West, who had been absent from St. Louis, returned the day after the capture of Camp Jackson. He preferred conciliation and made a truce with Price, who had been appointed commander of all the State forces of Missouri.

8. Blair succeeded in having Harney relieved from command. Lyon was made Brigadier-General and appointed in his place. He put an end to the truce with Price, and took measures to drive Price and Jackson out of the State. Lyon sent Sweeny and Sigel to the Southwest with 3,000 men to cut off the retreat of Price, and marched himself upon Jefferson City. The legislature and governor were obliged to flee. Leaving a garrison there, Lyon pushed on to Boonville, and on June 17th routed some State troops and drove the governor southward. Price, who had gone

to Lexington to organize several thousand militia there assembled, was obliged to retreat now to the southwest in order to unite with General McCulloch, who was advancing at the head of a Confederate force from Northwestern Arkansas. Price ordered Brigadier-General James S. Rains to move with the State troops to unite with the force under the Governor, while he with a small escort made his way to McCulloch in order to hasten the march of that officer.

9. On July 5th at Carthage, Sigel attacked the forces of the Governor commanded by General Rains. The fight did not last long, for Sigel was greatly outnumbered and driven from the field. Though retiring in order his retreat continued for forty miles.[1]

10. Price and McCulloch succeeded in uniting their forces, and began an advance (July 31st) toward Springfield. Their force was something over 10,000. Some of these were without arms and others had only squirrel rifles. Lyon advanced against them with about 5,400 men, inferior in numbers, but well organized and equipped. The two armies met at Oak Hill, or Wilson's creek, on the morning of August 10th. Here one of the bloodiest battles of the war took place. The part of Lyon's force commanded by Sigel was routed, but the troops under his immediate command were at first successful. At the crisis of the battle Lyon was killed while leading a charge. The Union army retreated, leaving the body of Lyon on the field. Two hours later it was delivered to a flag-of-truce party that had been sent to ask for

---

[1] How any one can call the fight at Carthage a Union victory is hard to understand.

it.[1] The next day Price occupied Springfield, and sent Rains with a mounted force to clear the western counties of the State of the plundering bands that had entered them from Kansas.

11. Price next moved to the northwest against Lexington, where there was a Federal garrison under Colonel Mulligan. After driving the Federals into their intrenchments Price proceeded to invest the place. In charging the Union position (September 20th) Price's men adopted the novel plan of rolling cotton bales before them as a sort of movable breastwork. On the next day Colonel Mulligan surrendered. The Missourians captured 3,500 prisoners, five cannon, 3 000 muskets, and valuable supplies of all kinds.[2]

12. General John C. Fremont, who now commanded the Union armies in the West, took the field against Price with over 40,000 men. Price sent his unarmed men home, and with about 7,000 marched quickly to Neosho, where Governor Jackson had convened the legislature (or what could be gotten together of it). The delegates present passed an ordinance of secession and allied the State with the Confederacy

13. Fremont's campaign against Price was brought to an end by his removal from command (March 2d). General Hunter, his successor, led the Union army back to St. Louis. Just before Christmas Price occupied Springfield, where the enlistment of Missourians into the Confederate army was begun.

[1] The losses in this battle were as follows: Union—killed, 223; wounded, 721; captured or missing, 291; total, 1,235. Confederate—killed, 265; wounded, 800; captured or missing, 30; total, 1,095.

[2] Price's force numbered 18,000 men, half of whom were unarmed.

14. The Confederates, however, never did get a firm hold in Missouri. While the people of Southern and Western Missouri were for the South the Union men were a majority of the whole State, and they were backed by strong Federal armies.

15. The last battle of the year in Missouri was at Belmont, in the southeast corner of the State. Here General Ulysses S. Grant attacked the Confederates under General Gideon J. Pillow. In the beginning of the fight Grant was successful; but the Confederates being reinforced defeated him and drove him to his gunboats.

16. In Kentucky an attempt was made by the State authorities to hold a position of neutrality between the States at war, but the attempt failed, as it had in Missouri. During the fall some of the people organized a provisional government, and tried to ally the State with the Confederate States. But the effort was a failure; for the regular State legislature and a large majority of the people of Kentucky sided with the Government of the United States. Both Kentucky and Missouri furnished many gallant soldiers to the Confederacy. But neither of these States seceded, and a majority of their people were undoubtedly on the side of the Union.

17. **Operations on the coast** were not very extensive during the year. On the 29th of August a Federal land force under General B. F. Butler and a fleet under Commodore Stringham captured the Confederate forts at Hatteras Inlet, off the coast of North Carolina. Another expedition, under General T. W. Sherman and Commodore Du Pont, captured the earthworks at Port Royal, South Carolina (November 7th).

18. The blockade of the Southern ports kept the products of the South cooped up at home, and interfered greatly with the obtaining of necessary supplies from abroad for the Confederate armies. Armed vessels were stationed before the leading Southern ports to prevent trading vessels from entering or departing

SCENE ON THE COAST OF NORTH CAROLINA.

from them. Many enterprising men, however, fitted out vessels manned by daring sailors to enter the bays, rivers and creeks, and even slip through the blockading squadron into the leading ports. If these vessels were caught they and their cargoes were confiscated. The adventures of these "blockade runners" form a very romantic part of the story of the war.

19. **Privateers** were fitted out by authority of the Confederate Government which captured merchandise to the value of many millions of dollars, and greatly crippled the foreign trade of the Northern States. The chief of these during 1861 were the Sumter and the Nashville, commanded respectively by Raphael Semmes of Alabama, and Robert B. Pegram of Virginia.

20. **The Trent Affair.**—Toward the latter part of the year two Confederate Commissioners, Mason and Slidell, were forcibly taken from the British ship Trent, by Captain Wilkes of the United States war-ship San Jacinto. The British government demanded reparation, and began preparing for war. The Government of the United States apologized for the act of Captain Wilkes and restored the embassadors to a British vessel. Thus war with England was avoided.

21. **The Close of 1861.**—As the year drew to a close the Confederates felt much encouraged. Though they had been disappointed in not securing the hearty co-operation of Maryland, Kentucky and Missouri, and had found unexpected opposition among the people of West Virginia, they had been victorious in the one great battle of the year and in most of the minor conflicts between the forces of the North and the South.

PART III.

The War Between the States and its Results.

Section II.—Events of 1862.

CHAPTER I.

SOME MINOR EVENTS BOTH IN THE EAST AND WEST IN THE BEGINNING OF 1862—THE WESTERN CAMPAIGN OF THE SPRING AND EARLY SUMMER.

LL through 1861 and in the first months of 1862 the Confederates were greatly embarrassed for lack of a sufficient supply of arms. Thus it happened that of something more than 300,000 troops enrolled, many thousands were in camps of instruction waiting for arms. By the 1st of January, 1862, the United States had in the field 600,000 well-equipped troops, and by the first of March many thousands more. The result was that in the first months of the year the Confederates were so greatly outnumbered that they could offer no effective resistance when the Union armies began to advance.

JACKSON'S WINTER CAMPAIGN.

2. In November, 1861, Stonewall Jackson was sent to command in the Shenandoah Valley. At that time the Union troops held Romney and occupied the north side of the Potomac in strong force. At first Jackson had only a small command, mostly militia. Toward the middle of the month his old " Stonewall Brigade" was sent to him, and still later the troops of Loring from West Virginia also joined him. In December an expedition was sent out by him which did considerable damage to the Baltimore and Ohio Railroad, and to the Chesapeake and Ohio Canal.

JACKSON PREPARING FOR BATTLE.

3. On the 1st of January, 1862, Jackson set out from Winchester with nearly 10,000 men on an expedition to clear his district of Union troops. The morning of that day was as beautiful and mild as a day in May, but before night the weather suddenly changed to be very severe. The snow and sleet made it impossible for the loaded wagons to keep up, and for several nights the soldiers bivouacked without tents or without a sufficient supply of blankets. Their sufferings were terrible, but they pressed on, drove the Federals out of Bath and across the Potomac (January 4th), occupied Romney (January 10th) and cleared the whole of Jackson's district of Union troops. On this march Jackson shared all the privations of his men.[1] At the last of the month the Confederates returned to Winchester and the Federals occupied their former positions.

SOME MINOR BATTLES OF 1862.

4. Union successes, both in the East and in the West, marked the first months of 1862. The most important of minor battles were Mill Spring in Kentucky (January 19th), where the Confederate General Zollicoffer was killed; Roanoke Island in North Carolina (February 8th); the capture of Fort Pulaski near Savannah, Georgia (April 11th), and of Fort Macon in North Carolina (April 26th).

---

[1] One morning near Bath some of Jackson's men, as they crawled out from under their snow covered blankets, began abusing him as the cause of all their sufferings. Jackson who was near by, heard it. Without noticing it he presently crawled out too, and shaking off the snow, made some jocular remark to the nearest men, who had no idea that he had ridden up during the night and laid down among them. This incident soon went through the army and reconciled the men to their hardships.

FORT DONELSON.

5. But these were trifling successes compared to the heavy blow dealt the Confederates at Fort Donelson. For months General Albert Sidney Johnston had kept three times his numbers at bay in Southern Kentucky. The Federal army in his front was under General Buell. Early in February General Ulysses S. Grant led a strong army into Tennessee, while Commodore Foote assisted him with a fleet of iron-clad gunboats. On February 6th they attacked and took Fort Henry on the Tennessee River.

6. General Grant now made ready to advance against Fort Donelson on the Cumberland, distant from Fort Henry about twelve or fourteen miles. Hearing of the approach of Grant, the Confederate General Albert Sidney Johnston sent reinforcements to the garrison at Fort Donelson. By the morning of the 13th, somewhere between 12,000 and 15,000 Confederates, under Floyd, Pillow and Buckner, had been concentrated at the threatened fort. That morning Grant appeared before Donelson, and with an army at first but little larger than that of the Confederates proceeded at his leisure to place his opponents in a state of siege.

7. After some manoeuvering of his troops, Grant discovered that he had not a force sufficiently strong to complete the investment. So he ordered up reinforcements. Why Floyd, the Confederate commander, made no attempt to prevent these movements of Grant is difficult to understand. General Lew Wallace, of the Union army, says: "A vigorous attack on the morning of the 13th might have thrown Grant back upon Fort Henry; but nothing occurred except slight skirmishing."

8. The morning of the 13th was calm and spring-like. By afternoon a fierce wind from the north brought upon both armies a storm of rain, snow and sleet. With heroic fortitude the volunteers of the North and of the South endured the pitiless tempest and waited for the morning, whose coming would usher in a still more dreadful storm of whistling bullets and shrieking shells.

MONTICELLO, THE HOME OF JEFFERSON.

9. On the morning of the 14th a gallant assault by the Union troops was gallantly repulsed. Then Foote with his gunboats attacked the water batteries Through the fierce fire of the Confederate guns the fleet pushed on, until when within 350 yards of the battery

a solid shot plunged through the pilot-house of the *St. Louis*, carrying away the wheel. About the same time the *Louisville* was disabled. The Confederates redoubled their energies. "A ball got lodged in their best rifle. A corporal and some of his men took a log fitting the bore, leaped out on the parapet, and rammed the missile home. 'Now, boys,' said a gunner in Bidwell's battery, 'see me take a chimney.' The flag of the boat and the chimney fell with the shot."[1] The Union fleet was obliged to retire out of range. With their repulse, the Confederates scored success number two, and communication by the river remained open to Nashville.

GENERAL SIMON B. BUCKNER.

10. That evening the Confederate leaders held a council of war. They knew that Grant was being heavily reinforced, and that his army had cut off land communication with Nashville. The following plan was adopted Pillow, with his division, was to attack the Union right at dawn. General Buckner, being relieved by troops in the forts, was to support Pillow by assailing the right of the Union

[1] "The Capture of Fort Donelson," by General Lew Wallace. Taken from the Century Company's War Book.

center. In case of success, he was to take post where he could cover the retreat. All night the troops made ready for the attack.

11. The decision of the Confederate leaders was heroic. Massing their troops on the Union right, they began the attack at dawn. Though bravely resisted, they steadily gained ground. The commands of Oglesby, Logan and W. H. L. Wallace were at last pushed aside, and Pillow's part of the programme was accomplished. The road was once more open. Buckner had faithfully performed his task, and was ready to cover the retreat. The Union general, Lew Wallace, says, that it may be said with strong assurance, that Floyd could have put his men fairly on the road to Nashville before Grant could have interposed an obstruction to the movement. The trouble was, now, that General Pillow, thinking he had defeated the whole of Grant's army, ignored the orders of Floyd, and attempted a pursuit of the Federals. This gave Grant an opportunity to bring forward the fresh divisions of C. F. Smith and Lew Wallace, renew the attack and recover his lost ground. So night found the Confederates hopelessly enclosed by a greatly superior army, which was being constantly reinforced.

12. It was now evident to the Confederate generals that Fort Donelson must be surrendered. As the river was still open to the Confederates, Floyd put his own brigade upon two steamboats (the only transportation on hand), and sailed away to Nashville. General Pillow accompanied him. General Buckner remained to share the fate of his troops. Colonel Forrest, the bold Tennessee trooper, declared that he could not and would not surrender. So, assembling

his men, all as hardy as himself, he plunged into a slough formed by a back water from the river. None but mounted men could have succeeded in such an attempt. After floundering about for a while in the icy water, they struck dry land and were safe. Buckner opened communication with Grant, who demanded unconditional surrender. As he could do nothing else, Buckner complied, and 9,000 Confederates laid down their arms.[1]

13. By this disastrous defeat Nashville was lost, and the Confederates had to take a new line, extending from Middle Tennessee to the border of Alabama and Mississippi. General Grant advanced to Pittsburgh Landing on the Tennessee, not far from the northern boundary of Mississippi. General Buell occupied Nashville, and prepared to join Grant for a still farther advance into the very heart of the Confederacy.

THE BATTLE OF SHILOH.

14. At Corinth, Mississippi, lay a Confederate force under General Beauregard. General Albert Sidney Johnston formed a plan to unite his force with that under Beauregard and attack Grant, with the hope of being able to crush him before the arrival of Buell. The union of the two Confederate armies was effected, and on the morning of April 3d they began their march against Grant.

15. The intention was to attack the Union army on the morning of the 5th. It was thought that this

---

[1] General Pillow states the Confederate loss in killed and wounded at about 2,000. General Buckner says in his official report that he surrendered 9,000 men. The total Union loss was 510 killed, 2,152 wounded, 224 missing—2,886.

could be easily done, as the distance to be marched
was only about twenty miles.   But the troops were not
moved as rapidly as had been hoped.   On the afternoon of the 4th there was some sharp skirmishing
within about six miles of the Union army.   Yet
Grant and Sherman did not seem to anticipate any
attack.   During the next day the Confederates advanced at their leisure, and formed line of battle
within easy striking distance of their enemy.

16. On the evening of the 5th at a council of war
Beauregard expressed the opinion that, as success
depended upon the surprise of the Federals, and as
they must now be fully aware of the presence and
design of the Confederates, it was best to abandon the
attack and return to Corinth   Polk and Bragg did
not agree with Beauregard.   After listening to the
views of each, Johnston closed the council with the
remark, "Gentlemen, we shall attack at daylight
to-morrow."

17. Grant and Sherman have claimed that they
were not surprised at Shiloh, but in their dispatches
of the 5th both of these officers expressed the opinion
that there would be no attack upon their lines.   Besides, the absence of the usual precautions for shield-
ing an army in the field proves that the attack at
Shiloh was, as Beauregard expressed it, one of the
most surprising of surprises.

18. On the morning of April 6th the Confederates
fell with resistless fury upon the Union troops, some
of whom were but half dressed.   Yet the Federals made
a gallant resistance.   In vain, however, were all the
efforts to stay the overwhelming onset of the Confederates led by Bragg, Polk, Hardee and Breckinridge.

BATTLE OF SHILOH.

Sherman and McClernand were forced back; Hurlbut, who with Prentiss and W. H. L. Wallace held so stubbornly the position called by the Confederates the "Hornet's Nest," was at last forced back to Pittsburgh Landing; Wallace, after giving the order to his division to retire, fell mortally wounded; and still later Prentiss, whose command had been the first to feel the shock of the battle in the early morning, after stoutly keeping the field until late in the afternoon, found himself completely surrounded, and was forced to surrender in person with about 2,200 officers and men.

19. The greater part of Grant's army had now been routed and driven entirely from the field, and those who maintained their organization could not have resisted a determined attack by the whole force in their front; thousands of his men had been killed and wounded, and the Union camps were in possession of the Confederates, with a rich spoil of artillery and military stores of every description. But General Albert Sidney Johnston had been killed, and Beauregard, thinking the victory complete, and that in the morning he could finish up what was left of Grant's army, stopped the fight. That very evening Lew Wallace reinforced Grant with 5,000 fresh troops, and during the night Buell came to his assistance with 25,000 more.

20. Early on the morning of the 7th these fresh troops and all of Grant's men that could be rallied and gotten into position (about 15,000 or 20,000) attacked the weary Confederates, who had not been reinforced by a single man. Unfortunately for them the Confederates, too confident of complete victory, had withdrawn from some of the high ground that

they had captured, in order to shelter themselves during the night from the fire of the gunboats. This high ground they expected to reoccupy in the morning and finish up the work so well begun. But Buell's troops occupied it during the night, and from this point of advantage advanced against the Confederates, who had spent the night in the captured Union camps.

21. Though now out-numbered and hard pressed, the Confederates bravely held their ground until after 2 o'clock in the afternoon. At that time Beauregard sent orders to the corps commanders to make a show of assuming the offensive, and then, taking advantage of the lull in the enemy's attack (which he hoped would occur in consequence of such a movement), to retire their commands behind a covering force of infantry and artillery, posted on elevated ground which commanded a wide view. These orders were executed with great skill, without apparently any perception on the part of the Federals that such a movement was going on.[1] Brigadier General Thomas Jordan, of Beauregard's staff, who had posted the protecting force, says: "There I remained until after 4 o'clock, or until the entire Confederate force had retired, General Breckinridge's troops being the last, and without seeing a single Federal soldier within the wide range of my eyes." The covering force then retired, carrying the caissons, loaded down with muskets and rifles picked up on the field. Many of the soldiers had also

---

[1] The Confederate retreat was discovered on some parts of the line, but no vigorous effort was made to interfere with them. An advance by two regiments, accompanied by General Grant, has been dignified into a charge led by that officer, although they advanced but a short distance, and encountered only a few skirmishers.

exchanged their arms for the superior ones of the Federals captured in the first day's battle. Besides this, the Confederates carried off with them 30 captured cannon, 26 stands of colors, and nearly 3,000 prisoners of war.[1]

22. Shiloh was the most terrible battle that had yet been fought during the civil war. The Confederate plan to destroy Grant's army had nearly succeeded. But the timely arrival of Buell with a fresh army had thwarted the plan and forced the Confederates to retreat. To this extent it had the effect of a Union

GENERAL ALBERT SIDNEY JOHNSTON.

victory. But to the Confederates Shiloh did not seem to be a defeat, but rather the disappointment of a hope

---

[1] The returns for the Union army, of April 4th and 5th, show present for duty 44,895. Grant claims that of this number there were only 33,000 effectives. According to some authorities, Buell and Lew Wallace brought in 31,000 reinforcements, according to others, 25,000, making a total of Union troops for both days of 64,000 or 58,000. The Union losses were 1,754 killed, 8,408 wounded, and 2,885 captured—in all 13,047 The aggregate of the Confederate forces engaged was, according to one authority, 39,323, but according to another, 40,335. The Confederate loss was, in killed, 1,728; in wounded, 8,012, and 959 in missing—in all, 10,699.

almost realized.   They knew that they had attacked
the victors of Forts Henry and Donelson, stormed and
spoiled their camp, and brought them to the verge of
ruin.[1] They even looked upon the second day's fight
as a victory for themselves, because they had fought a
fresh army assisted by the remnant of the one defeated
on the day before, and when they found the odds too
great had retired without the least attempt at pursuit
on the part of their foe, carrying with them much
of the spoil of the captured camp.

23. When on the 14th of April General Halleck
arrived in camp and took command he said to Grant,
"your army is not now in condition to resist attack."
One of the best evidences of the stunning blow dealt
the Union army is seen in the dispatch of Grant to
Halleck the day after the battle : " It would be demoral-
izing upon our troops here to be forced to retire upon
the opposite bank of the river, and unsafe to remain
on this many weeks without large reinforcements."
Buell's army was still with him.

24. But for the battle at Shiloh on April 6th, the
Union armies would have overrun the whole Southwest

---

[1] The Confederates always believed that but for the death of Albert
Sidney Johnston, Grant and his army would have been forced to an unconditional surrender before the night of the 6th of April. General
Buell says that of Grant's army "there were not more than five thousand
men in ranks and available on the battle-field at nightfall.   .   . the
rest were either killed, wounded, captured or scattered in hopeless confusion for miles along the banks of the river." General Nelson describes
them as "cowering under the river banks.   .   . frantic with fright
and utterly demoralized." Had not Beauregard ordered the fight to
cease for the night, the general testimony of Confederate officers and
soldiers on that part of the field is to the effect that the remnant of Grant's
army would have been forced to surrender. Buell shows how absurd is
the statement of Grant that the arrival of Lew Wallace's division would
have been enough to secure victory.

by the middle of the summer of 1862. The brilliant Confederate victory of that day, notwithstanding their enforced retreat on the 7th, by reason of the arrival of Buell's fresh army, caused the future movements of the Federals to be much slower and more cautious than they had hitherto been. Had the plan of the Confederates fully succeeded, they would have recovered all that they had lost by their disaster at Donelson. The failure of their plan made Shiloh a drawn battle with complete victory for neither side.

25. One week after Halleck's arrival General Pope, flushed with his victories at New Madrid and Island No. 10,[1] reached Pittsburgh Landing and united his army with those of Grant and Buell. General Curtis, who had defeated Van Dorn at Elkhorn, in Arkansas, also sent reinforcements to the same point. By the last of April Halleck had assembled on the banks of the Tennessee an army of 100,000 men.

CORINTH.

26. After the battle of Shiloh Beauregard had led his army, reduced by the casualties of that fierce conflict to 30,000 men, back to Corinth, which place he proceeded to fortify against the attack which he knew would soon come. Here he was reinforced by troops from across the Mississippi under Price and Van Dorn and by forces from other quarters until his army numbered 80,000 men.

27. Halleck advanced cautiously, intrenching every time that he halted. Fresh troops were constantly added to his force, so that by the time he appeared

---

[1] Pope captured at these places about 6,000 men and seventy cannon.

before Corinth he had 110,000 fighting men. By reason of sickness arising from the pestilential air and unwholesome water Beauregard's force had now been reduced to 53,000 effectives. Accordingly, as soon as the Confederate commander was certain that Halleck was nearly ready to open his siege guns and assault his works, he made preparations to retreat. The evacuation was conducted with the utmost secrecy and skill. The troops were ordered to the front with three days' rations in their haversacks, and told that

GENERAL G. J. PILLOW.

they were going to attack the enemy. The sick were sent away, and all military supplies were sent off by the railways. During the night of May 29th there was a great running of cars, and the Confederates were ordered to cheer whenever a train arrived, so as to make Halleck believe that they were being reinforced. Before daybreak of the 30th Beauregard's whole army, except his cavalry, had been withdrawn from Corinth.

28. Halleck had been completely deceived. A short while before daybreak Pope had informed Halleck that he expected to be attacked in heavy force at daylight. Halleck, therefore, disposed his army for defense and not for attack. When he discovered his mistake and marched into Corinth, Beauregard's army was already safe behind the Tuscumbia. Beauregard retreated to Tupelo, about fifty-two miles from

Corinth. The official records show that he lost less than 4,000 men during these operations, and many of these came in after a few days.

29. Halleck now planned a campaign for the capture of Chattanooga and the conquest of East Tennessee. As soon as Beauregard, whose health had been seriously impaired, was satisfied that he would not be attacked at Tupelo he turned over the command for a time to General Bragg (June 17th), and went to Mobile. President Davis then relieved Beauregard and placed Bragg in command of the department. Halleck at Corinth and Bragg at Tupelo now employed themselves in reorganizing their armies and getting ready for a new campaign.

New Orleans, Memphis and Vicksburg.

30. While all these events were occurring the Union fleets along the Mississippi were likewise busy trying to bring the whole river under Federal control.

31. **The capture of New Orleans** was another severe blow to the Confederates. Towards the last of April Commodore David G. Farragut (far-ra-gu), with a powerful fleet of armed vessels, after bombarding for six days Forts Jackson and St. Philip, which defended the passage to the city, boldly ran past their guns and attacked the small Confederate fleet of rams and fire-rafts. After passing the forts Farragut's chief difficulty was at an end. The Confederate fleet under Commodore Mitchell consisted nominally of fourteen vessels and forty guns, but only four of these vessels with twelve guns were completed and ready for action, while the Union fleet numbered forty vessels with 302

guns.[1] So Farragut gained an easy victory over the Confederate fleet. As he approached the city the Confederates retired and New Orleans was occupied by the Union troops under General Benjamin F. Butler (April 28th).

32. **The capture of Memphis,** on June 6th, was another heavy blow to the Confederate cause in the West. On that day Colonel Charles Ellet's fleet of steam rams attacked the Confederate fleet and destroyed it. The result was the occupation of Memphis by the Union forces.

33. **The first attack upon Vicksburg** renewed the hopes of the Confederates. The Union fleets from New Orleans and Memphis now united before that important post and demanded its surrender. But the city was stoutly defended by the garrison under General Van Dorn. On July 15th the Confederate ram *Arkansas*, under Captain Isaac N. Brown, came down from the Yazoo River, ran the gauntlet of the upper fleet, defeating every vessel that tried to impede its progress, and anchored under the guns of Vicksburg. After sending some of their best ships to destroy the *Arkansas*, and meeting signal defeat, both Union fleets gave up the siege of Vicksburg and sailed away. For several months thereafter the "heroic city" was left undisturbed.

ENERGY OF THE CONFEDERATES.

34. During all these months the Confederate Government had been putting forth wonderful energy.

---

[1] In the Confederate forts were 126 guns. Seventy per cent. of the Confederate guns were thirty-two-pounders and below, while sixty-three per cent. of the Union guns were of heavier caliber. As the passage was open, so that the fleet was not long under fire of the guns, the forts had no advantage over the ships.

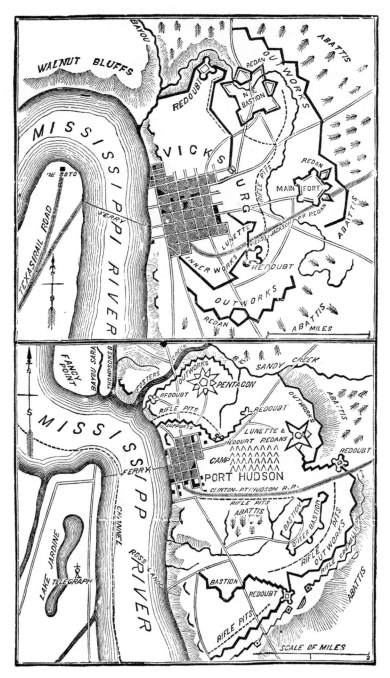

MAP OF VICKSBURG.

A law was passed bringing into the field every man between the ages of eighteen and thirty-five. Blockade
runners brought in large supplies of arms from Europe,
and newly-built work shops were busy making arms
and ammunition. From every available point reinforcements were brought to the hard pressed Confederate army of the West. From standing on the defensive they prepared to assume the offensive, and advance
all along the line. Brilliant successes in Virginia
greatly encouraged them to this change of tactics.
We will in the next chapter turn to the East and note
the progress of events in that quarter.

CHAPTER II.

FROM THE BEGINNING OF THE CAMPAIGNS OF 1862 IN
VIRGINIA TO THE CLOSE OF THE CAMPAIGN OF THE
SECOND MANASSAS.

THE campaign in Virginia did not begin as early as that in the West. When McClellan with his great army began to advance towards Manassas (March 10th) the out-numbered Confederates, under Joseph E. Johnston, could do nothing but retire. McClellan now determined to advance upon Richmond by what he considered a shorter and better way. So he moved his army to Fortress Monroe, with the view of advancing by way of the Peninsula, as that part of Virginia lying between the York and James rivers is called.

2 **The first battle of iron-clads** occurred just before the beginning of these movements of the armies.[1] When the Federal authorities abandoned the navy-yard at Norfolk in April, 1861, they sank the *Merrimac*, which was at that time undergoing repairs.[2] This vessel was raised by the Confederate authorities during the summer of 1861, and rebuilt as an iron-clad according to plans suggested by Lieutenant John M. Brooke, who had resigned from the old navy and joined that of the

[1] Some battles of iron-clads have already been described in the previous chapter on the western campaign. But the battle between the *Virginia* and *Monitor* was the first one fought between vessels of which each was a fully equipped iron-clad.

[2] At the navy-yard the Confederates captured 1,200 heavy guns, which during 1861 were distributed over all the South and mounted on fortifications from the Potomac to the Mississippi. Why the Federals abandoned Norfolk and the navy-yard it is impossible to understand. There was certainly no need for it.

BATTLE BETWEEN THE MONITOR AND THE MERRIMAC.

Confederates.   The vessel when rebuilt was named the *Virginia*.   It was not ready for service until March 8th, 1862.   On that day it steamed down the Elizabeth river, and headed for Newport News.   The intention was to attack the Union fleet in Hampton Roads.

3. Right gallantly did the fleet receive the onset of the iron-plated monster.   All in vain, however.   After a fierce conflict, the *Cumberland* was sunk, the *Congress* was captured and burned, the *Minnesota* ran aground, and the rest of the fleet was scattered.   The *Virginia* waited until morning to finish the work so well begun.

4. But at daylight the men on the *Virginia* noticed a strange looking craft lying between their ship and the *Minnesota*.   This proved to be Ericsson's *Monitor*, a vessel, little of which showed above the water except its revolving iron turret, armed with heavy rifled cannon.   Keeping between the *Minnesota* and the *Virginia*, the *Monitor* received the attack of the latter. Though the fight of the iron-clads was a drawn battle, doing no damage to either, yet the saving of the remnant of the Union fleet gave color to the Federal claims of victory in this second day's fight.

5. But the Virginia continued to be a terror to her foes.   When on April 11th she came out again, the Monitor and the fleet kept out of the way under the protection of the guns of Fortress Monroe.   One month later (May 8th) the *Monitor* with two other iron-clads and a number of heavy ships began to shell the Confederate batteries at Sewell's Point.   The *Virginia* went out and made directly for the *Monitor*, whereupon that vessel and all the other Union vessels ceased

firing and retreated below the forts. For some hours the *Virginia* remained in the Roads, defiantly sailing up and down, but her foes did not venture out from under the protection of the guns of the batteries.

THE PENINSULA CAMPAIGN.

6. McClellan's advance was delayed in front of Yorktown until early in May. For a time Magruder, with only 11,000 men, held him at bay, and finally the Confederate army from Manassas, under Joseph E. Johnston, was placed in his front. When at last McClellan's greatly superior force began to move forward the Confederates retired before him. In consequence of their retreat Norfolk was abandoned, and the iron-clad *Virginia* was destroyed to prevent its falling in to the hands of the Federals. At Williamsburg (May 5th) a sharp but indecisive battle occurred between Johnston's rear guard and McClellan's advance. At Drewry's Bluff the crew of the *Virginia* defended Fort Darling against five Federal iron-clads completely repulsing them and thus saving Richmond from capture by the Union fleet.[1]

7. **The Battle of Seven Pines or Fair Oaks** was fought in consequence of the discovery by General Johnston, that part of the Federal army under Casey and Couch, was in an exposed position. The Confederates utterly defeated the Federal left at Seven Pines (May 31st), capturing their camp with ten cannon, 6,000 muskets and a quanity of tents and camp equipage. The Union right at Fair Oaks held its ground, thus making the

[1] The Confederates afterwards built the James River Squadron, one of the best vessels of which was the new *Virginia*. This fleet bore an important part in the defense of Richmond.

battle indecisive. General Johnston was so badly wounded that he had to retire from active service for several months. On the next day (June 1st) there was some heavy fighting, the Confederates being commanded by General G. W. Smith; but nothing decisive was accomplished.[1] However McClellan's advance was completely checked by this battle. General Robert E. Lee was now put in command of the Confederate army of Northern Virginia.

JACKSON'S VALLEY CAMPAIGN.

8. When McClellan with 120,000 men began his Peninsula campaign the Federal plan of operations was that Fremont should come down from the northwest, Banks from the Shenandoah Valley, and McDowell from Fredericksburg, thus increasing the army of McClellan by more than 60,000 men. They confidently expected to capture Richmond and drive the Confederates out of Virginia. But Stonewall Jackson, who had been left in the Shenandoah Valley, by one of the most brilliant campaigns recorded in history, kept the co-operating armies too busy to carry out their part of the programme.

9. At the beginning of March Jackson did not have over 5,000 men of all arms for the defense of his disdrict, which began to swarm on every side with ene-

---

[1] The largest number closely engaged in this battle was on the first day, 21,000 on the Union side, and 18,000 on the Confederate. On the second day not more than 14,000 Union troops were engaged, and only 8,300 Confederates. The losses on the Union side were 790 killed, 3,594 wounded and 647 captured or missing—5,031.

On the Confederate side the losses were 980 killed, 4,749 wounded, and 405 missing—6,134. Other portions of the army were under fire, but not closely engaged.

mies outnumbering his own forces ten to one. Most men under the same circumstances would have despaired of being able to accomplish anything against such odds, and, abandoning the district, would have fallen back toward Richmond. But Jackson was not like most men.

10. About the middle of March he learned that the Federals had begun to withdraw some of their troops from the Valley with the design of reinforcing McClellan. This he resolved to stop, if possible. Moving forward with a little more than 3,000 men he encountered the army of Shields, 7,000 strong, near Kernstown, about four miles south of Winchester (March 23d). A fierce battle was fought, in which Jackson was repulsed   But this bold movement caused the Union authorities at Washington to greatly overestimate his strength and to stop the withdrawal of troops from the valley.

11. So well pleased were the Richmond government and General Johnston that they sent to Jackson the division of General Ewell, raising his force to about 15,000 men. Soon after Jackson retreated to the east of the Blue Ridge through Brown's and Swift Run Gaps. General Turner Ashby with 1,000 cavalry alone remained behind, and moving from point to point kept Jackson informed of the movements of his enemies.

12. Jackson's foes and friends alike thought that he was in full retreat for Richmond. Reaching the Virginia Central he placed his men upon the cars. All felt gloomy at the thought of abandoning the Valley, when lo! the train moved to the westward, and in a few hours brought them to Staunton. With a part of

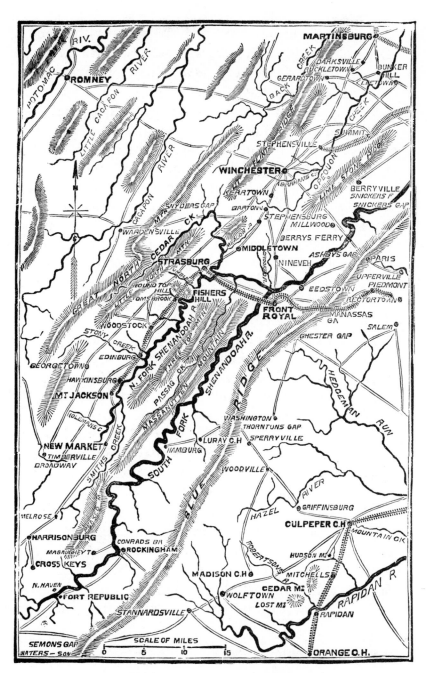

MAP OF SHENANDOAH VALLEY.

his force Jackson hastened to unite with General Edward Johnson, who was threatened with an attack by the army of Fremont advancing from Franklin.

13. Near the little village of McDowell the advance divisions of Fremont under Milroy and Schenck were encountered at Bull Pasture mountain (May 8th). After a desperate conflict the Federals were repulsed and fell back towards Franklin, with their flanks protected from Ashby's pursuing cavalry by the high mountains which skirted the valley through which lay their retreat. On the next morning Jackson sent the following dispatch to Richmond: "God blessed our arms with victory at McDowell yesterday." This was the first of the brilliant series of victories which have linked in undying fame the names Stonewall Jackson and Shenandoah Valley.

14. Jackson, leaving part of Ashby's cavalry under Captain Sheetz to menace Fremont near Franklin, marched with his main force down the Valley[1] for the purpose of attacking Banks. That officer had the larger part of his force well fortified near Strasburg, with a detachment at Front Royal, eight miles distant, and facing the Luray Valley. Reaching New Market Jackson left the main valley so suddenly that friends and foes were again mystified.

15. At Front Royal (May 23d) he suddenly turned up and swooped down upon the detachment under Colonel Kenly. After a fruitless resistance the Federals fled, with Jackson at their heels. The Confederate cavalry, under Colonel Flournoy and Lieutenant-Colonel Watts, captured great numbers of them. Gen-

[1] As the Shenandoah river flows northward, "down the Valley" means northward.

eral Banks at Strasburg hearing of Kenly's overthrow, began a rapid retreat upon Winchester.

16. At Newtown Jackson struck his flank (May
24th), capturing many prisoners and much spoil.   At
Winchester Banks attempted to make a stand, but,
after a sharp engagement with Ewell's division (May
25th), he fled again.   As the pursuing Confederates
pushed on through Winchester the ladies of that
patriotic little city, regardless of the bullets which
still occasionally fell around them, rushed from the
houses into the streets, greeting with delight their
Southern friends.   To Jackson's men it was a glorious
day.

17. Banks continued his retreat across the Potomac,
and then sent a dispatch congratulating his government that he at last had his army safe in Maryland.
Jackson then advanced to Harper's Ferry, and threatened the force there under General Saxton with an
assault, staying long enough to allow the rich spoils
captured at Winchester to be sent away toward Staunton.   Then he returned to Winchester.

18. Banks's defeat caused great consternation at
Washington.   Fremont and Shields were ordered to
unite their forces and cut off Jackson's escape.   General Imboden, who had been ordered by Jackson to
secure the gaps giving Fremont the nearest approach
to the Confederate rear, performed his part so well
that Fremont's advance did not reach Strasburg until
Jackson had passed.   But Shields was marching upon
Jackson from another direction, and the Federals were
confident that they would "bag" him.   But the skillful
Confederate passed between the converging armies
and escaped.

19. As the Confederates retired before their pursuers the cavalry, under the dashing Ashby, were ever impeding the Federal advance. This knightly Virginian, always in the front of battle, fell in a skirmish near Harrisonburg (June 6th)

20. At Cross Keys Jackson turned upon Fremont (June 8th), and after a long and bloody conflict remained master of the field. Leaving one division under Ewell to watch Fremont, Jackson with the rest of the army marched to Port Republic, on the Shenandoah river, to meet Shields. Here he gained the crowning victory of the campaign, attacking the advance of the Federals under Tyler, and driving them completely from the field. Fremont, hearing the noise of the battle, attempted to go to the rescue of Shields; but Ewell, after delaying him for some time, succeeded in getting across the river and burning the bridges. When Fremont came in sight of the battle-field the Federals had already been routed, and it was impossible for him to get across the river to assist his friends. Two days later Fremont and Shields succeeded in joining their forces, but not as victors. By the third day after the battle of Port Republic they were retreating to Luray Valley, where they could better protect Washington from the dreaded advance of Stonewall Jackson.[1]

[1] In this wonderful campaign Jackson's maximum strength was never more than 17,000. The lowest Union estimate of their forces in the Valley, including the troops at Harper's Ferry, is 52,000. But these are not all that could have been brought against Jackson. In the three departments of Fremont, Banks and McDowell. there were 80,000 men that could have been united against Jackson but were not. That Jackson was able to so far out-general them as to strike his enemy in almost every instance with superior numbers shows matchless skill. The total Union loss was 4,609, of whom 3,199 were captured. Jackson's total loss was 1,878, of whom only 232 were captured or missing.

21. General Lee, who was now in command of the Confederate army at Richmond, had sent Whiting's division to reinforce Jackson, and at his suggestion the Richmond papers had announced that Lee was sending men enough to the Valley to enable Jackson to advance upon Washington. Lee's design was to so mystify the Federal Government and its commanders as to bring Jackson to himself without their finding it out, and thus defeat McClellan before the other Union armies could march to his assistance. In Jackson Lee had a man who knew well how to carry out this plan. Sending Imboden with a small force of infantry and cavalry to keep up a clatter in the neighborhood of Fremont and Shields, and thus make them expect his own advance, Jackson on the 17th of June began his march for Richmond.

The Seven Days' Battles.

22. **Stuart's ride around McClellan** was made between the time of the battle of Port Republic and the beginning of Jackson's movement toward Richmond. In this daring raid Stuart made the entire circuit of McClellan's army, bringing in prisoners and booty and much important information. Lee was now ready, so soon as Jackson should join him, to strike the blow which he had been preparing for from the time that he took command of the Army of Northern Virginia.

23. **The Attack Begins.**—About two hours before sunset on the 26th of June Jackson's signal guns announced to General A. P. Hill that he had reached the outposts on the Union right. Hill had already crossed the Chickahominy near Meadow Bridge. As he and D. H. Hill advanced the whole plateau about

Mechanicsville was yielded to the Confederates, and the Federals retired behind Beaver Dam Creek, which was strongly fortified. The brigades of Ripley and Pender assaulted this strong position just at dark, but were repulsed.

24. **Gaines's Mill and Cold Harbor.**—Next morning, as the Confederates advanced, the whole Federal line fell back to Gaines's Mill and New Cold Harbor. The

SCENE IN THE CHICKAHOMINY SWAMP.

entire Union army before Richmond numbered at this time 105,000 effectives, of whom about 40,000 were under General Fitz John Porter, behind Powhite Creek, in the fortified lines at Gaines's Mill and Cold Harbor, and on the north side of the Chickahominy river. On the south side of that stream was Mc-Clellan with the greater part of the Union army. The Confederate army, including the reinforcements under Jackson, numbered about 80,000 effectives. Of this number Lee led 50,000 to attack Porter's position, and left Magruder with the balance to prevent Mc-Clellan's advance upon Richmond.

25. As the Confederates under Lee advanced, A. P. Hill first struck the Federal line; then Longstreet came into action. Jackson, with his own troops and those of D. H. Hill, formed the Confederate left, and advanced to turn the Union right, while Whiting's division was sent by Jackson to the help of Longstreet, on the Confederate right and opposite Porter's left center. From early in the afternoon until nearly sundown the Confederates made charge after charge only to be repulsed. On the success of their attack hung the fate of Richmond, and it seemed as though the day was about to go against them. Just as the sun was setting the whole Confederate line from right to left swept forward in one grand charge. On the Confederate right Whiting's division, consisting of Law's and Hood's brigades, with trailed arms and without firing, rushed forward down a slope and towards a ravine opposite that part of the Union line.[1] At every step the Federal artillery tore great gaps in their ranks. But swiftly and silently they swept on. As they approached the ravine and saw the desperate nature of the work before them they answered with a wild yell the roar of the Union musketry, and rushed for the works, sweeping out the first Federal line, which, in its flight, carried with it the second line also. On the extreme Confederate left the troops of D. H. Hill also out-flanked and broke the Union right, and

---

[1] Law's Brigade embraced the Second and Eleventh Mississippi, the Fourth Alabama, and the Sixth North Carolina. Hood led into the charge the Fourteenth Texas and Eighteenth Georgia.

the whole Confederate line, from one end to the other, moving forward in a resistless charge, occupied the Federal intrenchments, and the hard-fought field was won.[1]

26. Meanwhile, on the south side of the Chickahominy, General Magruder had so skillfully performed his part that he kept each of the Union corps commanders in momentary expectation of attack, and thus not only prevented McClellan from advancing upon Richmond, but also kept him from sending reinforcements to Porter. Thus Porter was overwhelmed, and the decisive Confederate victory of Gaines's Mill (or Cold Harbor) compelled McClellan to give up the siege of Richmond.

27. McClellan's retreat to the James was marked by the battles of Savage's Station (June 29th), Frazer's Farm and White Oak Swamp (June 30th), and Malvern Hill (July 1st). The last-named battle was fought with great desperation on both sides. It began late in the afternoon, and lasted until the darkness prevented farther fighting. The Confederates were repulsed, but remained close to the Federal works with the intention of renewing the battle in the morning. During the night some of Jackson's officers expressed the opinion that in the morning McClellan would assume the aggressive. "No," replied Jackson, "I think he will clear out in the morning." The Federals were gone before morning, and owing to the belief that Longstreet and A. P. Hill were making a march between Malvern Hill and Harrison's Landing, this retreat was attended with much disorder.

[1] In this grand charge were engaged troops from every Southern State, from Virginia to Texas.

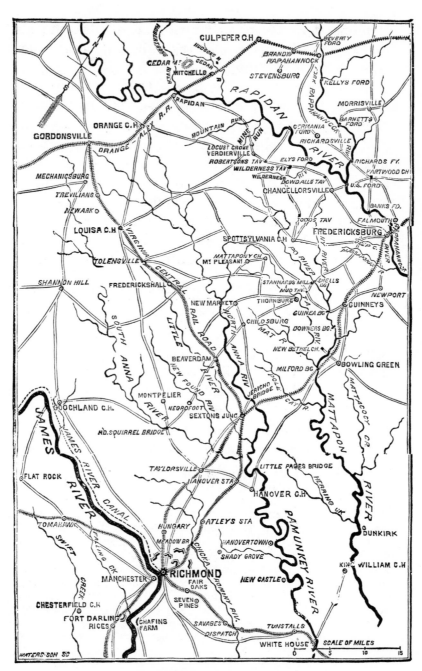

MAP OF NORTHERN VIRGINIA.

Wagons were abandoned by the Federals, who also
threw away knapsacks, cartridge-boxes, clothing and
rifles by the thousand.

28. The result of the Seven Days' Battles was a
complete Confederate victory. Lee had attacked his
enemy heavily intrenched, and had driven him to the
shelter of his gunboats, capturing from him 52 cannon,
more than 35,000 small arms, an immense amount of
army stores, and ten thousand prisoners, of whom
over six thousand were unwounded. The siege of
Richmond was raised and the discouragement at the
North was as great as after the battle of Manassas.
President Lincoln issued a call for 300,000 more men.[1]

CAMPAIGN OF THE SECOND MANASSAS (BULL RUN.)

29. On the very day that Lee was fighting the battle
of Gaines's Mill or (Cold Harbor) General John Pope,
who had made some reputation in the West, took command of the defeated armies of Banks, Fremont and
Shields, and uniting them into one force, began to
make ready for an advance upon Richmond. Before
Pope's army could be concentrated, the decisive defeat
of McClellan before Richmond compelled an alteration

[1] According to the official records "the effective force of the Union army
in these battles was 105,000." McClellan reports his losses as follows:
1,734 killed, 8,062 wounded, and 6,053 captured or missing—15,849. Other
authorities put the Union loss at 20,000, and this is probably nearer the
correct figures. President Lincoln visited the army at Harrison's Landing and found 86,000 men there. Thousands of McClellan's wounded fell
into the hands of the Confederates and were counted by them as among
their prisoners. The Confederate records are imperfect, many of them
being lost at the evacuation of Richmond in 1865. As near as can be
ascertained Lee's effective force in these battles was 80,000. His losses
were 3,286 killed, 15,909 wounded, and 940 captured or missing—20,135.
As the Confederates in every instance attacked strongly entrenched
lines, their losses in killed and wounded were much heavier than those of
the Federals.

BATTLE OF MALVERN HILL.

of the whole plan of campaign. In order to secure proper co-operation between McClellan and Pope, it was decided by the government at Washington to call Halleck from the West and make him commander-in-chief. This calling of Halleck to Washington stopped for a while all aggressive movements of the Federals in the West. So decisive was the great Confederate victory before Richmond, that it broke up the Union plan of operations for 1862, both in the East and in the West.

30. Halleck now ordered McClellan to send his army around by Aquia Creek, that it might be united with the force under Pope, and that a new advance upon Richmond might be made. Lee was uncertain as to what course the Federals would adopt, and was anxious to force the army of McClellan to abandon its position upon the James river and go northward to the defense of Washington. With the double purpose of effecting this result and of checking the advance of the army under Pope, Lee sent Stonewall Jackson to Gordonsville and kept Longstreet near Richmond to engage McClellan, if he should attempt another advance upon the Confederate capital. Jackson had with him his own and Ewell's division, and later on that of A. P. Hill was also sent to him.

BATTLE OF CEDAR (OR SLAUGHTER) MOUNTAIN.

31. Near Cedar (also called Slaughter) Mountain Jackson encountered Pope's advance under Banks, and the battle of Cedar Run was fought. At first outnumbered, the Confederates were forced back, but being reinforced they finally succeeded in driving the

GENERAL LEE AT THE SOLDIERS' PRAYER-MEETING.

Federals from the field.[1]   As soon as Lee became convinced that Richmond was in no danger from Mc-
Clellan he left four divisions to watch the movements
of the Union army on the James, and ordered those
divisions to move northward and join him as soon as
it was certain that the Federals had left that vicinity.
Lee himself commenced a vigorous campaign against
Pope.

32. Finding that the Union commander had placed
his army in a weak position between the Rapidan and
the Rappahannock rivers Lee determined upon prompt
action.   But before he could carry out his design a
dispatch that had been sent to General Stuart fell into
Pope's hands, and that general hastened to withdraw
his army to a safe position behind the Rappahannock.
While Lee was trying to find a good way to turn the
Federals out of their strong position Stuart, by a
charge upon Pope's headquarters' train, captured official papers which gave information that McClellan's
army on the James was being withdrawn for the
purpose of reinforcing Pope.

33. Lee, relieved now of all fear for the safety of
Richmond, sent Jackson northward and far to the
rear of the Federal army.   Stonewall, moving with
his usual rapidity, was soon many miles in rear of
Pope's army, and between it and Washington, having
gone without serious opposition from the Rappahannock close up to the field of Manassas, where the first

---

[1] In this battle the whole Union force engaged was 17,900. After their
defeat they were joined by a fresh division and by Pope in person, but it
was then too late. Jackson's force from first to last numbered about
20,000. The Union loss was 314 killed, 1,445 wounded and 622 captured
or missing—2,381. The Confederate loss was 241 killed, 1,120 wounded
and 4 missing—1,365.

great battle of the war had been fought. Jackson sent a force which captured Manassas Junction, taking eight cannon, a lot of prisoners, and a vast amount of all sorts of military supplies. Many a hungry Confederate feasted that day on dainties to which he had long been a stranger. Jackson took such of the supplies captured at Manassas as the Confederates could use and burned the rest. Then on the old battle-field of the previous year he waited for the Federals!

34. When Pope first took command in Virginia he announced to his army that he had come from the West, where he had always seen the backs of his enemies; that he wished them to discard such phrases as " taking strong positions and holding them," " lines of retreat," and "bases of supplies." He warned them that "success and glory are in the advance," and that "disaster and shame lurk in the rear." Notwithstanding this fine proclamation, his troops on their first encounter with Jackson at Cedar Run had been forced to retreat, and now the unexpected and brilliant move of Jackson convinced Pope that he must be looking after "the danger that lurked in the rear."

35. Leaving his strong position, Pope led his whole army against Jackson, hoping to crush that daring general before Lee could rejoin him. This was exactly what Pope ought to have done, and it was just what Lee thought that he would do. But the Confederate commander believed that Jackson could hold out, even against odds, until Longstreet, with the other wing of the army, should come to his assistance. This Longstreet hastened to do, forcing his way through Thoroughfare Gap, and coming to the support

of Jackson on the afternoon of August 29th. All that day Jackson had been fighting tremendous odds, but, as at the first Manassas, his men had stood like a solid wall of rock against the surging masses of the Federals.

36. Next morning (August 30th) Pope's whole army pressed up against Jackson, as if to crush him with an overwhelming mass. The Union commander did not seem to be aware of the presence of Longstreet, who, at the critical moment, fell with resistless power upon the Federal left. Then the whole Confederate line, moving forward, forced back the Federals across Bull Run, and the second Manassas was added to the list of Southern victories.[1]

37. Pope retreated to Centerville, where he was re-inforced by Sumner's and Franklin's commands from McClellan's army. Porter's corps, from the same army, had joined him in time to take part in the battle of the 30th. Lee spent the 31st in caring for his killed and wounded, and gathering up the spoils of the battle-field. On the next day (September 1st,) finding Pope strongly posted, Lee sent Jackson to flank his position. The Federal commander there-upon resumed his retreat towards Washington. At

---

[1] A careful review of the official records justifies the conclusion that in this great battle the effective strength of the Union army was 63,000 of all arms, and of the Confederate army 54,000. The Union losses were stated at 1,747 killed, 8,452 wounded, and 4,263 captured or missing—14,462. About 3,000 of their wounded fell into the hands of the Confederates, thus making their capture of prisoners amount to over 7,000 men. The Confederate loss is stated at 1,553 killed, 7,812 wounded, and 109 missing—9,474. They had captured during the campaign 30 cannon and more than 20,000 small arms. Horace Greeley, in his "American Conflict" (page 189), says that Pope's loss, if we include stragglers who never returned to their regiments, must have been fully 30,000 men.

Chantilly, or Ox Hill, his rear guard was attacked by Jackson, and there occurred a sharp conflict, in which the Union generals Stevens and Kearny were killed. Pope continued his retreat until his whole army was within the fortifications of Washington. Then he resigned his command, and McClellan was again called upon to save the Union capital.

38. The grand armies of the North, which had been so carefully organized and drilled, so splendidly equipped and so confidently sent forth for the conquest of Virginia and the South, had been driven back to the starting point, outgeneraled, baffled and defeated by armies greatly inferior in numbers, but greatly superior in the skill of their leaders.

CHAPTER III.

THE MARYLAND AND KENTUCKY CAMPAIGNS.

AS the summer of 1862 drew to a close, the fortunes of the Southern Confederacy were at full tide. On the very day that Lee gained the second battle of Manassas (August 30th) the Confederates under Kirby Smith won a brilliant victory near Richmond, in Kentucky, almost annihilating the opposing force. While the Confederate army of northern Virginia was entering Maryland, the western army of the Confederacy was sweeping everything before it in Kentucky. We will first notice events in the East.

THE MARYLAND CAMPAIGN.

2. As soon as Lee had cleared Virginia of invaders, he resolved on entering Maryland. He would thus afford the people of that state an opportunity to ally themselves with their Southern friends, and could also for a time at least, relieve the pressure upon the South. His army at this time numbered about 45,000 effectives. Many had been lost in battle, and many others had been so exhausted by long and rapid marches with insufficient supplies of food and want of shoes, that they had been unable to keep up with their stronger comrades. But the army, though greatly reduced in numbers, and suffering great hardships, was inspirited by its recent victories and felt capable of doing almost anything. On the 5th of September while the bands played the

popular air " Maryland, my Maryland,"[1] Lee's veterans,
whose hearts beat high with hope, crossed the Potomac.

3. Lee advanced to Frederick and there issued a
proclamation to the people of Maryland inviting them
to join the Southern cause.   There were already in the
Confederate army valiant sons of Maryland, who upon
the Federal occupation of their State had fled to Virginia to share the fortunes of the South.   They hoped
that thousands of their fellow-citizens would flock to
Lee's victorious standard.   But they were doomed to
disappointment.   The mass of Southern sympathizers
in Maryland were beyond the section of the State
occupied by the Confederates.

4. While at Frederick Lee found out that Harper's
Ferry was still garrisoned by the Federals.   Considering it dangerous to leave this strong post on his line of
communications in the hands of his enemies he determined to send Jackson with a force sufficient for its
reduction.   In order to do this it was necessary to
divide his army, already much weaker in numbers
than the now united forces of Pope and McClellan.
Lee believed that Harper's Ferry could be reduced,
and that his own forces could be united before Mc-
Clellan would be ready to press him.

5. Jackson, moving with his usual rapidity, recrossed the Potomac into Virginia and marched upon
Harper's Ferry from that side, while Major-General
Lafayette McLaws, with his own and Anderson's
divisions, moved for the purpose of seizing Maryland

[1] This noted Confederate war song was written by James R. Randall,
a native of Maryland. It is a feeling appeal to his State to ally herself
with the Southern Confederacy. It was written in the Parish of Pointe
Coupée in Louisiana in April, 1861.

A FULL-DRESS RECEPTION AT THE CONFEDERATE WHITE-HOUSE.

Heights, and Major-General John G. Walker recrossed the Potomac and occupied Loudon Heights. The garrison at Harper's Ferry found itself completely trapped.

6. Meanwhile an event occurred which came near thwarting Lee's whole plan and bringing ruin upon his army. Up to September 12th McClellan had been moving with great caution, but on that day a lost copy of Lee's order directing the movements of the Confederate army fell into the hands of the Union commander. Immediately he abandoned his cautious policy and moved with energy and rapidity, with the double purpose of relieving Harper's Ferry and crushing Lee's divided forces before they could reunite.

GENERAL HOWELL COBB.

7. At **Crampton's Gap** General Howell Cobb with three brigades of McLaws' division was posted, with orders to hold that pass until Harper's Ferry had surrendered, "even if he lost his last man in doing it." McClellan sent General Franklin to force his way through this pass. But it was so gallantly defended that Franklin did not succeed in getting through until the morning of the 15th, and then he was too late.

8. **Upon South Mountain at Boonsboro Gap** another Confederate force was posted under General D. H. Hill. Against this position McClellan sent the main body of his army (September 14th). Hill and his brave men

held their ground with their usual intrepidity. At the critical moment Longstreet arrived with his corps and saved Hill from being overwhelmed by the superior numbers of the enemy. McClellan succeeded by night in carrying part of the Confederate line. During the night the Confederates retired. By 10 o'clock next morning they were safely in position at Sharpsburg in a place where they could be easily joined by Jackson. Lee had baffled McClellan's plan to crush him, and had gained all the time needed for the success of Jackson's movement.

9. **Harper's Ferry** had meanwhile been closely invested by the forces under Jackson. During the 14th the summits of all the heights commanding the Federal position were crowned with artillery, which was ready to open fire by dawn of the 15th. After two hours' bombardment, the garrison of about 12,000 men surrendered. The Confederates captured also 73 cannon, 13,000 small arms, 200 wagons, and a large quantity of military stores. Leaving A. P. Hill to receive the surrender, Jackson again crossed into Maryland with the greater part of his force, and hastened to join Lee at Sharpsburg. McLaws and Walker did likewise.

10. At **Sharpsburg,** behind **Antietam Creek,** in a well-selected position, Lee's army, less than 40,000 strong, awaited the onset of McClellan's 87,000. Though the Union General appeared before this position on the afternoon of the 15th, he did not attack. He spent all the following day making preparations for the battle. On the morning of the 17th the corps of Mansfield and Hooker advanced to the attack. They were met by the divisions of Hood and Anderson, re-

inforced by Evans's brigade and D. H. Hill's division.
After a fierce conflict, in which Mansfield was killed
and Hooker wounded, their troops were completely
broken.   The fresh corps of Sumner and Franklin
now coming up forced back for a while the lately victorious Confederates, but Jackson's corps, consisting
of the veterans of Early, Trimble, Lawton and Starke,
held their ground until the timely arrival of the divisions of McLaws and Walker enabled the hard-pressed
Confederate left to repulse the Federals at every point.
Jackson had met and defeated the ablest generals in
the Federal army.

11. Burnside, with 20,000 men, had been ordered
by McClellan to assail the Confederate right, but he
had been held in check for several hours at a bridge
which crossed the Antietam by Toombs's brigade,[1] of
D. R. Jones's division.   Not until 4 o'clock in the
afternoon did Burnside get across, and it was an hour
later before he was ready to advance.   Then, by a
charge, he drove back Jones's division, gaining the
crest of the ridge south of the town.   At that moment
the division of A. P. Hill, 4,500 strong, arrived from
Harper's Ferry, and, falling upon the flank of Burnside's troops, drove them back across the Antietam.
As the sun went down the battle closed, with Lee's
army still in possession of the field.

12. All the next day Lee offered battle, but McClellan, though reinforced by 15,000 fresh troops, did not
attack.   On the night of the 18th, Lee, who had no
reinforcements near, recrossed the Potomac unmolested.   Porter's troops were sent across the Potomac

[1] Numbering about 600 men.

after Lee, but A. P. Hill drove them back at **Shepherds-town**, with heavy loss. Thus ended the Maryland campaign.

13. The Confederates had been disappointed in their hope that large numbers of Marylanders would join their standard. The ac- cident by which Lee's order of march fell in- to the hands of Mc- Clellan placed that part of the Confederate army still in Mary- land in great peril. But their desperate fighting against great odds at South Moun- tain and Crampton's Gap rescued them, in part, from the danger that threatened, and enabled their comrades investing Harper's Ferry to capture that post with its rich spoil.

LIEUT.-GENERAL JUBAL A. EARLY.

Their delay of McClellan also enabled Lee to reunite his divided army in time for the battle of Sharpsburg (or Antietam). In that great battle, so magnificent was the fighting of the Southern troops against great odds, that McClellan was not only repulsed, but was even impressed with the idea that Lee had more men than himself. The result was that Lee, after main- taining a defiant front all the next day, retired on the **night of the 18th across** the Potomac, carrying off in

safety his great train of artillery and wagons, leaving
" not a single trophy of his nocturnal retreat in the
hands of his enemy." Lee's men well knew the
odds against which they had fought, and ever afterwards felt that, though their enemy might sometimes be too strong for them to drive, yet they
could hold their ground against any force, however great, that might attack them.

14. Two inci-
dents of the battle
of Sharpsburg
(Antietam) are
worth special men-
tion. At one time,
when the Confed-
erate centre had
been stripped of
troops to help their
hard-pressed left,
General Longstreet
noticed that a
strong column of
the enemy was ad-
vancing against
this very point,
held by one small

GENERAL BURNSIDE.

regiment, Cooke's Twenty-seventh North Carolina, who
were without a cartridge. Two pieces of the Washington artillery were there, but most of the gunners
had been killed or wounded. Longstreet and his
staff[1] dismounted and served these guns until help

[1] These staff officers were Majors Fairfax and Sorrell and Captain
Latrobe.

reached them, and the Federals were repulsed. The other incident is related by Colonel Henry Kyd Douglas. At the time of Burnside's advance and before the arrival of A. P. Hill a section of the Rockbridge artillery was hurried over from the left to the right to check the Federal advance. As the horses drawing the guns galloped rapidly by where Lee was standing the general's youngest son, Robert E. Lee, Jr., a private soldier black with the long day's fight, stopped a moment to salute his father and then rushed after his gun. Is it any wonder that Lee's soldiers were such heroes?[1]

15. General Lee remained in the neighborhood of Shepherdstown for a few days and then took up a position between Bunker Hill and Winchester. Here the war-worn Confederates enjoyed several weeks of undisturbed repose. While in the camp several distinguished British officers visited Lee's headquarters, among whom was General Garnet Wolseley, since prominent in history. The monotony of camp life was also relieved by visits from the ladies and gentlemen of Winchester and the neighborhood.

16. During this season of rest General Stuart with 1,800 cavalry crossed the Potomac above Williamsport, pushed on to Chambersburg in Pennsylvania, where

---

[1] In the battle of Sharpsburg (or Antietam) McClellan states his strength at 87,000. Lee states his force at less than 40,000. The loss of the Union army in all the battles of the campaign from September 3d to September 20th, exclusive of Harper's Ferry, was 2,629 killed, 11,583 wounded, and 991 captured or missing—making a total of 15,203. The Union loss at Harper's Ferry was 44 killed, 173 wounded, and 12,520 captured—12,737. Total Union loss in the campaign, 27,940. The Confederate loss in all the battles (South Mountain, Crampton's Gap, Harper's Ferry, Sharpsburg and Shepherdstown) was 1,890 killed, 9,770 wounded and 2,304 captured or missing—13,964.

he destroyed a large amount of supplies; then passing entirely around McClellan's army he recrossed into Virginia below Harper's Ferry. In this raid Stuart captured 1,000 horses. He lost in the whole expedition only three wounded and three missing.

17. While the army was resting, its strength was steadily increasing, chiefly by the return of absentees, who had recovered from sickness or from wounds. By the middle of October its strength amounted to 60,000 men, full of spirit and ready for any enterprise.

The Kentucky Campaign.

18. We will now turn our attention to the West and notice the course of events in that quarter. After the evacuation of Corinth by the Confederates, General Halleck made a new distribution of the Union armies of the West. He kept 65,000 with himself, he ordered General Buell to move toward Chattanooga and attempt the conquest of East Tennessee, and the rest of his force he sent across the Mississippi to the help of General Curtis in Arkansas.

19. In Northern Mississippi the Confederates had a force under Van Dorn and Price, leaders, whose enterprise compensated in some measure for the inferiority of their numbers. The army at Tupelo under General Braxton Bragg, a man of nerve and ability, was eager to be led against the Federals. General E. Kirby Smith commanded the Confederate force in East Tennessee. The occupation of Cumberland Gap by a Union force under Brigadier General George W. Morgan, and the advance of Buell toward Chattanooga greatly endangered Smith's department.

20. Bragg sent Major-General John P. McCown's division to Chattanooga (June 27th). He also sent to Tennessee cavalry expeditions under Colonels John H. Morgan and Nathan B. Forrest. Morgan advanced into Kentucky, captured Lebanon and Cynthiana with 1,200 prisoners and returning to Tennessee, captured Clarksville with a very large amount of military stores. Forrest crossed the Tennessee river at Chattanooga early in July, and captured McMinville and Murfresboro with the garrison of the latter place.

GENERAL E. KIRBY SMITH.

21. Bragg now ordered the march of his whole force from Tupelo to Chattanooga. The Union army in North Mississippi was at this time under General Grant. Halleck had been summoned to Washington after McClellan's defeat before Richmond, and placed in command of all the Union forces. In order to prevent Grant from marching against Tupelo, Bragg had sent Col. Joseph Wheeler into Middle Tennessee. This officer spent a week behind the Union lines, attacking important posts, destroying bridges, and creating the impression of a general advance. Bragg left Van Dorn and Price to confront Grant, and with

Lis army marched to Chattanooga to join Smith. He now, with Kirby Smith, arranged for an advance into Middle Tennessee and Kentucky.

22. By the 14th of August Smith started north-ward by way of Rogers's Gap. General Heth, with another part of his force, marched through Big Creek Gap, and General Stevenson advanced to Cumber-land Gap, which was still occupied by the Federals under General George W. Morgan. Smith hastened forward toward the rich blue grass region of central Kentucky. Colonel John S. Scott, with 900 cavalry, preceded the column.

23. Near the town of Richmond Scott discovered the Federals drawn up in line of battle to prevent any farther advance of the Confederates. Although Smith had with him only the two divisions of Cleburne and Churchill, he resolved on immediate attack, believing that boldness was the surest road to victory. Cleburne opened the fight (August 30th)[1] and Churchill joined in the attack. The Federals, under General Manson, were soon routed. Farther on they found reinforce-ments under General William Nelson, who now took command and tried to stay the Confederate advance. All in vain. Attacked in front and flank, and rear, the Union troops at last gave way in utter rout. Over 1,000 of them were killed and wounded, and more than 4,000 were captured.[2]

24. Reinforced just after the battle by Heth's divi-sion, the victorious Confederates moved on and occu-pied Lexington. Heth, going northward to Coving-ton, alarmed the North for the safety of Cincinnati.

[1] The same day on which Lee gained the battle of Manassas.
[2] The Confederates also captured nine cannon and 10,000 small arms.

25. The Union General Morgan at Cumberland
Gap, becoming alarmed at these movements in his
rear, abandoned his position and retreated with his
force of nearly 9,000 men through Eastern Kentucky
to the Ohio river. The Confederate General Stevenson with about an equal force now occupied the Gap.

26. Meanwhile Bragg at Chattanooga organized his
army of about   0,000 men into two wings—the right
under General Leonidas Polk, the left under General
William J. Hardee. Flanking Buell's army he moved
northward and entered Kentucky on the 5th of September (the same day that Lee entered Maryland).
Reaching Mumfordsville he captured a Union fort and
its garrison of 4,000 men before Buell could go to their
assistance (September 17th).[1] Bragg moved forward
until he had occupied Frankfort, the capital of Kentucky. There he inaugurated Richard Hawes as Confederate Provisional Governor of that State (October
4th).

27. Buell, who had now reached Louisville and received heavy reinforcements, began to advance upon
Bragg. The Confederates had hoped to receive large
accessions to their numbers in Kentucky; but those
who joined them did not make up for their losses by
the dropping out of broken-down men, a character of
loss which always attends a rapidly moving army.

28. When Bragg found that Buell was advancing in
overwhelming force he began to retire. Buell's advance was so conducted that Bragg, instead of calling
Smith to his assistance, sent a large part of his force
to the help of Smith. The result was that Buell's

---

[1] Among the trophies were ten cannon and 5,000 small arms.

main army came up with Bragg's diminished forces at Perryville on the evening of October 7th.

29. **The Battle of Perryville** was opened by the advance of Cheatham's division of Polk's wing (October 8th). Cheatham was at once supported by Cleburne and Bushrod Johnson of Hardee's wing, and soon the whole Confederate line from right to left was advancing steadily, forcing back the Federals. During this fierce struggle the Confederates advanced nearly a mile, capturing prisoners, guns and colors. At length darkness came, and they rested on the field so bravely won.

30. As the darkness which ended the conflict came on, it was evident to the Confederate commander that

GENERAL FITZHUGH LEE.

the Federals were massing in overwhelming force. The soldiers themselves only knew that they had been successful in the fight of that day, and hence they were surprised when at midnight they were withdrawn. General Buell in his account of the battle says that Bragg " captured some artillery that he did not carry off, though he exchanged some of his pieces for better ones." Bragg states that he captured fifteen guns.[1]

31. Buell ordered Crittenden, commanding his right

corps, to renew the fight at 6 o'clock the next morning, but, through a misunderstanding, the advance did not begin until 9 o'clock. Then the Federals found out that the Confederates had retired, and that only three divisions had been engaged in the attack upon them on the afternoon of the previous day. Buell also admits

LIEUTENANT-GENERAL JAMES LONGSTREET.   that this battle had enabled Bragg "to perfect his junction with Kirby Smith at Harrodsburg, as originally intended." [2]

32. After concentrating his forces near Harrodsburg, Bragg waited two days for Buell's attack. As the Union army showed no disposition to do this, but

---

[1] According to the official record the Union army at Perryville numbered 54,000 men, of whom about half were present in time for the battle. The Union loss was 845 killed, 2,851 wounded, and 515 captured or missing—4,211. The whole Confederate force of all arms numbered only 16,000. The Confederate loss was 510 killed, 2,635 wounded, and 251 captured or missing—3,396.

Buell's own statement, in volume III. of "Battles and Leaders of the Civil War," page 49.

seemed inclined to await its own time for battle, unless Bragg should attack, the Confederate general being fully aware of the inferiority of his force, determined to withdraw from Kentucky. Accordingly, Kirby Smith and Colonel Wheeler were entrusted with the task of covering the retreat and holding the Federals in check. The long train of captured stores made the progress of the army very slow, sometimes only five miles a day.

33. So well were the Federals held in check that nothing was lost. Before the pursuit was abandoned, at Rock Castle, Wheeler's cavalry had been engaged twenty-six times. His vigilance was so well known by the infantry that they never feared a surprise. Early in November Wheeler and Forrest were ten miles south of Nashville with the cavalry, and Breckinridge was with part of the army at Murfreesboro. Here, towards the last of the month, the whole Confederate army was concentrated.

34. The Kentucky campaign was over. Buell was deprived of his command for not having defeated Bragg. On the other hand, the Southern people found great fault with Bragg for not having destroyed the army of Buell.

35. Nevertheless the Kentucky campaign was attended with great results to the Confederacy. General Wheeler sums them up thus: " Two months of marches and battles by the armies of Bragg and Smith had cost the Federals a loss in killed, wounded and prisoners of 26,530. We had captured 35 cannon, 16,000 stands of arms, millions of rounds of ammunition, 1,700 mules, 300 wagons loaded with military stores and 2,000 horses. We had recovered

Cumberland Gap and redeemed Middle Tennessee and North Alabama."

36. When Bragg marched into Kentucky he left Van Dorn and Price in Northern Mississippi to prevent Grant and Rosecrans from reinforcing Buell, and with the hope that Price might be able to move to his aid.   **At Iuka** in Northern Mississippi, Price fought an indecisive battle (September 19th).

37. **At Corinth** on the 4th of October the united forces of Van Dorn and Price, numbering 22,000, attacked an equal number of Federals under Rosecrans in a strongly fortified position.   Notwithstanding the most desperate valor the Confederates failed completely.[1] Thus neither Price nor Van Dorn had been able to go to the help of Bragg, while Grant had been able to reinforce Buell.   Thus, though the lack of sufficient numbers had prevented complete Confederate success, yet the Kentucky campaign had recovered much lost ground, and also prevented the advance of the Federals all along the line.

[1] The Union loss in this battle was 355 killed, 1,841 wounded and 324 captured or missing—2,520.

The Confederate loss 505 killed, 2,150 wounded, and 2,183 captured or missing—4,838.

CHAPTER IV.

FREDERICKSBURG, SECOND ATTEMPT UPON VICKSBURG, MURFREESBORO.

FREDERICKSBURG.

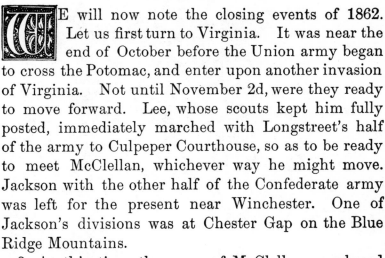E will now note the closing events of 1862. Let us first turn to Virginia. It was near the end of October before the Union army began to cross the Potomac, and enter upon another invasion of Virginia. Not until November 2d, were they ready to move forward. Lee, whose scouts kept him fully posted, immediately marched with Longstreet's half of the army to Culpeper Courthouse, so as to be ready to meet McClellan, whichever way he might move. Jackson with the other half of the Confederate army was left for the present near Winchester. One of Jackson's divisions was at Chester Gap on the Blue Ridge Mountains.

2. At this time the army of McClellan numbered 145,000, and that of Lee about 72,000. Yet neither Lee nor his soldiers expected anything but victory, whenever or wherever the next battle might be fought. A stanza of one of the favorite camp songs of the Confederates expresses well their confidence:

> Lee formed his line of battle,
> Said, "Boys, you need not fear,
> For Longstreet's in the centre
> And Jackson's in their rear."

3. McClellan's movements were not rapid enough to suit the authorities at Washington. So on the 5th of November President Lincoln wrote an order re-

ATTACK ON FREDERICKSBURG.

moving him from command and putting General Ambrose E. Burnside in his place. But the disastrous failures of McClellan's successors ought to make his critics less severe in their judgment of that officer.[1]

4. Burnside formed his army into three grand divisions. About the 19th of November Lee received information that Sumner's grand division was moving towards Fredericksburg. At once two of Longstreet's divisions were sent to that place, and on the 21st reached the hills which surrounded that little city. A few days later the rest of Longstreet's corps came up. As soon as it was known that all of Burnside's army was on the march for Fredericksburg Jackson's command was also brought down from the Shenandoah, and Lee's whole force was once more concentrated in front of the Federal hosts.

5. After several weeks of careful preparation Burnside began the crossing of the Rappahannock (December 11th). But Barksdale's single brigade of Mississippians kept up such a hot fire along the river front that they defeated nine different attempts of the Federals to construct their pontoon bridges. Then the powerful artillery of the Union army from Stafford poured a terrific iron hail upon the gallant Mississippians and the town of Fredericksburg. But the defense was kept up until all the Confederate troops had been able to take their proper positions, and then Barksdale's men were withdrawn from their perilous post. Their heroic fight had long delayed the crossing of Sumner's grand division, and had caused

---

[1] Meade did not one bit better after Gettysburg, and even Grant was repeatedly defeated by Lee, and would have succeeded no better in the end but for the complete collapse of the Confederate power in the West.

Franklin's grand division, which had crossed farther down, to return to the Federal side of the river to await the result of Sumner's efforts. Thus Lee secured twenty-four hours to prepare for the assault, and also had full notice of the points of attack.

6. During the 12th the vast army of the Federals was massed and prepared for the assault. Heavy skirmishing of the outposts continued all day long. On the 13th came the shock of battle. Franklin's "left grand division" assaulted Jackson's lines near Hamilton's Crossing. As they moved forward in their bright blue uniforms, with bayonets glistening in the sun, they presented a magnificent spectacle, in striking contrast with the butternut suits of Jackson's grim veterans, who silently waited their approach. Soon Stuart's horse artillery under Major John Pelham, a brave officer and almost a boy in years, opened upon the dense masses of Federals. When they came near enough Jackson's men opened a terrific fire, which hurled them back. A part of Franklin's men penetrated a gap between Archer's and Lane's brigades, but Gregg's troops checked them, though their leader fell mortally wounded. Taliaferro's and Early's divisions increased their disorder. Pender's and Law's brigades joining in the fight and Jackson's second line advancing, the defeat of the Federal left was made complete.

7. The most desperate fighting of the day was on the Confederate left. In dense masses Sumner's right grand division and Hooker's centre grand division advanced against the Confederate lines on Marye's Hill, held by Thomas R. R. Cobb's Georgians, Kershaw's South Carolinians and Ransom's North Caro-

linians. The Confederate artillery had been so arranged by General E. P. Alexander as to sweep every approach to Marye's Hill.[1] That officer had said to Longstreet, the commander of this wing of Lee's army: "We cover that ground so well that we will comb it as with a fine-tooth comb." As the dense masses of the Federals advanced the Confederate artillery ploughed through them front, right and left. But with determined bravery that deserved success they pressed on, until the withering fire of infantry added to that of the artillery at last drove them back. Six of these desperate charges were made by the Federals, all with the same result. Meagher's (Marr's) Irish brigade left their dead within twenty-five paces of the stone wall, behind which stood the troops of Cobb and Kershaw and Ransom. Cobb was mortally wounded, and General Cooke of Ransom's division was borne from the field severely wounded. After the sixth charge, which occurred just at dark, the Federals withdrew, leaving the ground heaped with their dead. The battle of Fredericksburg was over, and Burnside had met with a terrible repulse.

8. Burnside wished to renew the attack on the 14th, but his officers protested against it. So, on the night of the 15th, the Union army recrossed the Rappahannock, and the Virginia campaign of 1862 was ended.[2]

[1] Among the most celebrated organizations of the Confederate army was the Washington Artillery Battalion of New Orleans. Some of the best artillery fighting of this day was done by them.

[2] According to Burnside's report, the Union army numbered on the morning of the battle 113,000. The Union loss was 1,284 killed, 9,600 wounded, and 1,769 captured or missing—12,653. The Confederate army numbered 65,000. Of this number less than 20,000 were engaged in the battle; so strong was their position. The Confederate loss was 608 killed, 4,116 wounded, and 653 captured or missing—5,377.

9. Two Incidents of the Battle of Fredericksburg.—General Lafayette McLaws, in an account of this battle, tells how a Georgia boy named Crumley, an orderly of General Kershaw's, seeing his chief's horse in a very exposed position, rode the animal up a slope, exposed to the hottest fire of the enemy, left him in a safe place, and returning by the same way with an inferior horse, rejoined the general, who, until his return, was ignorant of Crumley's daring feat. Rev. J. Wm. Jones, in his "Christ in the Camp," relates another thrilling incident of the same battle. On the day after the fearful slaughter of the Federals in front of Marye's Hill, and while Burnside's forces were still within about 200 yards of the Confederate position, a brave young South Carolina boy, Sergeant Kirkland, asked permission of General Kershaw to give water to the wounded Union soldiers lying just outside the Confederate works. The general hesitated, because of the great danger to be incurred, but to the earnest entreaties of Kirkland finally yielded, exclaiming, "May God protect you." The noble boy gladly sprang over the stone wall, and going to his wounded foes gave them the water which they so much craved. After a few shots, which missed their mark, the Federal sharpshooters became aware of the Christ-like errand which had carried the young Confederate into this dangerous position, and greeted him with shouts instead of bullets. Having performed his errand of mercy, the gallant Kirkland returned in safety to his friends.

VICKSBURG.

10. Now let us turn to the West again. About the middle of October General John C. Pemberton was

RICHARD KIRKLAND CARRYING WATER TO THE WOUNDED.

appointed commander of the Department of Mississippi and East Louisiana, and near the same time General Grant was placed in supreme command of all the Union forces in north Mississippi. Grant at once began efforts to capture Vicksburg. He planned an advance from Memphis and Grand Junction toward Grenada. This was defeated by the raids of Van Dorn and Forrest upon Grant's communications. The former captured Holly Springs, with 2,000 prisoners, and destroyed Grant's depot of supplies. Thus Grant was compelled either to retire or starve. He accordingly retreated, and gave up his expedition for the present.

11. General Sherman, who was to co-operate with him by an attack upon the rear of Vicksburg, advanced against the Confederate position at Chickasaw Bayou[1] with 30,000 men. He was repulsed with heavy loss by General Stephen D. Lee with one brigade of the Vicksburg garrison. So Vicksburg was let alone for a while longer.

MURFREESBORO.

12. About the 26th of December Wheeler, now a general of cavalry, reported to Bragg at Murfreesboro that Rosecrans was advancing from Nashville. The Confederate army was at once concentrated and made ready for battle. On Tuesday (December 30th) Rose-

---

[1] The effective strength of the Union army at Chickasaw Bluff was 33,000, of which about half were engaged. The Union loss was 208 killed, 1,005 wounded, and 563 captured or missing—1,776. The total effective strength of the Confederates, near Vicksburg, at this time was 25,000. Not more than 3,000 were in the battle of Chickasaw Bluff (or Bayou). Total Confederate loss, 63 killed, 134 wounded, and 10 missing—207.

crans appeared in front of the Confederate position. His plan was to throw forward his left and center at daylight the next day, crushing Breckinridge on the Confederate right, and then wheeling rapidly, to fall with overwhelming force on the Confederate center, and, sweeping through Murfreesboro, to push the Southerners from their line of retreat, and thus destroy or capture their army.

12. But Bragg had formed a similar plan, designing to throw his own left against the Union right, and by a constant right-wheel to crush it back upon the center, and thus interpose between the Federals and their supplies.

13. At daylight (Wednesday, December 31st) Hardee, with Cleburne's and McCown's divisions, attacked McCook's corps of the Federal army, who, though surprised, resisted bravely. But Polk, with Wither's and Cheatham's divisions, joining Hardee, drove the Federals a distance of between three and four miles, bending them back upon their center, until their line was at right angles to its original position. In vain had Sheridan, Negley and Davis tried to stay their brilliant and resistless onset.

14. But Rosecrans, learning of the disaster to his right, hurried forward reinforcements to that wing, and massed his artillery upon the favorable rising ground, to which his line had been driven back. These movements were concealed by a thick grove of cedars. This new position was held against the desperate assaults of the Confederates until night closed the fight. The Confederates held the greater part of the battle-field, with many prisoners, cannon, small arms, wagons,

a great quantity of ammunition, and the dead and wounded of both armies.

GENERAL ROBERT RANSOM.

15. All the next day (January 1st, 1863) the two armies remained quiet. On the night of the 31st Rosecrans had retired his left to a more advantageous position. Bragg took this for a retreat of the Union army, and telegraphed to Richmond, "God has, indeed, granted us a happy New Year." Polk's right was advanced to occupy the ground vacated by the Union army on the west side of the Stone river.

16. On the 2d of January Bragg noticed that Beatty's Federal brigade on the right of Stone river enfiladed Polk's line in its new position. Bragg ordered Breckenridge to take his division and dislodge these troops. It was intended to seize the crest of the hill, and there intrench. But when that had been carried, the ardor of the troops could not be restrained. Pushing beyond support, the Federal batteries massed on the west of the river opened on them, and drove them back with great slaughter. This fight was between only a part of each army.

17. All day of the third both armies remained quiet. Bragg hearing that Rosecrans was being heavily reinforced from Nashville, retired during the night, and took up a new position at Tullahoma.[1] He carried off with him his prisoners and the spoil of the battle of December 31st. Had he remained firm the Federals would probably have retreated themselves. As it was the Union army was so shattered that it did not resume operations for five months.[2]

[1] It is said that General Rosecrans was himself meditating retreat when he received news that the Confederates were retiring. Turning to his officers, he said: "Bragg is a good dog, but Holdfast is a better one." He remained where he was, and laid claim to Murfreesboro as a Union victory,

[2] The Union army in the battle of Murfreesboro numbered 43,400. Its loss was 1,730 killed, 7,802 wounded, and 3,717 captured or missing— 13,249. The Confederate army numbered 37,712. Its loss was 1,294 killed, 7,945 wounded, 1,027 captured or missing—10,266. They captured and carried off 30 cannon, 6,000 small arms, and over 6,000 prisoners, including those captured by cavalry in rear of the Union army. Wheeler's cavalry also captured and burned 800 wagons.

PART III.

The War Between the States and its Results.

Section III.—Events of 1863.

CHAPTER I.

THE EMANCIPATION PROCLAMATION—THE ADMISSION OF WEST VIRGINIA—EARLY MILITARY OPERATIONS OF 1863.

THE EMANCIPATION PROCLAMATION.

A FEW days after the close of the Maryland campaign (September 22d, 1862), Mr. Lincoln issued a proclamation declaring that on the 1st day of January, 1863, the slaves in all the States or parts of States then in "rebellion against the United States" should become free and so remain forever. Some attributed to this proclamation the success of the opposition candidates in many of the State and congressional elections held during the fall of 1862, by which the adminstration majority of 41 in the House of Representatives was changed into an opposition majority of 10.

2. Horace Greeley in his "American Conflict" seems inclined not to take this view. He thinks that the strength of the opposition party was due to an unwillingness to suffer the hardships involved in a continuance of the war, and that this unwillingness was owing to the ill-success of the Union arms. Mr. Greeley also says that, leaving out the vote of the soldiers in the field, which had not yet been authorized, " it is quite probable that had a popular election been held at any time during the year following the 4th of July, 1862,[1] on the question of continuing the war or

---

[1] This was the year between the Confederate triumph at Richmond in the Seven Days' Battles and their defeats at Gettysburg and Vicksburg.

OLD ST. JOHN'S CHURCH, RICHMOND, VA.

arresting it on the best attainable terms, a majority would have voted for peace; while it is highly probable that a still larger majority would have voted against emancipation."

3. However this may be, on the first day of January, 1863, Mr. Lincoln issued another proclamation giving freedom to all the slaves in the Confederate States. Although the President had no right under the Constitution to adopt such a measure, his friends justified it on the plea of military necessity. The design was to weaken the Confederacy and strengthen the cause of the Union both at home and abroad. Of course Mr. Lincoln well knew that this proclamation would amount to nothing unless the Union arms should be successful.

THE FORMATION AND ADMISSION OF WEST VIRGINIA.

4. It has already been mentioned that a large majority of the people in many of the counties of Northwest Virginia refused to abide by the action of Virginia in seceding from the Union. A convention was held at Wheeling (June 11th, 1861) and steps taken to bring about a separation from old Virginia. Such members of the legislature of Virginia as lived in those counties met soon afterwards and claiming to be the loyal legislature of Virginia gave permission to themselves to separate from Eastern Virginia and form the new State of West Virginia.

5. Toward the latter part of 1862 the West Virginians formed a provisional government and applied for admission into the Union. This application was granted by the Congress of the United States. West Virginia was recognized as a State

April 20th, 1863, and was fully admitted two months
later.

Early Military Operations of 1863.

6. The year 1862, sometimes called "The year of
Battles," had come to a close with the Confederates
greatly encouraged and the Federals correspondingly
discouraged. Several battles occurred in the early
months of 1863 which added to the confidence of the
Confederates, since they were successful in most of
them.

7. **Galveston** in Texas had been occupied by a Union
land and naval force. General John B. Magruder,
commanding the Confederate forces in Texas, determined to recapture this important post. He secured two ordinary steamboats, protected them with
cotton bales piled from the main deck to the hurricane
roof, manned them with Texas cavalry and volunteer
artillery, and placed them under the command of Captain Leon Smith of the Texas navy. Both boats were so
frail that the only chance for success was to get close
enough to a Union ship for the Texans to board her.
Between night and morning of January 1st Magruder
with the land force got into Galveston. In the early
morning he attacked the garrison, while his two gunboats made for the *Harriet Lane*, the strongest of the
Federal ships. One gunboat was speedily disabled,
but the other closed in with the *Harriet Lane*, which
the Texans immediately boarded and captured. The
Union flag-ship *Westfield* got aground and was blown
up by the order of Commander Renshaw, who with
fifteen of his men perished on account of the explosion's occurring before they could get far enough
from the vessel. The *Harriet Lane*, two barges and a

schooner were captured. The rest of the fleet escaped. The garrison surrendered to Magruder. The most remarkable thing connected with this brilliant victory of the Texans was the successful cavalry charge upon a fleet.

8. **Capture of the Hatteras.**—Not far from Galveston, on the afternoon of January 11th, Commodore Semmes of the Confederate war steamer *Alabama* attacked and captured the Union war steamer *Hatteras* and her crew of 118 men. In ten minutes after her capture the *Hatteras* sank, and was thus lost to the victors.

9. **Sabine Pass.**—On the 21st of the same month, at Sabine Pass, Major O. M. Watkins with two Confederate gunboats chased out to sea and captured a Federal gunboat and schooner with 13 cannon, 129 prisoners, and $1,000,000 worth of stores.

10. **Arkansas Post.**—As a partial off-set to these brilliant Confederate victories, a Union army of 30,000 men, under Generel John McClernand, assisted by Admiral Porter's fleet, after a desperate fight of five hours' duration, captured Arkansas Post with its garrison of 5,000 men, commanded by General T. J. Churchill, besides seventeen cannon, 3,000 small arms, and a great quantity of munitions and commissary stores.

11. **Battles in Charleston Harbor.**—On the 29th of August, 1862, General Beauregard had been appointed commander of the Department of South Carolina and Georgia, with headquarters at Charleston. Though his resources were very limited, he at once went to work to put his department into a good state of defense. Several months before (June 16th, 1862) a Federal force had been defeated in a fierce fight at

Secessionville, on James Island, and a little more than a month after he assumed command another Union force was defeated at Pocotaligo (October 22d, 1862) in an effort to seize the Charleston and Savannah railroad.

.12. The Federal government was busy making the most formidable preparations for the the capture of Charleston. Meanwhile, a rigid blockade of the port was kept up by the Union fleet. The Federal preparations were on such a grand scale that they consumed much more time than had been anticipated. This gave Beauregard a better opportunity to prepare againt them. There were at that time two Confederate iron-clad gun-boats in Charleston Harbor, the *Palmetto State*, commanded by Lieutenant John Rutledge, and the *Chicora*, by Captain John R. Tucker. General Beauregard and Commodore Duncan N. Ingraham, after consultation, decided that a bold night attack on the wooden Union fleet might cause considerable damage, and compel it to leave its anchorage outside the bar. It was also concluded that this must be done before the threatened arrival of the Federal monitors.

13. On the early morning of January 31st, the attack took place. The *Palmetto State*, on which was Commodore Ingraham himself took the lead. The attack was successful. The *Palmetto State* captured the *Marcedita*, and the *Keystone State* surrendered to the *Chicora.* The rest of the Union fleet steamed out to sea, leaving the outer harbor in full possession of the two Confederate rams. Not a Federal sail was visible, even with spy-glasses, for more than twenty-four hours. Though the blockade of Charleston was

BATTLE OF CHARLESTON HARBOR.

soon renewed, it never was complete.   Both before and after this naval battle blockade-runners frequently entered the port of Charleston.   In fact lines of blockade running steamers entered and left that port at regular intervals up to nearly the very close of the war.

14. Just the evening before Commodore Ingraham's brilliant victory there took place another notable event. The entrance of Stono River had been left unguarded, and Federal gunboats were in the habit of passing as near Fort Pemberton as their own safety allowed and harassing the Confederate camps on James and John's Islands by the fire of their long-range rifled guns.   Desirous of putting a stop to this practice General Beauregard instructed General R. S. Ripley to have masked batteries erected at designated points along Stono River near where the Union gunboats were in the habit of passing, and where they sometimes stayed over night.   The instructions were, that if one of these gunboats should come along, the men at these masked batteries should let her steam by unmolested as far as she might choose to go.   Then they were to open fire and cut off her retreat.   The command of these masked batteries was given to Lieutenant-Colonel Joseph A. Yates, of the First South Carolina Artillery.   On the evening of January 30th the *Isaac Smith*, carrying nine heavy guns, all unconscious of danger, sailed up the Stono, and leisurely anchored just above the masked batteries.   Fire was at once opened upon her.   She returned the fire and tried to make her escape, but was so roughly handled that she dropped anchor and surrendered.   The Confederates repaired her, and under the name of the

Stono she served as a guard-boat in Charleston harbor, with Captain H. J. Hartstene as commander.

15. About the 1st of April the long heralded iron-clad Union fleet appeared before Charleston. It consisted of nine vessels, armed with thirty-three guns of the heaviest caliber ever used in war up to that time—15 and 11-inch Dahlgren guns and 8-inch rifled pieces. In the Confederate forts and batteries sixty-four cannon and five mortars were brought into action, none of heavier caliber than the 10-inch Columbiad. The Union fleet was supposed to be invulnerable. The vessels came up in line, one following the other (April 7th, 1863). First came the *Weehawken*, the *Passaic*, the *Montauk*, and the *Patapsco*, four single-turreted monitors. Next came the frigate *New Ironsides*, the flag-ship of the fleet, and the mightiest. On it was Rear-Admiral Du Pont, the commander of the fleet. Then came the *Catskill*, the *Nantucket*, and the *Nahant*, three other single-turreted monitors. The double-turreted *Keokuk* closed the line. All the vessels were commanded by experienced and gallant officers. Confidently and bravely the fleet advanced to the attack upon Fort Sumter, which, with all the other batteries in range, opened fire upon the Union vessels. It was a grand spectacle, this fight between forts and floating batteries. The citizens of Charleston, with intense interest and anxiety, watched the progress of the fight from balconies and house-tops, and from their beautiful promenade known as the " Battery." After a fierce fight of two hours and a half, the fleet withdrew with half of its turret ships in part or wholly disabled. And yet they had encountered only the outer lines of defense. The *Keokuk* was destroyed. Thus

ATTACK ON FORT SUMTER BY THE MONITOR FLEET.

the grand naval attack, from which so much had been expected, came to naught.[1]

16. **Fort McAllister.**—Previous to this great battle in Charleston Harbor the Federals had made three separate attacks on Fort McAllister at Genesis Point on the Ogeechee river below Savannah, Georgia. The first of these was on February 1st, 1863, when the monitor *Montauk*, accompanied by three gun-boats and a mortar boat, approached within a short distance of the work and opened fire. After a four-hours' fight the monitor and its companions drew off defeated. Another attack was made on this fort (February 28th) by four iron-clad gunboats under Commodore Worden, and still another on March 3d by four ironclads and three mortar schooners, commanded by Admiral Du Pont.[2] The Union vessels were repulsed on each occasion, and after that saved their ammunition by letting Fort McAllister alone.[3]

17. These many successes of the Confederates in the first months of 1863 added greatly to their confidence and produced a corresponding depression in the feelings of the Federals.

[1] Admiral Du Pont's own statement   See "Battles and Leaders of the Civil War," vol. IV., page 40.

[2] Though repulsed by the fort on February 28th, the Union fleet succeeded in burning the Confederate steamer *Nashville*, which was anchored near by.

[3] In one of these attacks a bursting bomb tore up the earth to such an extent as to cover up completely one of the gunners. The man scrambled out from under the earth that had been heaped upon him like a mound, wiped the sand from his mouth and called out "All quiet along the Ogeechee to-day."

CHAPTER II.

CHANCELLORSVILLE AND GETTYSBURG.

CHANCELLORSVILLE.

AFTER his disastrous defeat at Fredericksburg Burnside was relieved and General Joseph Hooker was put in command of the Union Army of the Potomac. This new commander went diligently to work to reorganize the Federal army and to bring it to a high state of discipline and efficiency. By the last of April Hooker was ready to begin his campaign. He was a favorite with his soldiers, who called him "Fighting Joe." The army with which he advanced numbered 132,000 effectives and had with it 404 cannon.[1]

2. Lee still occupied the heights around Fredericksburg with 60,000 effectives and 170 cannon. Hooker had no intention of attacking the Confederates in this strong position, but decided to move to their left. In order to mask his real design Hooker sent a force of 10,000 cavalry under General Stoneman to operate upon Lee's communications with Richmond, and sent General Sedgwick to take position just below Fredericksburg. Then, with the balance of his army, he crossed the Rappahannock, and by the afternoon of April 30, with four corps, he occupied the position

---

[1] Before Hooker was ready for this advance he had sent General Averill across the Rappahannock at Kelley's Ford with a strong body of cavalry. Fitz. Lee encountered this force and Stuart came to his assistance when Averill was defeated and compelled to recross the river. In this fight Major Pelham, the boy artillerist, was killed. Lee always spoke of him as the gallant Pelham.

around Chancellorsville,[1] ten miles southwest of Fredericksburg.

3. Hooker was so delighted with the progress made up to this time that he issued an address to his troops, in which he said: "The operations of the last three days have determined that our enemy must either ingloriously fly or come out from his defenses and give us battle on our own ground, where certain destruction awaits him." To some of his officers Hooker remarked: "The Confederate army is now the legitimate property of the Army of the Potomac. They may as well pack up their haversacks and make for Richmond, and I shall be after them."

GENERAL JOSEPH HOOKER.

4. Lee's position was indeed a critical one. Sedgwick was in front of his lines at Fredericksburg with 30,000 men, Hooker with 90,000 was on his flank at Chancellorsville, and Stoneman with 10,000 cavalry was marching to intercept his retreat upon Richmond.

[1] Chancellorsville was not a town or village, but simply a farm house with the usual buildings, situated at the edge of a small field, surrounded by a dense thicket, which extends for miles in every direction, and from its wild aspect has been called the Wilderness.

Longstreet was absent in Southeast Virginia with 15,-000 men, and it was impossible to bring him to his aid in time. Thus, with barely 60,000 men of all arms, he must thwart and beat back the vast host that was trying to overthrow him.

5. Leaving Early with his division, Barksdale's brigade, and the reserve artillery under General Pendleton, 9,000 men in all, to watch and fight Sedgwick, he

LEE AND JACKSON PLANNING THE BATTLE OF CHANCELLORSVILLE.

marched with the balance of his force to do what Hooker never imagined he would do—attack the Federal army. The very boldness of this move disconcerted Hooker. He had sent forward General Sykes who encountered McLaws and Anderson and was driven back. Though Couch with Hancock and Warren had moved to Sykes's support, Hooker became uneasy and ordered his whole line back to Chancellorsville, giving up to Lee the ridges, whose crests that general quickly seized and crowned with his artillery. Thus Hooker lost his opportunity, and his army was thrown upon the defensive in a position where its superior numbers could not be used to the best advantage. Lee had outgeneraled him at the very outset.

6. Lee resolved to strengthen his position so as to keep Hooker in check, while Jackson, with 22,000 men, should march to the rear of the Federal position by a road sufficiently remote to prevent discovery. General Stuart was to cover the movement with his cavalry. Early on the morning of May 2d, Jackson's column was in motion, and after making a circuit of fifteen miles reached the desired position. At one time during the day a part of Jackson's column was seen by some of the Federal officers and the fact was reported to Hooker who concluded that Lee was retreating towards Gordonsville. He accordingly sent part of Sickles's corps and Pleasanton's cavalry to gain information, but Colonel Thompson Brown, with his battalion of artillery, supported by Jackson's rear guard, not only checked the Federals near Catharine Furnace, but also kept them in uncertainty as to the real movements of the Southern troops.

7. When Jackson had reached the desired point, he rode forward with General Fitzhugh Lee and obtained such a view of the enemy (Howard's Eleventh corps) as to show him that the Federals were all unconscious of the thunderbolt about to fall upon their heads. Returning to his troops Jackson formed Rodes's division in the front line, Colston's in the second, and A. P. Hill's in the third. Then at about 6 o'clock in the afternoon (May 2d) turning to Rodes, Jackson

asked, "Are you ready?"   "Yes, sir," said Rodes,
eager for the fray.   "You can go forward then," said
Jackson.   Suddenly the woods rang with the bugle
call, which was answered from right to left along the
line.   Then the skirmishers sprang forward, followed
by the eager line of battle, whose enthusiastic "Rebel
yell" re-echoed through the forest for miles around.[1]

8. Howard's corps, taken completely by surprise,
was routed and communicated its panic to the troops
through which it passed.   Jackson's men pressed on,
routing line after line until the close of day.   After
his troops had halted Jackson went forward to recon-
noitre, when his party was mistaken in the darkness
for a party of Federal scouts and fired upon by the
Confederates.   The first volley killed some of his at-
tendants and the second wounded Jackson himself.
As he was about to be borne from the field General
Pender expressed fears of not being able to hold his
advanced position.   "You *must* hold your ground,
General Pender! you must hold your ground, sir!"
replied Jackson.   And this was his last order upon the
battle-field.

9. Early on the next morning the Confederates renewed the attack.   Stuart led Jackson's men, everywhere conspicuous in the thickest of the fight, singing
as he led the charging columns, "Old Joe Hooker, will
you get out of the Wilderness?"   McLaws and Anderson with their divisions supported him.   Hooker had
restored order during the night, and the Federals
fought bravely until 10 o'clock.   Then they gave way
at every point before the onward rush of the Confede-

---

[1] See Rev. James Power Smith's account of "Stonewall Jackson's Last
Battle," in Battles and Leaders of the Civil War, vol. iii.

JACKSON ATTACKING THE RIGHT WING AT CHANCELLORSVILLE.

rates led on by the leaders already named, nobly seconded by Rodes, Heth, Doles, Pender and others.
General Lee accompanied the troops in person, and as
they emerged from the tangled Wilderness in which
they had been fighting, driving the enemy before
them, he appeared in their midst. His presence was
greeted with "One long, unbroken cheer, in which the
feeble cry of those who lay helpless on the earth
blended with the strong voices of those who still
fought, rose high above the roar of battle and hailed
the presence of the victorious chief."[1]

10. While these events were transpiring at Chancellorsville, Early had detained Sedgwick at Fredericksburg until the 3d, when that general, by a determined
attack, drove Early back, carried Marye's Hill, and
marched towards Chancellorsville. Lee being informed of what had happened, sent Wilcox with his
brigade, who checked Sedgwick at Salem Church until
McLaws and Anderson could come up. Lee, leaving
his other generals to look after Hooker, went to meet
Sedgwick, against whom he directed a combined attack by McLaws and Anderson in front and Early in
the rear. Sedgwick was defeated, and driven back
across the Rappahannock (May 4th). Next day Lee
gathered all his troops in Hooker's front for the purpose of giving him the finishing blow; but the Federal general, under cover of a dark and stormy night,
effected his retreat. Thus the series of battles around
Chancellorsville ended in a most astonishing victory
for the Confederates.

[1] Address of Colonel Charles Marshall at a soldiers' memorial meeting
in Baltimore.

11. But the joy of the victors was turned into mourning by the loss of Stonewall Jackson. At first his wound was not supposed to be mortal; but pneumonia set in, and on May 10th, at a quarter past

GENERAL "STONEWALL" JACKSON.

3 P. M., he breathed his last. A short while before his death he aroused from a state of unconsciousness, and "spoke out very cheerfully and distinctly the beautiful sentence which has become immortal as his last: 'Let us cross over the river, and rest under the

shade of the trees.'"[1–2] General Howard, of the Union army, after describing the rout of his corps by Jackson at Chancellorsville, says: "'Stonewall' Jackson was victorious. Even his enemies praise him; but, providentially for us, it was the last battle that he waged against the American Union. For, in bold planning, in energy of execution, which he had the power to diffuse, in indefatigable activity and moral ascendancy, Jackson stood head and shoulders above his confreres, and after his death General Lee could not replace him."

Gettysburg.

12. After their great victory at Chancellorsville the Confederates returned to their old quarters at Fredericksburg. The month of May was spent in recruiting and reorganizing. The infantry of the army was now formed into three corps of three divisions each. The first corps was commanded by Lieutenant-General James C. Longstreet, the second by Lieutenant-General Richard S. Ewell, and the third by Lieutenant-General Ambrose P. Hill.

13. By the first of June the Army of Northern Virginia was the best disciplined, the best organized and the most high-spirited army that had ever been seen on American soil. The successful campaigns through which it had recently passed had inspired it with such

---

[1] "Life of Stonewall Jackson," by his wife.

[2] According to the official returns, the Union army at Chancellorsville numbered 132,000 men. Its losses were 1,606 killed, 9,762 wounded, 5,919 captured or missing—17,287. The Confederate army numbered about 60,000. Its losses were 1,649 killed, 9,106 wounded, and 1,708 captured or missing—12,463. Besides those mentioned as captured from the Union army thousands of wounded fell into the hands of the Confederates, who also captured thirteen cannon, and 20,000 small arms.

ardor and enthusiasm that it felt capable of doing almost anything.

14. General Lee did not believe in sitting down quietly and waiting the movements of his enemy. He believed that the best way to defend Richmond was to so employ his army as to keep the Federals alarmed for the safety of their own capital and country. He believed that an advance into Pennsylvania would, if it accomplished no other good, prevent another advance against Richmond for that year at least. General A. L. Long, at one

LIEUTENANT-GENERAL R. S EWELL.

time his military secretary, says that Lee had no idea of going to Philadelphia, but that he hoped, that if the Federal army could be decisively defeated somewhere in the vicinity of Gettysburg, the Confederates might get possession of Maryland, besides making a diversion in favor of their Western Department, where the affairs of the Confederacy were on the decline.[1]

[1] Grant was at this time pressing the siege of Vicksburg, which was in great danger.

15. Early in June Lee's army began to move. Hooker, uncertain as to Lee's intentions, sent General Pleasanton across the Rappahannock to get information as to the movements and position of the Confederates. At **Fleetwood,** near Brandy station, Pleasanton encountered Stuart (June 9th), and the greatest cavalry battle of the war took place. After several hours hard fighting the Federals were forced to recross the river, leaving three of their cannon as trophies to the Confederates.[1]

16. When Hooker ascertained that Lee was actually moving northward, and that there were but few troops in Richmond, he proposed to the Federal authorities that he should be allowed to march at once upon that city, but they were too uneasy about Washington to consent to Hooker's proposition.

17. Meanwhile Ewell, with his corps, leaving Brandy Station (June 10th), reached Cedarville two days later, whence he sent Rodes and Jenkins to capture Martinsburg, while he, with Early's and Edward Johnson's divisions marched directly upon Winchester. On June 14th Ewell captured Winchester and Rodes captured Martinsburg. These brilliant operations resulted in the expulsion of the Federals from the Valley, the capture of 4,000 prisoners and their arms, 28 pieces of superior artillery, 300 wagons and as many horses, and a large amount of all sorts of military stores. The entire Confederate loss was 47 killed, 219 wounded, and three missing. On the 23d of June Ewell, with the advance of Lee's army, crossed the Potomac.

[1] In this affair there were 10,981 Federals. The Confederate cavalry under Stuart numbered 10,292, but all were not present in the fight. The Union loss was 907, of whom 421 were killed and wounded. The Confederate loss was 485, of whom 301 were killed and wounded.

18. On that very day General Lee wrote a letter to President Davis urging him to gather all troops that could be spared from the Carolinas and Georgia and place them at Culpeper under the command of General Beauregard, believing that the presence of that officer would give magnitude even to a small demonstration. On the 25th he wrote again to Mr. Davis urging the same views, but the Confederate President did not see how he could do this with the troops at his disposal.

19. On the 24th of June Longstreet and Hill followed Ewell, and three days later reached Chambersburg. It was expected that General Stuart would give notice whenever the Federal army should cross the Potomac. But that officer had unfortunately moved in a direction which made it impossible for him to keep Lee as well posted as usual. Orders were therefore issued to move upon Harrisburg. Ewell's corps moved to execute these orders. Two of his divisions, Rodes's and Johnson's, entered Carlisle, while Early occupied York, and sent Gordon's[1] brigade to get possession of the bridge across the Susquehanna at Wrightsville. But the bridge was burned by some Federal cavalry, and Gordon's men aided the citizens to save the town from the flames. Lee had given strict orders that there should be no pillaging, and that his soldiers should not annoy the inhabitants in any way. These orders were strictly obeyed. The conduct of the Confederates in Pennsylvania was in striking contrast to that of the Federals in Virginia.

[1] General John B. Gordon, a Georgian, had entered the army as a captain in an Alabama regiment. He had now risen to the rank of brigadier-general.

20. The Union army had now crossed the Potomac, and was moving into Pennsylvania for the purpose of encountering Lee. On account of a disagreement between Halleck and Hooker, the latter requested to be relieved of the command. His request was granted, and Major-General George G. Meade was placed in command of the army moving against Lee.

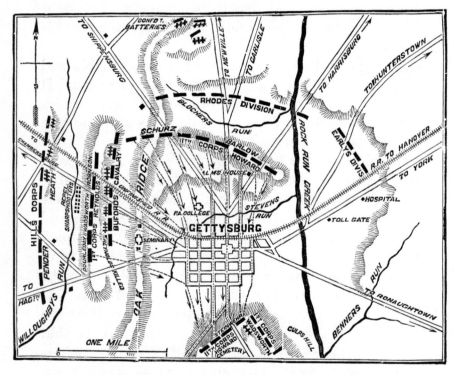

MAP SHOWING POSITION OF TROOPS THE FIRST DAY AT GETTYSBURG.

21. **The First Day.**—Lee recalled Ewell's corps, and proceeded to concentrate his army for battle. On the morning of July 1st, as Hill was advancing toward Gettysburg with the divisions of Heth and Pender, **his skirmishers encountered Buford's dismounted**

troopers. Archer, commanding one of Heth's brigades, pushed on too far, when Federal reinforcements coming up, overwhelmed him, capturing Archer himself and several of his men. Heth formed for battle, and, being joined by Pender, moved forward, pressing back the Union troops, breaking two of their lines and advancing against the third. These two divisions were now engaged with the two corps of John F. Reynolds and Howard. Just as the fight was at its height General Reynolds was killed. Ewell came up at an opportune moment with Rodes's division, and Early soon afterwards joined him. Then the whole Confederate line advanced. The Federals were routed and driven through Gettysburg with the loss of more than 5,000 prisoners, exclusive of the wounded. Two brigadier-generals were among the captured. The Confederates also captured three of their cannon and several colors. The Confederates had gained a brilliant success. The defeated troops retreated to Cemetery Hill, where they found reinforcements. General Lee did not wish to bring on a general engagement until his whole army was up. He sent word to hasten the march of Longstreet's corps.

22. **The Second Day.**—Lee wished to attack as soon after daylight as possible, before all of Meade's troops could get up. But all the dispositions for attack were not made until 4 P. M. Had the attack been begun as Lee intended, it would have struck the Federals before their whole force was concentrated, and judging from what was accomplished when the attack was made, must have resulted in a decisive success for the Confederates. In the battle of the 2d Longstreet's blow fell mainly upon Sickles's corps, which was driven

from its position with heavy loss, its commander being severely wounded.[1] Hood tried to seize Little Round Top, but failed, though he did capture part of the line assailed. McLaws was also in part successful. Wilcox's, Wrights and Perry's brigades pressed up close to the Federal line. Wright broke through and seized the Union batteries, but not being supported was driven back. "At the close of the day the Confederates held the base of the Round Tops, Devil's Den, its woods, and the Emmettsburg road, with skirmishers thrown out as far as the Trostle House; the Federals had the Round Tops, the Plum Run Line and Cemetery Ridge."[2] Horace Greeley, in his American Conflict, says that the ground on which Reynolds had fallen was now in the centre of the Confederate army. "They held that also on which Howard had been cut up, and that from which Sickles had been driven in disorder. True they also had lost heavily, but they had reason for their hope that the morrow's triumph would richly repay all their losses."[3]

23. **The Third Day**—Lee says in his report: "The result of this day's (July 2d) operations induced the belief that with proper concert of action, and with the increased support that the positions gained on the right would enable the artillery to render the assaulting column, we should ultimately succeed, and it was accordingly determined to continue the attack." The general plan of battle was the same as on the second.

[1] The Confederates lost in this fight Generals Barksdale, Pender and Semmes.

[2] Account of the second day at Gettysburg by the Union General Hunt in Battles and Leaders of the Civil War, vol. 3.

[3] In the battle of the second day the Confederates had captured four cannon. several hundred prisoners and two regimental flags.

General Longstreet, who had been reinforced by
Pickett's division, was ordered to attack next morning,
and General Ewell was to assail the Federal right at
the same time. General Longstreet was not ready as
soon as had been hoped. The consequence was that

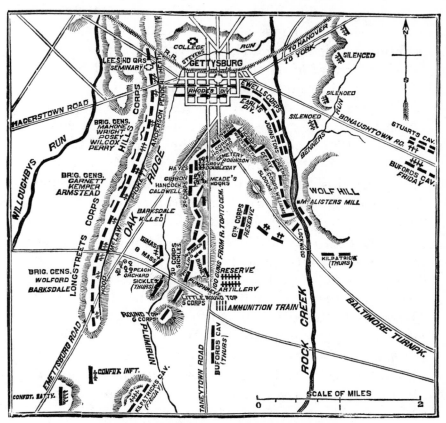

POSITION OF TROOPS THE SECOND AND THIRD DAYS.

General Edward Johnson of Ewell's corps, who had
captured part of the works on the Union right, was,
after a fight which lasted several hours, obliged to retire to his original line. Lee now changed his plan
of assault. The Union center presented a weak point,

upon which an attack could be made with a reasonable hope of success. Lee determined to attack at this point. Longstreet was to conduct the assault, while Hill and Ewell were to support him. One hundred and forty-five cannon were massed to cover the advance of the attacking column. After one of the most terrific and prolonged cannonades ever witnessed, the assaulting column consisting of Pickett's division, supported on the left by that of Heth under Pettigrew, and Scales's and Lane's brigades under Trimble, and on the right by Wilcox's brigade of Anderson's division, appeared from behind the ridge, and marching over the crest, descended into the depression which separated the two armies. A thrill of admiration ran through the Union army as this magnificent array of fifteen thousand men moved onward with the steadiness of a review. Then they opened upon the attacking column such a withering fire that the Confederates, after breasting the pitiless storm for a great part of the distance recoiled and fell back, with the exception of Pickett's division, who continued the charge alone. The divisions of Hood and McLaws had not been sent forward, and were not near enough to lend their aid at the critical moment. Yet the gallant Virginians rushed forward, broke through the Federal lines, and with shouts of victory planted their banners on the captured guns. Now was the time for their supports to rush in and secure the triumph so bravely won. But Heth's division had not been able to force its way, and the other supports were too far off to be of timely aid. From every side the Federals rushed upon Pickett's men, who at last were compelled to retire, leaving the greater **part of their number killed, wounded or prisoners.**

PICKETT'S CHARGE AT GETTYSBURG.

The great attack had failed, but Pickett had made one of the grandest charges recorded in history.[1]

24. Lee took all the blame of the failure upon himself, but his soldiers never have looked upon it that way. Every officer upon the field exerted himself to restore order, and the men of all the commands so promptly obeyed that the whole line was soon established. General Meade has been blamed for not making a counter-attack upon Lee. But General Henry J. Hunt, chief of artillery of the Union army, bears testimony to the fact that it was in no condition to attempt such a thing. Other Union officers also state that an attack by the Federals would have resulted in disaster to them.

25. Some have criticised Lee for attacking Meade at all in his strong position, and suggested many moves that he might have made that they think would have been better. The same General Hunt who has been quoted before says: "A battle was a necessity to Lee, and a defeat would be more disastrous to Meade, and less so to himself at Gettysburg than at any point east of it. With the defiles of the South Mountain Range close in his rear, which could be easily held by a small force, a safe retreat through the Cumberland Valley was assured. It is more probable that General Lee was influenced by cool calculation of this nature than by hot blood, or that the opening success of a chance battle had thrown him off his balance."[2]

---

[1] Of Pickett's three brigade commanders, General Armistead and R. B. Garnett were killed, and General Kemper was badly wounded.

[2] Meaning the first day's battle at Gettysburg. "The battle of Gettysburg closed with a sharp but indecisive cavalry combat, participated in by the brigades of Wade Hampton, B. H. Robertson, Fitzhugh and W. H. F. Lee, A. G. Jenkins, and W. E. Jones, all under the command of Stuart."

A decisive victory at Gettysburg would probably have secured Southern independence, and thus have

saved to the South the blood and suffering of nearly two years more, with final defeat. With such a prospect in view it was worth the risk.[1]

26. Anything short of a decisive victory while in the enemy's country amounted

MAJOR-GENERAL GEORGE E. PICKETT.

to a decisive defeat under the circumstances which surrounded Lee. It would be very difficult for him to procure supplies, and fresh Federal troops might be sent to cut off his army from the fords of the Potomac. He

[1] The maximum of Meade's army at Gettysburg was 101,679, of which 93,500 were engaged. Its losses were 3,072 killed, 14,497 wounded, and 5,434 captured—23,003. Some 1,500 of the wounded were paroled by the Confederates. The Confederate army numbered 70,000 of all arms. Its losses were 2,592 killed, 12,709 wounded, and 5,150 captured—20,451. Of the wounded 6,802 fell into the hands of the Federals.

remained at Gettysburg during the 4th, waiting to see if Meade would attack, and feeling perfectly able to repel any assault. All that day the Confederates busied themselves in burying their dead, and in moving such of their wounded as were in a condition to be moved. On the night of the 4th the Confederate army began to retire, but the rear of the column did not leave Gettysburg until after daylight on the 5th. The Confederate wagon and ambulance train had been sent ahead of the army under the escort of General Imboden, who also had in charge nearly 5,000 prisoners. Lee's army retired by way of Fairfield, and so managed that Meade was obliged in following to make a circuitous march through the lower passes. This makes manifest the strategic advantage to Lee and disadvantage to Meade of Gettysburg. The Union general could not pursue to advantage.

27. Early on the morning of the 6th, at Williamsport General Imboden received news that 7,000 Federal cavalry under Buford and Kilpatrick were advancing to attack him. Imboden had but 2,100 men. He increased his strength by organizing 700 wagoners into companies of a hundred men each under the command of wounded line officers, quartermasters and commissaries. He had with him also eight guns of the famous Washington Artillery of New Orleans, under the command of Major Eshleman. With this force he held the Federal cavalry in check until Fitzhugh Lee came up from one side and Stuart from the other. Then the Union troopers were routed and chased for several miles. From the gallant conduct of the Confederate wagoners on this occasion, this has been called the "Wagoner's Fight."

28. On the 7th of July the Confederate army reached the Potomac. Finding the river so much swollen that the trains with the wounded and prisoners could not be got across, Lee took up a position extending from Williamsport to Falling Waters, and waited for the subsiding of the river and the construction of bridges. When Meade appeared before this position he called a council of his officers, who declared that the Confederate position was too strong to be attacked. Lee's soldiers were eager for battle, confident of retrieving their repulse at Gettysburg. Meade did not attack but fortified his own position. On the night of the 13th, Lee withdrew his army across the Potomac

GENERAL W. H. F. LEE.

into Virginia without serious interruption by the Federals.[1]

29. In this whole campaign the Confederates had captured 38 cannon. The Federals had captured

[1] A sad loss was sustained, however, in the death of the brave General Pettigrew who received his mortal wound in a skirmish with some Federal cavalry.

no cannon in battle, but had secured three guns
which got stuck in the mud and were abandoned at
the crossing of the Potomac.   The Southerners had
failed at Gettysburg ; but, as the Union General Hunt
says, " Right gallantly did they act their part, and their
failure carried no discredit with it.   Their military
honor was not tarnished by their defeat, nor their
spirit lowered, but their respect for their opponents
was restored to what it had been before Fredericksburg
and Chancellorsville."

30. The Confederate army retreated at its leisure.
On the 23d of July it was still near Winchester.   When
Meade at last advanced toward Culpeper Courthouse, Lee moved rapidly southward passing entirely
around Meade's right flank, and appeared in front of
the Union army, when it again looked across the Rappahannock.   Notwithstanding the failure at Gettysburg Lee's army had lost none of its spirit.   Its confidence in itself and its leader was unabated.   But the
Confederacy had been struck an almost fatal blow in
the West.   This was the capture of Vicksburg by the
army under Grant on the same day that Lee was preparing to retreat from Gettysburg (July 4th, 1863).
We shall read about this in our next chapter.

CHAPTER III.

VICKSBURG, CHICKAMAUGA, CHATTANOOGA AND MISSIONARY RIDGE.

Vicksburg.

SEVERAL attempts to capture Vicksburg and their failure have already been mentioned. Near the 1st of February, 1863, General Grant appeared before Vicksburg. An immense Union fleet under Porter occupied the river, and Grant concentrated a large army on the Louisiana shore. During the next two months he made repeated attempts to capture the city.

2. His first attempt by Williams's Canal was a failure. Then came an expedition by Lake Providence and Bayou Maçon, which was defeated by natural difficulties. Next an expedition was sent by way of Yazoo Pass, which was stopped by Fort Pemberton. This was a fort made of cotton bales by Captain P. Robinson of the Confederate States Engineers. It was situated on the overflowed bottom-lands of the Tallahatchie and Yallabusha rivers, near their junction. Here General Loring, with three cannon and 1,500 men, defeated a fleet and land force. In the hottest of the fight Loring stood upon the cotton-bale parapet and shouted to his men, "Give them blizzards, boys! give them blizzards!" From this time his men nicknamed him "Old Blizzards." The last of these flanking expeditions was led by General Sherman and Admiral Porter by way of Steele's Bayou to

reach the Sunflower and Yazoo rivers above Haynes's
Bluff.   This, too, was a failure.

3. Grant then adopted a bold plan.   This was to
send his army down the west bank of the Mississippi

AN "INTELLIGENT CONTRABAND."

River to a point opposite Grand Gulf, and to have his
transports run past the Vicksburg batteries to the
same point.   His design was to cross the Mississippi
below Grand Gulf, and, moving up from that point,
attack Vicksburg from the rear.   At the same time a
force under General Sherman was again threatening
Haines's Bluff, and the Union General Grierson was
on a very destructive raid with a large cavalry force
in Northern Mississippi.   Most of Pemberton's cav-

alry had been sent to Bragg at Tullahoma, and the rest of it was looking after Grierson. Thus he could not ascertain any thing about the movements of the Union army.

4. Before Pemberton could determine which was the real point of attack Grant had silenced the batteries at Grand Gulf and passed that point with his fleet. On the 30th of April he crossed the river at Bruinsburg. Then he marched rapidly forward, defeated Bowen at Port Gibson (May 1st) and Gregg at Raymond (May 12th). Two days later Sherman captured the city of Jackson. The evening before the capture of Jackson General Joseph E. Johnston had sent the same dispatch by three different messengers to Pemberton, directing him to fall upon Sherman's rear. One of the messengers was a Union man, who had been expelled from Memphis by the Union General Hurlbut for uttering disloyal sentiments. But the expelled man and Hurlbut understood each other. The whole thing was a sham to deceive the Confederates. The expelled man was received into favor by them and was one of Johnston's messengers on this occasion. Instead of taking the dispatch direct to Pemberton, he took it first to the Union General McPherson. This enabled Grant to thwart the whole plan.

5. On the 16th Grant defeated Pemberton at Champion Hill, near Baker's Creek, and on the next day routed his forces at the Big Black. Pemberton retreated towards Vicksburg. He now received a dispatch from Johnston, telling him to abandon Vicksburg and make a junction with him. Under the circumstances, this was the right thing to do. But Pemberton had also received a dispatch from Mr. Davis,

telling him to hold Vicksburg to the last, assuring him that if besieged, he should be relieved.

6. Pemberton retired into Vicksburg with 30,000 effectives. Grant's skillful and brilliant movements had completely succeeded. When he first crossed the Mississippi Pemberton, by a rapid concentration of forces, could have crushed him. But, instead of that, the Confederates met Grant in small detachments, and were defeated in detail. Grant's force through his whole department numbered, by his report of June 30th, 103,000 effectives of all arms. As soon as he had driven Pemberton into Vicksburg he concentrated his troops around the doomed city, until he had present for duty with him 75,000 effective soldiers. With these he not only pressed the siege of Vicksburg, but fortified his own position, so as to be secure against assault, unless attacked by an overwhelming force. Besides his army, Grant had his great fleet, of which he says: " Without its assistance the campaign could not have been successfully made with twice the number of men engaged."

7. On the 19th of May an assault was made on the Confederate lines, which was repulsed. On the 22d another and much more determined assault was made with the hearty co-operation of such able officers as Sherman, McPherson, and McClernand. But the assailants were completely repulsed. Grant now determined to starve the garrison into a surrender. Vicksburg was full of people who were in great danger from the shells which were thrown into the city by the fleet night and day. Many citizens found safety for their families by making underground rooms, some of which were carpeted and neatly furnished. The Federals

ran parallels, which gradually approached nearer and nearer to the Confederate works. Their sappers also dug mines for the purpose of blowing up the works of the defenders. The Confederates tried to defeat these efforts by counter-mining.

GENERAL JOSEPH E JOHNSTON.

8. While these things were going on at Vicksburg General Banks advanced from New Orleans with 15,000 men and began a close siege of Port Hudson, which was defended by 6,000 Confederates under General Gardner. On May 27th Banks assaulted the Confed-

erate works, but was repulsed with the loss of 3,000 men, while the Southerners did not lose 300 in all.

9. The Confederate Government was now making efforts to assemble an army under General Joseph E. Johnston for the relief of Vicksburg and Port Hudson. Some divisions were sent from Bragg's army and some from Beauregard's department. General Richard Taylor, on the Louisiana side, also attempted a diversion in favor of Port Hudson. On the 22d of June he captured Brashear City, with 1,000 prisoners, ten large cannon, and supplies valued at $6,000,000. But his force was not strong enough to make Banks let go his hold.

10. On the 1st of July General Johnston sent a note to Pemberton, telling him that on the 7th he would make a diversion to enable him to cut his way out. But Pemberton was a prisoner before the message reached him. On the 4th of July he surrendered to Grant the stronghold of Vicksburg, with 172 cannon and 29,000 prisoners, including the sick and wounded. Not more than 15,000 of them were at that time able to fight. When Pemberton first asked for terms, Grant demanded an unconditional surrender. To this Pemberton would not accede. Then Grant agreed that, as soon as paroles could be signed by officers and men, they should be allowed to march out, the officers taking with them their side-arms and clothing, and the field, staff and cavalry officers one horse each. The rank and file were to be allowed all their clothing, but no other property. The victors did not cheer at the surrender, except that one Federal division gave three cheers for the gallant defenders of Vicksburg.

11. On the 9th of July Port Hudson, which had been bravely defended to the last, surrendered to General Banks, with nearly 6,000 prisoners and 51 cannon. Only 3,000 of the garrison were well and able to fight.

12. The surrender of Vicksburg and Port Hudson was a terrible blow to the Confederacy, made much worse by the defeat at Gettysburg. Some have said that instead of marching into Pennsylvania Lee should have sent a part of his forces to the West. But if they had not been managed any better by the officers then commanding in Mississippi than were the troops that they did have they would only have been thrown away for naught. It is probable that Lee did the best thing with them that could have been done, taking all things into consideration.[1]

CHICKAMAUGA.

13. For nearly six months after the battle of Murfreesboro (Stone River) Bragg's army lay at Tullahoma, and that of Rosecrans at Murfreesboro. The cavalry of the two armies, however, kept busy, On the 5th of

---

[1] The effective force of the Union army in the operations against Vicksburg ranged from 43,000 at the beginning to 75,000 at the close of the campaign. In the whole department Grant had 103,000 effectives. Its total loss in all the battles of the campaign was 1,514 killed, 7,395 wounded, and 453 captured or missing—9,362. Pemberton's greatest available force, including those at Raymond and Jackson, numbered 40,000. After the battle of Champion Hill Loring, with his division, marched eastward. while Pemberton entered Vicksburg with 23,000 effectives. The total number surrendered, including wounded, sick, and the non-combatants, was 29,491. In all the battles of the campaign the Confederates lost 1,260 killed, 3,572 wounded, and 4,227 captured or missing—9,059. Of course, to this should be added the number surrendered at Vicksburg. By June 4th Johnston had assembled 24,000 men with which to attempt the relief of Vicksburg.

March a cavalry force under Van Dorn captured the
Federal Colonel Coburn, with 1,300 men, at Spring
Hill, in Middle Tennessee.   Still later (May 8th) Colonel Streight, who had been sent with about 2,000
Union cavalry on a raid into Georgia to destroy mills
and machine shops, was captured near Rome by Forrest and Roddy.

14. About the last of June Rosecrans began to
advance on Bragg, whose army had been very much
weakened by the transfer of troops to Mississippi. On
the afternoon of July 3d Bragg retreated southward,
and the Union army entered Tullahoma.   Bragg continued his retreat until he had crossed the Tennessee
and entered Chattanooga.   On the day appointed by
Mr. Davis for fasting and prayer (August 21st), while
the people of the town were in church, the Union
army appeared opposite Chattanooga and began to
throw shells into the town.   Some women and children
were killed by the shelling.

15. On the 7th of September Rosecrans sent
McCook and Thomas to cross the mountains to the
south of Chattanooga and take such positions as would
completely flank the Confederate stronghold.   On the
next day Bragg abandoned the town and retired
southward.   Several days of marching and counter-
marching now occurred, during which Bragg missed
one or two excellent opportunities of beating the
Union army in detail.   The Confederate Government
seeing Bragg's need sent him Longstreet with part of
his corps.   Receiving this reinforcement Bragg began
to advance against Rosecrans, who was concentrating
his troops at Lee and Gordon's Mills, twelve miles
south of Chattanooga.

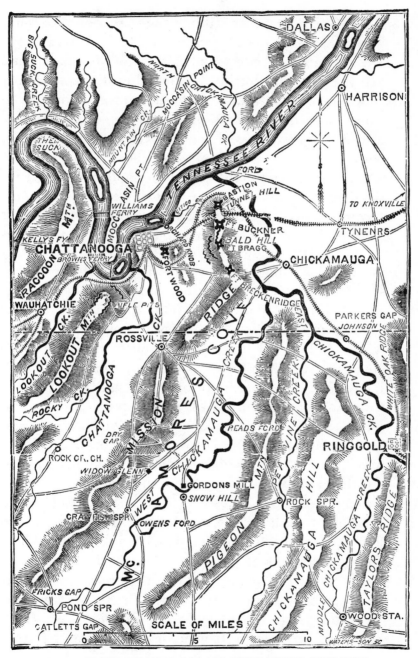

CHART OF THE CHICKAMAUGA AND CHATTANOOGA CAMPAIGNS.

16. On September 19th Bragg attacked General Thomas, a Virginian by birth, who had adhered to the Union, and who commanded the left of Rosecrans's army. As Bragg hurled division after division against this wing, Rosecrans sent successive divisions to Thomas. The battle was hotly contested, and battery after battery was taken and retaken. The day closed without decisive advantage to either side.

17. During the night each commander prepared for the decisive conflict, which all believed that the morrow would bring. Bragg placed General Leonidas Polk in command of his right wing, consisting of the corps of D. H. Hill and William H. T. Walker, the division of Cheatham and the cavalry of Forrest ; to Longstreet he gave the right wing, embracing the corps of Buckner and Hood, the division of Hindman and the cavalry of Wheeler. Each wing was well supplied with artillery. Thomas so arranged his line as to cover the Rossville (or Chattanooga) and the Dry Valley roads. It began four hundred yards east of the Chattanooga road on a crest which was occupied from left to right by four divisions: Baird's of Thomas corps, R. W. Johnson's of McCook's, Palmer's of Crittenden's, and Joseph J. Reynolds's division of Thomas's corps. On the right of Reynolds came the divisions of Brannan and Negley. Across the Chattanooga road toward Missionary Ridge came the divisions of Sheridan and Jeff C. Davis of McCook's corps, with Wood's and Van Cleve's divisions of Crittenden's corps, in reserve.

18. Bragg's plan of battle was successive attacks from right to left. When the battle commenced Breckinridge's and Cleburne's divisions of Hill's corps fell with such fury upon the Union left that

Thomas was obliged to call for help. Rosecrans kept sending troops to the help of Thomas, as that wing was pressed by troops hurried to the help of Breckinridge and Cleburne. At length, through some misunderstanding, a gap was left in the Federal line of battle. Into this Longstreet pushed the eight brigades of Bushrod Johnson, McNair, Gregg, Kershaw, Law, Humphrey, Benning, and Robertson, sweeping completely from the field Sheridan's entire division, two brigades of Davis's division and one of Van Cleve's. Longstreet now disregarded the order of the day, wheeling to the right instead of the left, capturing batteries, wagon-trains, prisoners, and

GENERAL BRAXTON BRAGG.

the headquarters of Rosecrans, who was borne away in the flight of his routed right. But Thomas held firm, and, assisted by Gordon Granger, who came to his support, held his ground until night-fall, when, under the combined attack of both wings of the Confederate army, he was obliged to give way and retire towards Rossville. From his firm stand on this day Thomas has been called "The Rock of Chickamauga." He had saved the Union army from utter ruin. Longstreet, by his prompt action in entering the gap in the Federal line had won the victory for the Confederates.[1]

19. The defeated Union army retreated to Chattanooga. Had Bragg pushed the pursuit next morning he could have reaped the full fruits of his great victory. The roads were full of disorganized masses of men trying to get on; batteries of artillery were mingled with trains of wagons; everywhere there was disorder and confusion. Forrest, in front with his cavalry, sent back word to Bragg that "every hour was worth a thousand men." Rosecrans spent the day and night of the 21st hurrying his trains and artillery out of town. Then, finding that he was not pressed, remained in Chattanooga with his army.

CHATTANOOGA AND MISSIONARY RIDGE.

20. Bragg spent the 21st in burying the dead and gathering up the captured stores. Among his trophies were fifty-one cannon and 15,000 small arms. On the 22d he moved forward, and during the next two days came slowly into position on Missionary Ridge and Lookout Mountain, which he connected by

[1] The official records are not clear as to the strength of the opposing forces at Chickamauga, on account of incompleteness in the returns. Hence conflicting estimates have been made. According to Colonel Archer Anderson's (Confederate) estimate the Union army numbered 59,000 infantry and artillery and 10,000 cavalry, while the Confederate army numbered 55,000 infantry and artillery and 11,000 cavalry. Another estimate (Federal) says that the whole Union force was 56,965. Major E. C. Dawes (Federal) estimates the Confederate army at 71,550 of all arms. But in order to arrive at this result he counts several commands which did not arrive until after the battle. The Union loss is stated at 1,656 killed, 9,749 wounded, and 4,774 captured—16,179. But General D. H. Hill says this is too small by more than 1,000 men. The Confederate loss was 2,389 killed, 13,412 wounded, and 2,003 captured or missing—17,804. The Confederates lost more, because they attacked the breastworks of the Federals.

a line of earthworks across Chattanooga Valley. Bragg sent a force into Lookout Valley, which commanded the twenty-six mile wagon road to Bridgeport. Thus he forced the Union army to draw its supplies by an almost impassable mountain road ot sixty miles to the same point. Knowing that it would be impossible to long subsist an army by this route, Bragg hoped to force the Union army into a surrender. Had the Confederate Government been able to accumulate superior numbers at other points this plan would undoubtedly have succeeded.

MISSIONARY RIDGE FROM THE CEMETERY AT CHATTANOOGA.

21. But relief came to the besieged. The two corps of Hooker and Howard were detached from the Union army in Virginia and sent to Tennessee. Grant was ordered to relieve the besieged army. He removed Rosecrans from command and put Thomas in his place. He ordered Sherman to come from Mississippi with another army. Under dispositions made by Grant the forces from Virginia and those in Chattanooga succeeded in concealing their movements until they had seized and fortified a position which gave them command of the Tennessee river from Lookout

Valley to Bridgeport.   The Federal army was no longer in danger of starvation, and the Confederate hope of effecting its capture was gone.

22. While Grant was concentrating everything available for the relief of the Union army in Chattanooga the Confederate authorities sent Longstreet away from Bragg with a force of about 15,000 men to drive Burnside out of East Tennessee.   That officer had captured Cumberland Gap in September, and soon afterwards occupied Knoxville.   As Longstreet advanced Burnside's forces, which were some distance south of Knoxville, were defeated at Philadelphia Station and Campbell's Station and driven into Knoxville, which place Longstreet proceeded to invest.

23. As soon as Sherman reached Chattanooga with his army, Grant resolved to attack Bragg's now weakened forces.   On the 24th of November Hooker's corps carried the works on Lookout Mountain, which point, through some bad management, was not properly defended.   On the 25th occurred the battle of Missionary Ridge.   In this battle General Hardee, who had resumed command of his old corps, commanded the Confederate right.   Breckinridge commanded the left [1]

24. Sherman's force was to attack the Confederate right, Thomas was to move against the center and Hooker against the left.   The Confederate right repulsed every attack, and Hooker was so delayed that he could not relieve the pressure upon Sherman. Bragg had moved one body of troops after another to

[1] There had been such serious dissension between Bragg and his two corp commanders, Hill and Polk, that the two latter had been assigned to duty elsewhere.

strengthen his right until his center was weakened. Grant, who from his position could see the movements of the Confederates, ordered Thomas forward. Im-

GENERAL W. T. SHERMAN.

mediately the divisions of Wood and Sheridan advanced with such impetuosity that they carried the lower Confederate line; then without waiting for orders pressed on and carried the crest. Bragg hurried forward General Bate's command to repair the breach, but it was too late. Soon the whole Confederate left was in utter rout. Hardee now threw a portion of

Cheatham's division directly across the path of the advancing Federals, and held his ground until darkness closed the fight. During the night Bragg's army retreated. Hardee in this battle did for the Confederate army what Thomas had done for the Union army at Chickamauga.

25. Grant had gained a great victory. He had captured 40 cannon, 7,000 small arms, and many baggage wagons. Bragg had weakened his army by sending off Longstreet to Knoxville and then had sent off another division just on the eve of battle. Thus he made it possible for Grant to capture what would have been an impregnable position if properly manned. Grant lost no time in following up his victory. He sent Hooker in pursuit of Bragg's retreating army, and Sherman to relieve Burnside at Knoxville.[1]

26. Hooker pressed the pursuit vigorously, but at a gap in Taylor's Ridge near the little village of Ringgold General Cleburne halted his division with the intention of holding the place long enough for Bragg's trains and artillery to get safely out of the way. When Hooker came up, he attacked Cleburne, but was repulsed, losing heavily. He was now ordered to discontinue the pursuit and return to Chattanooga.

27. Longstreet, who had commenced a siege of Knoxville, made an assault upon the Union works

---

[1] Grant says that he had in this battle about 60,000 men. But the official records show that he had at and around Chattanooga 80,822 effectives present for duty. The Union loss was 752 killed, 4,713 wounded, 350 captured or missing—5,815. The Confederate army numbered less than 40,000 of all arms. Their loss was 361 killed, 2,180 wounded and 4,146 captured or missing—6,687. Most of the wounded fell into the hands of the Federals and thus increased their list of prisoners.

(November 30th). He failed, being repulsed with heavy loss. He now learned of Bragg's defeat and Sherman's approach. He accordingly abandoned the siege, and retired towards Virginia.

28. By their double defeat at Chattanooga and Knoxville the Confederates had lost all the fruits of their magnificent victory at Chickamauga. Bragg felt that his army had lost all confidence in his ability to command it, and asked to be relieved. This was done, and Lieutenant-General William J. Hardee was placed in command. He, however, requested to be left in command of his own corps, and asked that General Joseph E. Johnston be appointed to lead the Confederate army of Tennessee. This was done, and the work of reorganization, which had been commenced as soon as the army halted at Dalton, went rapidly on. The spirits of the men revived, and every day their efficiency was improved.

CHAPTER IV.

OTHER IMPORTANT EVENTS OF 1863.

MORGAN'S OHIO RAID.

ONE of the most thrilling episodes of the war is the celebrated cavalry raid of General John H. Morgan into Ohio during the summer of 1863. This remarkable man was a Kentuckian who embraced with all his heart the cause of the South. He had entered the Confederate army as a captain in 1861, and by his daring exploits had rapidly risen to the rank of brigadier-general. A short while before Bragg's Kentucky campaign Morgan, leaving Tennessee with less than a thousand men, penetrated a country in the hands of the Federals, captured seventeen towns, and destroyed all government supplies and arms in them, dispersed 1,500 home guards, and paroled nearly 1,200 regular troops. In subsequent campaigns he was equally successful.

GENERAL JOHN H. MORGAN.

2. Morgan's most wonderful exploit was his great raid through Kentucky, Indiana and Ohio, which be-

gan on the 2d of July, 1863, when, with near 2,000 horsemen and four cannon, he crossed the Cumberland river near Burksville. Moving rapidly forward, he met and defeated Wolford's Kentucky Union command. At Brandenburg, on the Ohio, Morgan's bold riders captured two steamboats. Then one-half of the command crossed the Ohio and attacked about a thousand men on the Indiana side, while Morgan, with the other half, turned his artillery on two gunboats that had come down the river to prevent the crossing, and drove them off. The rest of the command then crossed over and dispersed or captured the whole Federal force.

3. Moving on, they captured Corydon and about 1,200 citizens and soldiers, who tried to defend it. All pillaging was forbidden as they passed through the country. Only provisions for men and provender for stock were taken. Every effort was being made to effect their capture. At last, after having passed through fifty-two towns—nine in Kentucky, fourteen in Indiana, and twenty-nine in Ohio—having captured nearly 6,000 prisoners, and damaged public property to the amount of ten million dollars, Morgan and his men were captured. Some were sent to Camp Morton, Indiana.

4. Morgan and some of his officers were taken to Columbus, where they were treated like common felons. Their heads were shaved, they were attired in prison garb and placed in stone cells, where they were carefully guarded day and night. But Morgan and six of his officers, with no tools but case-knives, cut their way through the solid stone, tunnelled under ground and made their escape. Morgan succeeded in

getting across Kentucky and Tennessee into North Georgia, and then went to Richmond, where he was received with every mark of honor and esteem.

RENEWED EFFORTS TO CAPTURE CHARLESTON.

5. On the 12th of June, 1863, General David Hunter, who had been commanding the Union army before Charleston, was superseded by General Quincy A. Gillmore, an engineering officer of great repute. On the 6th of July, Admiral Dahlgren succeeded Admiral Du Pont. On the 10th the Federals effected a landing on the south end of Morris Island and captured a small Confederate work at that point. At the same time demonstrations were made against the Confederate works on James Island. Beauregard was glad that the Federals made the attack by way of Morris Island, which he considered far less dangerous to Charleston, than an advance by James Island.

6. On July 11th, an assault was made upon Battery Wagner, which was easily repulsed. On the 18th, after a furious bombardment from the Union fleet and land batteries, about 6,000 men under General Thomas Seymour under cover of darkness made an impetuous assault upon Battery Wagner held at the time by 1,000 men under General W. B. Taliaferro. The Federals were repulsed with a loss of more than 1,500 men, among whom was General C. C. Strong After this defeat the Federals kept up a constant bombardment of the fort.

7. Among the most remarkable incidents of this period of the seige was the seven days' bombardment of Fort Sumter (August 17th to August 23d). It was a desperate attempt to force the surrender of the fort

FORT MOULTRIE, S. C. FORT SUMTER IN THE DISTANCE.

and of the city of Charleston. Sumter was made a mass of ruins on the side facing the Union batteries, so that its guns could no longer be of assistance to the Confederate works on Morris Island (Wagner and Gregg). These would soon become untenable. But Beauregard was busy constructing interior defenses, on which guns taken from Fort Sumter were mounted. Until these interior defenses should be ready, Wagner and Gregg were held with determined valor by the brave garrison, commanded in turn by Taliaferro, Hagood, Alfred Colquitt, Clingman, Graham, Harrison and L. M. Keitt.

8. Colonel Rhett, with his regulars, was placed in command of the interior defences. Major Stephen Elliott, with an infantry command of troops selected from various regiments, was put in charge of the ruins of Fort Sumter for the purpose of holding it against any storming party and to give the morning and evening salutes to the Confederate flag, which still floated to the breeze from the ruined fort. Then, during the night of September 6th, the garrisons of Gregg and Wagner were withdrawn and Morris Island was occupied by the Federals. But it proved a barren victory, for it did not enable them to take Sumter or Charleston.

9. Major Elliott (afterwards lieutenant-colonel) continued in command of Fort Sumter until May, 1864, when he was succeeded by Captain John C. Mitchell, who lost his life there (July 20th, 1864), and was succeeded by Captain T. A. Huguenin, who remained in command until the evacuation of Charleston (February 17th, 1865), just before the close of the war.

10. Two nights after the evacuation of Wagner and Gregg, Admiral Dahlgren attempted to take Fort Sum-

Jno. C. Calhoun.

Old Presbyterian Church at which Calhoun Worshiped.

The Calhoun Homestead at Fort Hill.

Calhoun's Grave in St. Phillip's Churchyard.

ter by a night attack. But the storming party, consisting of troops in boats, was repulsed with heavy loss. The ruins of Sumter were held and repaired, so that early in October Elliott mounted in the northeast casemates two ten-inch columbiads and one seven-inch rifled cannon. In the following January he mounted in the northwest casemates one eight-inch and two seven-inch rifled cannon. Under the diligent efforts of officers and men Fort Sumter, from a mass of shapeless ruins, at length became a powerful earthwork, which for eighteen months endured the constant fire of the Federals, and "for a hundred days and nights their utmost power—even supporting the other works at the entrance of Charleston harbor with six guns of the heaviest caliber."[1]

11. From the Swamp Angel and (after that had exploded) from other guns Gillmore threw shells into Charleston. But all his efforts on land and water availed nothing against the skill and valor of the defenders.

SABINE PASS.

12. One gallant exploit near this little fort on the Texas coast has already been recorded. Another yet remains to be told. In September a Federal land force of 4,000 men under General Franklin, assisted by a fleet, was sent to effect a landing at Sabine Pass, and from thence to operate against Galveston and Houston. On the 8th of September four Union gunboats attacked Fort Grigsby, which was defended at the time by forty-two men and two lieutenants, with an armament of six cannon. The officers and men were all Irishmen,

[1] From an article on "The Confederate Defence of Fort Sumter," by Major John Johnson, "Battles and Leaders of the Civil War." Vol. iv.

and the company was called the "Davis Guards."
The captain (F. H. Odlum) was not present, and the
company was commanded at the time by Lieutenant
R. W. Dowling.   For an hour and a half this gallant
little band was subjected to a terrific bombardment.
The result of the fight was the repulse of the gunboats, two of which were captured with their armament—eighteen guns and 150 men.   Just at the close
of the battle a reinforcement of 200 men under Captain Odlum arrived, and enabled the gallant defenders
to secure the gunboats and prisoners.   The success of
this defence caused the Federals to magnify the strength
of the Confederate works and the number of their
troops.   So the fleet of twenty vessels minus two gunboats sailed away with Franklin's command without
making any farther attempt   Besides the prisoners
the attacking party lost fifty killed and wounded.   Not
a man of the garrison was hurt.   The victory was as
decisive of the attempted invasion of Texas as if it
had been a great battle.

LEE'S FLANK MARCH IN OCTOBER.

13. After it became certain that Longstreet, with a
large part of his corps, had gone to the West, General
Meade made ready for an advance against Lee.   But
the defeat of Rosecrans at Chickamauga and the peril
of the Union army in Chattanooga, as we have already
seen, caused the government to take two corps from
Meade's army and send them to the West.

14. Lee then determined upon an advance against
Meade, hoping to bring that general to battle.   As
soon as Lee commenced his flank march the Union
army, which had seemed so anxious for another battle,

at once retreated, going back as far as Centreville, near Washington. Lee, after destroying the railroad on which Meade depended for his supplies, returned to his former position on the Rappahannock. He had inflicted on the Federals a loss of 3,000 men, mostly prisoners, while his own loss was not half so many.

15. Soon after the two armies had taken up their former positions General Russell of Meade's army, by a brilliant dash, captured an exposed Confederate work at Rappahannock Station, taking four cannon and 1,600 prisoners.

THE MINE RUN CAMPAIGN.

16. In the latter part of November Meade determined to advance, hoping to find Lee's army divided in their winter quarters. Lee, however, discovered this move, and, rapidly concentrating his troops, took up a strong position behind a little stream called Mine Run. Meade was greatly disappointed. After some skirmishing, which satisfied him that Lee's position was too strong to be attacked, he withdrew on the night of December 1st, and returned to his old camp north of the Rapidan.[1]

SUMMARY OF THE YEAR'S FIGHTING.

17. During 1863 the Federal Government had recovered control of the Mississippi river, had overrun the State of Tennessee, and had regained almost all of

---

[1] In the Mine Run campaign the Union army lost 173 killed, 1,099 wounded, and 381 captured or missing—1,653. The Confederate loss was 98 killed, 610 wounded, and 104 captured or missing—812.

Arkansas, and portions of Louisiana, Mississippi and
Florida.   Hence the people of the North were ready
to continue the war.   On the other hand, the Confederates had gained some brilliant victories, and were
equally determined to fight it out to the end, whatever
that might be.

PART III.

The War Between the States and its Results.

Section IV.—Events of 1864.

CHAPTER I.

EVENTS IN THE EAST AND THE WEST IN THE FIRST MONTHS OF 1864.

AS has been seen in the last chapter, the year 1863 had closed with the South disappointed, yet determined, and the North hopeful and confident. The events of the first half of 1864 revived again the hopes of the Confederates and produced in the minds of their enemies the same depression and doubt as to the final result which had prevailed during the period between the defeat of McClellan at Richmond and the Federal victories at Vicksburg and Gettysburg.

2. The year 1864, the fourth of the war, was also the year for the election of a President of the United States. It was considered desirable that some of the Southern States should be brought so completely under the control of the Union army as to enable such of the inhabitants, white and black, as might desire to do so to form "loyal" State governments and be re-admitted to the Union. This would be looked upon as a practical success of the Union arms. Florida seemed to offer a good prospect of success in an undertaking of this sort.

INVASION OF FLORIDA.

3. This State had within its limits only a few scattered Confederate troops, its coast was completely at

WINTER SCENE IN FLORIDA.

the mercy of the Union fleet, and it was hoped that the Union army could overrun it before a sufficient force could be concentrated for its defence. Accordingly General Gillmore, who commanded the Department of the South, sent General Truman Seymour, with 7,000 troops, to take possession of Jacksonville and march from thence into the interior. The fleet of Admiral Dahlgren accompanied the expedition.

4. Jacksonville was occupied without opposition February 7th. Then General Seymour promptly marched inland, forcing Colonel McCormick, with a small body of Confederate cavalry, to retire before him. After passing a few miles beyond Baldwin, Seymour was obliged to halt for the lack of transportation. From Hilton Head, South Carolina, Gillmore issued a proclamation announcing the occupancy of Florida, which he said would not be again abandoned.

5. As soon as General Joseph Finegan, the Confederate commander of East Florida, heard of the landing of Seymour's force at Jacksonville, he telegraphed to Savannah and Charleston for reinforcements, which were immediately sent to him. By the 13th a Confederate force of about 5,400 men was concentrated near Lake City. It consisted of two brigades, one under General Alfred H. Colquitt and the other under Colonel George P. Harrison, Jr., all from Georgia and Florida.[1]

[1] Colquitt's brigade consisted of the Sixth, Nineteenth, Twenty-third, Twenty-seventh, and Twenty-eighth Georgia regiments, the Sixth Florida, and the Chatham Artillery of Savannah. Harrison's brigade consisted of the Thirty-second and Sixty-fourth Georgia volunteers and the First Georgia regulars, First Florida battalion, Bonaud's infantry battalion and Guerard's light battery. The cavalry was commanded by Colonel Caraway Smith.

6. On the 20th of February Seymour advanced against the Confederates, with 5,500 men. His force was divided into three brigades, each commanded by a colonel. Hawley's brigade consisted of Connecticut and New Hampshire troops and one regiment of colored troops ; Barton's brigade consisted of New York, and Montgomery's of Massachusetts regiments.

GENERAL A. H. COLQUITT.

7. About two miles east of **Olustee** the Federals encountered Colquitt's brigade, and the battle commenced. Just at the right moment Colquitt was reinforced by Harrison. The two armies were nearly equal and the battle was an open, square fight. The result was a complete Confederate victory, which brought to an end the Federal scheme for the conquest and reconstruction of Florida. The year 1864 had opened with a brilliant Confederate success.

SHERMAN'S EXPEDITION.

8. About the same time the Confederates gained another important success in Mississippi. On the 3d of February General Sherman set out from Vicksburg with two columns of infantry 20,000 strong under Generals McPherson and Hurlbut, with the purpose of breaking up the Mobile and Ohio and the Jackson and Selma railroads. He expected the co-operation of

10,000 cavalry from Memphis under General William S. Smith. As Sherman advanced General Polk, whose force was not strong enough to offer effective resistance, retired before him. Sherman advanced as far as Meridian and even contemplated an attack upon Mobile from the rear.

9. Smith had been expected to start from Memphis on the 1st of February, so as to meet Sherman at Meridian on or near the 10th. Sherman himself did not reach that place until the 14th. There he waited six days to hear from Smith. As no tidings came from that officer, he abandoned his expedition and went back to Vicksburg.

10. The reason for Smith's failure to appear was that he did not get ready to start until the 11th. After marching nine days almost unopposed he found the forces of Forrest drawn up to dispute his advance. The next day he began to retreat. Forrest pursued, and near **Okalona** made a vigorous attack (February 22d), in which that dashing Confederate cavalryman gained a complete victory, driving Smith back to Memphis, capturing prisoners, six cannon, and thirty-three stands of colors.[1]

FORREST'S RAID.

11. After his victory over Smith, Forrest marched northward through West Tennessee, captured Union City, with 450 prisoners ; occupied Hickman, Kentucky, and made an attack upon Paducah, which failed. Then he turned southward, and on the morning of April 12th appeared before Fort Pillow, forty miles above Memphis.

[1] Smith had with him 7,000 men and Forrest only 2,500.

12. Forrest attacked the fort and captured the outer line of works. The gunboat New Era joined in the defence. Forrest sent a demand to the Union commander for a surrender of the fort and garrison. Major Booth, the first in command, had been killed in the opening of the fight, and Major Bradford, who succeeded him, refused the demand for a surrender. The Confederates then carried the fort with a rush. The Federals, half of whom were colored troops, fled towards the river, firing as they ran. The result was that at least half the force were killed and wounded. Fortunately for those of the Federals who still survived, one of Forrest's men pulled down the flag that was still flying over the fort, when at once the firing ceased. The failure of Sherman's expedition, and the fact that the Confederate forces in north Mississippi could hold their own, and at the same time send out successful expeditions, aroused the hope that Vicksburg was not so fatal a blow as had been supposed.

THE RED RIVER EXPEDITION.

13. Confederate hopes were destined to be raised still higher by what was on their part one of the most brilliant campaigns of the war. It has already been mentioned that in the early part of 1863, Arkansas Post was captured by a Federal land and naval force (January 11th). The subsequent capture of Helena (July 4th, 1863), and the capture of Little Rock (September 10th) had placed all of Arkansas, except a small region in the southwest under the control of the Union army. A large part of east Louisiana was also in the hands of the Federals.

BURNSIDE'S EXPEDITION CROSSING HATTERAS BAR.

14. When Sherman returned to Vicksburg after his expedition to Meridian, a large part of his army was sent to General Banks, the Union commander in Louisiana. In co-operation with General Steele, the Union commander at Little Rock, General Banks arranged a plan by which he expected to drive the Confederates entirely out of Louisiana and Arkansas, and complete their overthrow in Texas.

16. General E. Kirby Smith, the Confederate commander of the Trans-Mississippi Department began preparation to meet this combined movement of Banks and Steele. Shreveport, Louisiana, was th capital of the Trans-Mississippi Department and the Headquarters of General Smith. While Banks moved forward with an army of 31,000 men Admiral Porter with his feet ascended the Red River.

16. General Richard Taylor, who commanded the troops in front of Banks, retired slowly before the advancing column until he reached Mansfield. Here, being reinforced until he had 11,000 men, he moved forward to **Sabine Cross-Roads.** Banks's army, now about 26,000 strong,[1] was stretched out to the length of almost a day's march, on a single narrow road, and encumbered with a long wagon-train.

17. Taylor saw that he had a fine opportunity to attack Banks while his army was so stretched out, that its superior numbers would be of no advantage. So, turning suddenly upon the advanced division, he routed it completely, capturing cannon, wagons, and over 2,000 prisoners (April 8th). The whole Union army now retreated. News of the disaster was sent to

[1] He had left 5,000 troops at Alexandria.

the fleet, which also ceased its advance and started down the river.

18. Taylor pursued, and on the next day came up with the Union army strongly posted at **Pleasant Hill.** The Confederates attacked, but were only partially successful. The Federal left repulsed them, but they held at the close of the day part of the Federal center and right. That night Banks continued the retreat.

19. Kirby Smith, leaving only a small force with Taylor to press the pursuit, started northward after Steele, who had occupied Camden. After two battles, one at **Marks's Mill** (April 25th), and the other at **Jenkins's Ferry,** on the Saline (April 30th), Steele retreated to Little Rock. Smith then sent most of his troops back to Taylor. But before they could get there Banks was gone.

20. Porter's fleet had been detained at the rapids above Alexandria on account of the falling of the river. It seemed at one time as though the fleet would have to be abandoned to its fate. But Lieutenant-Colonel Joseph Bailey, of the Fourth Wisconsin, at that time serving on General Franklin's staff as chief engineer, succeeded in constructing a dam which raised the water sufficiently to float the vessels over the falls. In this way the fleet was saved.

21. General Taylor's force was only large enough to annoy, but not to attack the Federal army. He had urged Smith to let Steele alone and concentrate everything against Banks, believing that Porter's whole fleet would be the rich prize that would fall into their hands by adopting such a course. But when the force that Smith had taken with him against Steele was returned to Taylor, both Banks and the fleet had

escaped.   The campaign, however, had been a great
triumph to the Confederates and a great disaster to
the Federals, who had lost in the whole campaign
8,000 men, over thirty cannon, 1,100 wagons, one
gunboat, and three transports.   The Confederates had
recovered large portions of Louisiana and Arkansas
hitherto occupied by the Federals.[1]

22. Taylor, who pursued Banks's retreating army
until it had crossed the Atchafalaya (May 19th), states
that "in their rapid flight from Grand Ecore to
Monette's ferry, a distance of forty miles, the Federals
burned nearly every house on the road."   He adds :
"In pursuit we passed the smoking ruins of home-
steads, by which stood weeping women and children."
General Taylor also says that General Banks and the
officers and men of the Nineteenth Corps (Eastern
troops) did all in their power to prevent these outrages.   He lays all the blame on A. J. Smith's command, from Sherman's army.

THE CAPTURE OF PLYMOUTH.

23. In the spring of 1864 the Confederate authorities decided to attempt the recapture of Plymouth, on
the Roanoke river in North Carolina.   In order to
effect the capture General Hoke was ordered to take a
division of troops and surround the town from the

---

[1] In the Red River campaign Banks's army numbered 31,603, and had
the assistance of Porter's fleet.   Its losses, including those lost on the
retreat from Alexandria, were 454 killed, 2,191 wounded and 2,600 captured or missing—5,244.   Steele's Union army in Arkansas numbered
13,000, and its total loss was 2,500.   Total Union loss, 7,744.   Taylor's
Confederate army at Mansfield numbered 11,000.   Its total loss in the
campaign was 3,976.   Kirby Smith led against Steele 14,000 men.   Half
of them were from Taylor's army and have already been counted.   His
losses were 1,200, making the total Confederate loss 5,176.

river above to the river below, so as to storm the breast-works as soon as the *Albemarle*,[1] a powerful Confederate iron-clad, should clear the river front of the Federal ships that protected the garrison with their guns.

24. The *Albemarle*, commanded by Captain J. W. Cooke, successfully passed the obstructions in the river and the fire of the Union fort ; then closing in with two ships that attacked her, she sank the *Southfield* and drove the *Miami* below Plymouth into Albemarle Sound.   (April 19th.)

25. Next morning General Hoke stormed and carried the Federal works, but not without heavy loss, Ransom's brigade alone loosing 500 killed and wounded in their heroic charge.   General Wessels, the Union commander, made a stout defence and surrendered only when farther resistance would have been madness.   During the attack the *Albemarle* held the river front and poured shot and shell into the Federal fort. The Federal loss by this capture was more than 2,000 men (1,600 of whom were effective), twenty-five cannon, 2,000 small arms and valuable stores.   In consequence of the loss of Plymouth the Union General Palmer soon after abandoned the little town of Washington[2] at the head of Pamlico Sound.

THE RAID OF KILPATRICK AND DAHLGREN.

26. Early in March there occurred in Virginia the great cavalry raid of General Kilpatrick and Colonel Ulric Dahlgren, the object of which was to capture

---

[1] The Albemarle was built by Gilbert Elliott according to the plan of Chief-Constructor John L. Porter.

[2] Horace Greeley in his "American Conflict" says that some of the Union soldiers disgraced themselves and their flag by arson and pillage before they left.

Richmond by a surprise and release the Federal prisoners. In order to secure the success of this expedition General Custer was sent with another division of cavalry on a raid towards Gordonsville. The whole plan came to naught, and Dahlgren was killed on the retreat. On Dahlgren's person were found papers ordering the burning of Richmond and the killing of Mr. Davis and his Cabinet. General Lee sent photographic copies of these papers to General Meade, who wrote to General Lee stating that no such orders were given by the United States Government, General Kilpatrick, or himself.

27. The result of this fruitless cavalry raid was the disabling for a time of three or four thousand of the very flower of the Union cavalry.[1] The reader of the events recorded in this chapter will see that before the opening of the two principal campaigns of 1864 the hopes of the Confederates had been again raised by signal triumphs in the East and in the West.

[1] This statement is made by General Martin T. McMahon of the Union army in " Battles and Leaders of the Civil War," Vol. IV., page 94.

CHAPTER II.

FROM THE OPENING OF THE VIRGINIA CAMPAIGN TO THE END OF JULY, 1864

IN March General Ulysses S. Grant was made Lieutenant-General and placed in command of all the forces of the United States. Two grand campaigns were now planned—one against Richmond, in Virginia, under Grant himself; the other against Atlanta, in Georgia, under the leadership of General William Tecumseh Sherman Grant had proved himself the ablest of all the Union commanders. He had out-generaled everybody in the West with the single exception of Albert Sidney Johnston.[1]

2. The plan of campaign adopted by Grant is best expressed in his own words: " to hammer continuously against the armed force of the enemy and his resources until, by mere attrition, if in no other way, there should be nothing left to him but an equal submission with the loyal section of our common country to the constitution and laws of the land." In other words, his plan was to press the fighting without regard to defeats or losses in the full confidence that the North, which could bring many more men into the field than the South, and which had vastly greater resources, would be sure to win in a struggle of this sort.

---

[1] Albert Sidney Johnston had out-generaled and beaten Grant at Shiloh. and but for his death would probably have destroyed the Union army. His death caused such delay that Buell got up and saved Grant's army from the ruin that threatened it.

3. It would have been well for the Confederate cause if at this time Robert E. Lee had been commander-in-chief of all the Southern armies, with full and absolute control of all their movements Against the policy that Grant proposed to pursue, it was only necessary to make a successful defence of the main points assailed, to wear out the patience of the North, and bring the war to a successful end; for Grant's plan involved such a fearful sacrifice of life that nothing but decided victory somewhere would make

GENERAL U. S. GRANT.

the people of the North willing to endure it. Lee had out-generaled every one who had been pitted against him. To him should have been committed full control of all the movements against Grant and all his lieutenants in every part of the country.

4. Grant's plan was that both the grand campaigns should begin on the same day, and that the Confederate armies in Virginia and Georgia should be kept so busy that neither could send aid to the other.   At the same time the Government was to keep a constant stream of reinforcements going to the front to supply the losses of the armies under himself and Sherman. On the 4th of May, while the Army of the Potomac was crossing the Rapidan, Grant seated on a log by the

GRANT WRITING DISPATCHES TO SHERMAN BEFORE CROSSING THE RAPIDAN.

side of the road, wrote a telegram to Sherman bidding him to start.

THE OVERLAND CAMPAIGN.

5. Grant left Meade in nominal command of the Army of the Potomac, but he made his headquarters with that army and directed its movements.   His plan for the Virginia campaign was that his own army

(140,000 strong) should advance from the north upon Richmond, while Generals Crook and Sigel were to capture Staunton and Lynchburg, moving from thence upon the Confederate rear, and General Butler, with a fleet and nearly 40,000 men, was to move up the James River, take Petersburg, and approach Richmond from the south.

6. The skill with which General Lee met this great combination would have made him famous if he had never done anything else. Grant crossed the Rapidan with 118,000 men of all arms, and with power to call for as many thousands more of reinforcements as he might need. Lee had but 64,000 men (according to the highest estimate) with which to meet this mighty array. General A. S. Webb, of the Union army, says:[1] "Grant's 118,000 men, properly disposed for battle, would have covered a front of twenty-one miles, two ranks deep, with one-third of them held in reserve; while Lee, with his 62,000 men similarly disposed, would cover only twelve miles. Grant had a train which he states in his "Memoirs" would have reached from the Rapidan to Richmond, or sixty-five miles.

7. On the 4th of May Grant made a feint towards Lee's left, and then crossed the Rapidan on his right at Germanna and Ely's Fords. This is exactly what Lee two days before had told a group of officers that Grant would do.[2] The Federal commander expected to pass around Lee's flank before he could concentrate his forces, and thus get between him and Richmond.

---

[1] " Battles and Leaders of the Civil War," Vol. IV., page 152.

[2] General E. M. Law, of the Confederate army, in "Battles and Leaders of the Civil War," Vol. IV., page 118.

Grant's passage of the Rapidan was unopposed, and he looked upon this as a great success. When Lee ascertained that the Union army was moving he prepared to advance upon its flank with his whole force as soon as it should clear the river and begin its march southward.

8. About noon on the 4th of May Lee started the corps of Hill and Ewell on the march against Grant, and ordered Longstreet, who was camped near Gordonsville, to move rapidly across the country and follow Hill.

9. Before describing the battle let us glance for a moment at the two armies who were about to close with each other in the fierce struggle in the Wilderness. The great superiority in numbers of the Union army has been already shown. The Union army was thoroughly equipped and well supplied with every thing needed in modern warfare. The Confederate army was scantily supplied with food and clothing. General E. M. Law of that army says: " a new pair of shoes or an overcoat was a luxury, and full rations would have astonished the stomachs of Lee's ragged Confederates. I have often heard expressions of surprise that these ragged, barefooted, half-starved men, would fight at all. But the very fact that they remained with their colors through such privations and hardships was sufficient to prove that they would be dangerous foes to encounter upon the line of battle."

10. Ewell's corps was the first to find itself in the presence of the Federals. As it advanced along the Orange Turnpike on the morning of the 5th of May the Federal column was seen crossing it from the direction of Germanna Ford. Ewell at once formed

CONFEDERATE GENERALS.

line of battle across the turnpike and notified Lee of
what he had done. General Warren, whose corps was
passing when Ewell came up, at onced faced towards
Ewell and made a vigorous attack. Sedgwick's corps
came to the help of Warren, but the Confederates
could not be moved from their position upon the
Union flank. Soon after Ewell became engaged, A.
P. Hill's advance struck the Federal outposts on the
Orange plank road at Parker's store on the outskirts
of the Wilderness. Heth's division in front, driving
these in, came upon Getty's division of Sedgwick's
corps, which was covering the junction of the Plank
road with the Stevensburg and Brock roads, on which
the Federal army was moving towards Spotsylvania.

11. Hancock's corps, which was already on the
march to Spotsylvania by the the way of Chancelors-
ville, was recalled and ordered to drive Hill out of the
Wilderness. Desperate was the fighting at close quarters in these tangled thickets, where officers could not
see the whole of their commands, and could tell only by
the firing whether their friends to the right or left
were advancing or being driven. Night closed with the
Confederate line still firmly held. Lee sent word to
Longstreet to make a night march, so as to reach the
battle-field by daylight of the next morning.[1]

12. As soon as it was light enough to see on the next
morning (May 6th) Hancock's troops swept forward
with such force as to hurl back Wilcox's division, of
Hill's corps, to the position of Poague's artillery, which
now opened upon the attacking force. For a few
moments things looked bad for the Confederates, but

---

[1] Among the killed in the battle of the 5th were General Alexander
Hays, of Hancock's corps, and General J. M. Jones, of Ewell's.

soon Longstreet's splendid corps was seen coming down the Orange plank road in a trot. They were in double column, and with ranks well closed they pushed their way onward. Kershaw, whose division first struck the Federals, checked their advance and drove them back to their first line of works. Then, urged on by Longstreet, the division charged and captured the works.

13. Nearly at the same moment Field's division moved forward on the left. In front was Gregg's brigade of Texans and Arkansans, behind which came Benning's Georgians, with Law's Alabamians next and Jenkins's South Carolinians following. General Law says : " As the Texans in the front line swept past the batteries, where General Lee was standing, they gave a rousing cheer for ' Mars' Robert,' who spurred his horse forward and followed them in the charge. When the men became aware that he was going in with them they called loudly to him to go back. ' We won't go on unless you go back,' was the general cry. One of the men dropped to the rear, and taking the bridle, turned the General's horse around, while General Gregg came up and urged him to do as the men wished. At that moment a member of his staff (Colonel Venable) directed his attention to General Longstreet, whom he had been looking for. With evident disappointment General Lee turned off and joined General Longstreet." Gregg's men then rushed forward. Benning's and Law's brigades came to their support, and the whole line swept over the first line of Federal works. In a fruitless effort to re-take this line the Federal General Wadsworth was killed.

14. Next Longstreet moved the brigades of Mahone, Wofford, Anderson, and Davis to the flank and rear of the Union line. Attacked in front, flank, and rear, the Federal left wing was rolled in confusion back upon the Brock road. Longstreet rode forward with Jenkins's fresh brigade, intending, with the support of Kershaw's division, to press the attack. Just then they were mistaken for enemies by some of the Confederates and fired upon. Jenkins was killed and Longstreet severely wounded. The wounding of Longstreet caused such delay that nothing more was effected on this part of the field.

GENERAL WILLIAM MAHONE.

15. Later in the day Gen. Ewell ordered a movement against the Federal right wing, and John B. Gordon, with two brigades, just at sunset made a sudden attack upon the right flank of Sedgwick's corps, driving the Federals from their works and capturing 600 prisoners, among whom were Generals Seymour and Shaler.

Night closed the **Battle of The Wilderness.** General Webb, of the Union army, says: "Grant had been thoroughly defeated in his attempt to walk past General Lee on the way to Richmond. Ewell had most effectually stopped the forward movement of the right wing of Meade's army, and Hill and Longstreet defeated our left, under Hancock "[1]

16. Both armies were now strongly intrenched and neither could afford to attack. Had the numbers and resources of the two generals been reversed Grant would have been obliged to retreat. He decided to make no farther attempt to drive Lee from his path, but to try by a flank march to go around Lee's army and seize Spotsylvania Courthouse, thus putting his own army between the Confederates and Richmond. The 7th was spent in skirmishing, each army waiting to see what the other would do.

17. Grant ordered Warren's corps to withdraw from The Wilderness after dark on the 7th of May, and to move by the left behind Hancock on the Brock road, with Sedgwick following him, and to march as rapidly as possible to Spotsylvania Courthouse. But Stuart had posted his cavalry across the Brock road and checked Sheridan's cavalry until Warren's corps came up. This caused some delay to the Federal column. Longstreet's corps, now commanded by R. H. Anderson, marched all night, and reached Spotsylvania by 8 o'clock on the morning of the 8th. The advanced troops of the Federals were driven back and the heights were seized by the Confederates. They had won the race, and had completely baffled Grant's design.

[1] "Battles and Leaders of the Civil War," Vol. IV., pages 162 and 163.

18. During the 8th there was considerable skirmishing as the armies got into position. No fighting of
importance occurred during the 9th, but on that day
Major-General John Sedgwick, of the Union army,
while bantering his men for dodging the balls of the
Confederate skirmishers, was himself shot in the head
and instantly killed.

19. Early in the morning of the 10th Hancock
crossed the Po beyond the Confederate left, but he
was met by Early, in command of Mahone's and
Heth's divisions, and forced back across the river with
severe loss. Another attack, made upon Field's division of Longstreet's corps, met with a complete repulse. In the afternoon another attack was made on
the same part of the line by Warren's corps, but again
"the Boys in Blue" were hurled back, leaving the
ground covered with their dead and wounded. Expecting a renewal of the assault, many of the Confederates went out in front of their works, and, "gathering up the muskets and cartridge-boxes of the dead
and wounded, brought them in and distributed them
along the line. If they did not have repeating rifles,
they had a very good substitute—several loaded ones
to each man."[1] At last the assault came, and in such
force that in one or two places the Federals broke
through the Southern lines, but they were driven out
again and forced back to the cover of their own works.
Generals James C. Rice and T. G. Stevenson were
among the Union dead in this day's fight.

20. The next day passed without serious fighting.
It was on that day Grant sent to Halleck his famous

[1] E. M Law in "Battles and Leaders of the Civil War," Vol. IV., page
129.

GENERAL ROBERT E. LEE.

dispatch, in which he stated his purpose "to fight it out on this line if it takes all summer."

21. On the 12th came the most determined effort of Grant to break Lee's line. During the night of the 11th Hancock's corps was massed in front of Edward Johnson's division, of Ewell's corps. These troops occupied an elevated point somewhat advanced from the general line, and known as the "Salient." At dawn (May 12th) Hancock's men, by a sudden rush, burst over the Salient, capturing Edward Johnson, with 2,800 of his men and twenty cannon. Then extending their line across the works on both sides of the Salient, they resumed their advance when Lane's brigade, of Hill's corps, which was on the right of the captured works, attacked Hancock's left wing, checked its advance, and forced it back. "Just at this time General C. A. Evans led Gordon's veteran brigade against Hancock's right, causing a momentary check. At nearly the same instant other Confederate reserves reached the field, and John B. Gordon, who was that day in command of Early's division, prepared to lead his own and the other brigades in a general advance." Just as the charge was about to commence General Lee rode up and joined Gordon, who protested earnestly against this exposure on the part of the commanding General, reminding him that these troops—Pegram's Virginians and C. A. Evans's Georgians—were men who had never failed and would not fail now. The men joined their entreaties by crying out, "Lee to the rear!" Seeing that his presence would only embarrass his troops, Lee remained where he was and let Gordon lead the charge. The opposing lines met in rear of the captured works, and after a fierce

BATTLE OF SPOTSYLVANIA COURTHOUSE.

struggle the Federals were driven back to the base of
the Salient. But Gordon's division did not cover the
whole front. So Rodes sent Ramseur to restore the line
between himself and Gordon. After Ramseur had
swept the trenches the length of his brigade, the gap
was still not entirely filled. Then three brigades from
Hill's corps were ordered up. Perrin's Alabamians,
who were the first to arrive, charging through a fearful fire, recovered part of the line, their brave leader
falling dead as they entered the works Harris's Mississippi and McGowan's South Carolina brigades rushed
through a like fearful storm of bullets and seized the
works on Ramseur's right.[1] The Confederates had
recovered all their line except a part of the Salient,
still held by the Federals. Here the men fought all
day long and until past midnight, neither side being
able to drive the other.[2] Grant during this fierce fight
at the centre pressed the attack all along the line, but
Wright's corps was repulsed by Anderson's (Longstreet's) troops, and Burnside was driven back by
Early. So the day closed with a Confederate victory.
To the Federals, who had been defeated at every other
point, the possession of the Salient was a fruitless success. The Confederates held the lines of Spotsylvania
as firmly as ever. The Salient, from the terrible fighting at that point, was called by both armies the
" **Bloody Angle**."

22. From the 12th to the 18th, there was no other
attack made upon the Confederates Never was re-

[1] Ramseur was severely wounded in this charge, but remained in the
trenches with his gallant North Carolinians. General Daniel, leading
another North Carolina brigade, was killed.

[2] So intense was the fire that an oak 22 inches in diameter was cut
down by the constant scaling of minnie balls.

spite more welcome, and never did hungry men enjoy with greater relish any luxuries, than did the weary Southerners the coffee and sugar obtained from the haversacks of the Federal dead. On the 18th Hancock's and Wright's (formerly Sedgwick's) corps made a last effort to force the lines of Spotsylvania; but Ewell's corps, which still held the lines in rear of the famous Salient, repulsed them and drove them back in disorder. This ended the series of **battles at Spotsylvania**.

23. Grant had been reinforced, but he decided to make no more attacks upon Lee's army at this point. He tried again (May 20th), just as he did after his repulse in the Wilderness, to get away unobserved, and place his army between Lee and Richmond. But when he reached the **North Anna,** he found that Lee had again thrown himself across his path. After spending two days in fruitless efforts to find a weak point in the Confederate lines, during which time the skirmishers of both sides were busy, Grant came to the conclusion that it was best not to attack the Confederates in this new position.

24. While the armies were still facing each other at Spotsylvania Sheridan started on a raid toward Richmond, hoping that he might be able to take that city by a sudden dash. General Stuart having part of the cavalry met him with only half his numbers at Yellow Tavern (May 11th), and checked him long enough for the works at Richmond to be manned. But this was Stuart's last battle. He was mortally wounded and was carried into Richmond, where he died next day. Thus another light of the Army of Northern Virginia had gone out for ever.

GENERAL J. E. B. STUART.

25. During the night of the 26th the Federal army again disappeared on another flanking march. Lee started again to head them off. On the afternoon of the 28th after a severe cavalry battle at Hawe's Shop, in which Hampton and Fitz Lee opposed the advance of Sheridan, the infantry of both armies came up and faced each other along the Totopotomoy. Grant decided that Lee's position was too strong to be attacked and tried another flank march towards Richmond.

26. But at **Cold Harbor** Lee was found still barring his way. To get to Richmond it was necessary for the Federal army to storm the position which two years before under McClellan they had been unable to hold. On the evening of June 2d, Grant gave orders that on the next morning at half-past 4 a general assault should be made along Lee's whole front. At the time appointed the attack was swiftly and gallantly made, and as swiftly and gallantly repulsed. General McMahon, of the Union army, says : " The time of actual advance was not over eight minutes. In that little period more men fell bleeding as they advanced than in any other like period of time throughout the war. A strange and terrible feature of this battle was that as the three gallant corps moved on each was enfiladed, while receiving the full force of the enemy's direct fire in front. No troops could stand against such a fire, and the order to lie down was given all along the line. At points where no shelter was afforded, the men were withdrawn to such cover as could be found, and the battle of Cold Harbor, as to its result at least, was over." Grant had met the most bloody and terrible repulse of the whole campaign. In that short but fearful battle he had lost 10,000 men, and Lee but

little over 1,000.   Later in the day orders were given by Grant for the renewal of the assault.   But not a soldier moved forward in obedience to the command.[1]

27. That night many of the Union wounded were gathered up and carried behind their lines.   Some of them, however, lay between the lines for several days, exposed to the summer sun.   Grant was unwilling to send a flag of truce asking permission to care for his wounded and bury his dead, since that would be a confession of defeat.   He did send a flag of truce at last, three days after the battle, when many of the wounded needed no farther care, and the dead had to be buried where they lay.

28. Grant's overland campaign, which ended with the battle of Cold Harbor, had been a dismal failure.   At no place had he gained a victory.   The nearness to his line of march of so many watercourses, patroled by Federal gunboats, enabled him to shift his base from one place to another, so that after a repulse he could retire from the front of the Confederates, and by a flank march take a position farther south.   First the Rappahannock, next the York and Pamunkey, and finally the James, furnished him a new base for the receipt of supplies and reinforcements, and a new line from which to renew his attack.   Grant's merit in this campaign lies in the fact that he saw what no Federal general before him seemed to appreciate, that an army so vastly superior in numbers and resources need not run away because it has met with a repulse from one so greatly inferior in these respects, especially when the defeated army, still superior in strength and with

[1] In the battle of Cold Harbor the brave General Doles of Georgia was killed.

BATTLE OF COLD HARBOR.

its base close at hand, can by entrenching make its position secure against attack and wait for reinforcements. Had the circumstances surrounding the two generals been reversed, Lee would have destroyed the army of Grant.

GRANT'S CO-OPERATING ARMIES—BUTLER'S EXPEDITION

29. The generals who were to co-operate with Grant had succeeded no better. On the 5th of May General Benjamin F. Butler landed at Bermuda Hundreds with 40,000 men, and, after leaving a small force at City Point, marched to the neck of land between the James and Appomattox rivers. The Confederate authorities, however, had suspected the approach of General Butler, and had hurriedly recalled General Hoke, with his division, from the outworks of Newberne, which they had already taken. Hagood's, Wise's, and Colquitt's brigades had also been summoned from South Carolina to assist in the defence of the Confederate capital. Hagood reached Petersburg just in time to baffle the assault of Butler's forces in their attack upon the Richmond and Petersburg railroad (May 6th and 7th). Hagood and his men were the heroes of the day, and were looked upon as the saviours of Petersburg.

30. Beauregard arrived on the same day with Hoke's command (May 10th), and three days later Whiting, with his command, came up from Wilmington. Beauregard bringing over Ransom's division also from the defences of Richmond, formed his troops into three divisions, and on the 16th of May defeated Butler at **Drewry's Bluff** and forced him to take refuge within his fortified lines.[1] Then the Confederates fortified a

[1] In this battle the Confederates captured 1,400 prisoners, five cannon, and five stands of colors.

line across Butler's front, thus for the present "bottling him up," as far as offensive operations in that quarter were concerned. As Grant approached Cold Harbor he called to his assistance the Eighteenth corps, from Butler's command.[1] Lee also requested that there should be sent to his aid for that battle a large part of Beauregard's forces. The Richmond Government hesitated, but finally granted his request.[2]

[1] Grant was able to order to his help whatever troops he wished, while Lee had to ask repeatedly for more troops before he received them, since his command did not at that time include Petersburg.

[2] The effective strength of the Union army in the Wilderness was 118,000 men of all arms. The losses (including those sustained by the reinforcements at Spotsylvania and Smith's corps at Cold Harbor) from May 5th to June 15th were as follows:

BATTLES, &c.	KILLED.	WOUNDED.	CAPTURED OR MISSING.	TOTAL.
The Wilderness.	2,246	12,037	3,383	17,666
Spotsylvania.	2,725	13,416	2,258	18,399
North Anna and Totopotomy	591	2,734	661	3,986
Cold Harbor and Bethesda Church. . .	1,844	9,077	1,816	12,737
Sheridan's First Expedition	64	337	224	625
Sheridan's Second Expedition	150	741	625	1,516
Grand total from the Wilderness to the James.	7,620	38,342	8,967	54,929

According to a table made up from the Official Records for "Battles and Leaders of the Civil War."

Butler's army on the James numbered during the same period 36,000 effectives. Its losses were 634 killed, 3,903 wounded and 1,678 captured or missing—6,215. This does not include the losses of Smith's corps at Cold Harbor, which are included in the above table. As Grant lost 40,051 up to the first of June and still had 113,875 in the battle of Cold Harbor, his total reinforcements during the campaign were 35,926, which, added to 118,000, gives 153,926 as the total effective force under his command during the campaign. According to General Humphreys, of the Union army, Lee's effective force at the opening of the campaign was 62,000. Colonel Walter H. Taylor, Lee's Adjutant-General, states that 64,000 of all arms would be a liberal estimate. The total reinforcements received

SIGEL'S EXPEDITION.

31. The conjoint movement of Crook and Sigel was also a failure. Grant had intended that all his co-operating armies should move at the same time that he advanced against Lee. Butler attempted to carry out these orders and was defeated. Sigel began his advance early in May with about 7,000 men. Crook with about the same force was to move from West Virginia and join Sigel. The ad-

SCENE ON THE JAMES RIVER NEAR DREWRY'S BLUFF.

vance of Sigel was delayed in consequence of the disastrous defeat of his cavalry by General Imboden. By the time he reached New Market Imboden had been joined by 2,500 veteran troops under General John C. Breckinridge, who now took command.

32. Breckinridge brought with him also 225 cadets from the Virginia Military Institute under Colonel Ship, one of their professors. The cadets were boys between the ages of 16 and 18. Breckinridge's whole

by Lee during the campaign were 14,400. So at the highest estimate all the troops engaged under Lee from the Wilderness to Cold Harbor inclusive amounted to 78,400 of all arms. During the whole campaingn his losses did not exceed 20,000. The losses in killed, wounded and missing are not separately stated, because many of the Confederate returns were lost. Beauregard's force in his campaign against Butler amounted to 20,000 effectives, of whom only 16,000 reached Drewry's Bluff in time for the battle of May 16th. The losses of this force were 490 killed, 2,708 wounded and 309 captured or missing—3,507.

force numbered nearly 5,000. Finding Sigel near the town of New Market he resolved to attack him. Breckinridge wished to hold the cadets in reserve, but the boys were eager to take part in the battle. First Sigel's cavalry force was routed, which exposed the flank of his infantry to the fire of McLaughlin's and McClanahan's artillery. Then under the energetic advance of the regulars of Wharton's and Echol's brigades, Smith's Sixty-second Virginia regiment and the cadets, Sigel's whole line was forced back half a mile. In this new position the conflict became fiercer than ever. There was a six-gun battery which gave the Confederates considerable trouble. This the Sixty-second and the cadets charged and captured, together with most of the gunners. Exultant shouts went up, when a cadet mounted one of the captured caissons and waved over it in triumph the flag of the Institute. At the same time with the capture of the battery Wharton and Echols charged and the whole Federal line gave way. After retreating three miles Sigel again tried to make a stand; but his men retired before a fresh advance of the Confederates, and did not again stop until they had placed the Shenandoah River between them and their pursuers, and burned the bridge behind them.[1]

33. General Imboden says of this battle: "If Sigel had beaten Breckinridge on the 15th of May, General Lee could not have spared the men to check his progress (as he did that of Hunter a month later) without exposing Richmond to immediate and almost

[1] In the battle of New Market the Federal army numbered 6,500, and its losses were 93 killed, 552 wounded and 186 captured or missing—831 The Confederates numbered 4,816, and their losses were 42 killed, 522 wounded and 13 missing—577. Of this loss the cadets had 8 killed and 46 wounded.

GENERAL JOHN D. IMBODEN.

inevitable capture. In view of these probable consequences, there was no secondary battle of the war of
more importance than that of **New Market**." The day
after the battle Lee called Breckinridge to him. Imboden was left with about 1,000 men to defend the
Valley as best he could.

Hunter's Lynchburg Expedition.

34. Toward the last of May General David Hunter
relieved Sigel in command of the Valley district. On
June 1st, with 8,500 men, he began his advance, driving before him the small command of Imboden.
That general telegraphed to Lee of his danger, whereupon Lee directed Brigadier-General William E. Jones,
then in Southwest Virginia, to go to the help of Imboden with all the men that he could collect. Brigadier-
General John C. Vaughn also joined him with his
Tennessee cavalry. Jones having the oldest commission took command.

35. Near the little village of Piedmont, Hunter met
this hastily-gathered army of about 5,000 men and
immediately attacked. After repelling two attacks, in
which Brigadier-General R. B. Hayes, afterwards President of the United States, bore a conspicuous part,
the Confederates were disastrously beaten by a flank
attack, losing 1,500 men and General Jones, who was
killed. By this victory Hunter was enabled to effect
a junction with the cavalry of Crook and Averill at
Staunton.

36. With their united forces 18,000 strong the Federals, led by Hunter, took up the line of march for
Lynchburg. At Staunton they burned, by Hunter's

orders, public and some private property.   At Lexington Hunter burned the Virginia Military Institute, the residence of Governor Letcher, and other private property.   But for the protests of his officers he would have also applied the torch to Washington College.

37. But Hunter's expedition was destined to come to an inglorious end.   After the decisive defeat of Grant at Cold Harbor, Lee felt strong enough to send Breckinridge with a few troops, and shortly afterwards Early with the Second corps, to the defence of Lynchburg.   To this place Breckinridge had retreated and Hunter had advanced.   Early prepared to attack Hunter at daylight on the 19th, but during the night of the 18th the Federal general retreated.   The Confederates pursued Hunter and chased him for more than sixty miles, capturing prisoners and artillery.   Hunter did not cease his flight until he had crossed the mountains into West Virginia.

SHERIDAN'S TREVILIAN RAID.

38. While Hunter was on his march Sheridan had been sent out with 8,000 cavalry to tear up the Virginia Central railroad, seize Gordonsville and Charlottesville, and then unite with Hunter.   Lee detecting this move, sent Hampton, now in command of the cavalry of the Army of Northern Virginia, to head Sheridan off.   Hampton, whose whole force did not exceed 5,000, hastened to carry out these instructions. Near Trevilian station, June 11th, Hampton was defeated and forced back.   Then Sheridan began the work of destruction, tearing up the railroad towards Louisa Courthouse.

39. In the fight of the 11th Hampton's forces were not all up and acting together; but on the 12th affairs were very different. There was more concert of action on the part of the Confederates. General M. C. Butler on this day led Hampton's division of South Carolina, Georgia and Virginia troops, and held the left of the Confederate line. Fitzhugh Lee led his own division of Virginians, and was on the right wing. Hampton commanded the whole. Several fierce assaults were made on Butler, but they were all repulsed, and a flank attack made by Fitzhugh Lee completed the discomfiture of the Federals. During the night Sheridan retreated. He stated as his reason for retiring that he had learned from prisoners that Hunter was not near Charlottesville, but was marching on Lynchburg, and that Breckinridge was at Gordonsville (a mistake). Had he not been defeated on the 12th Sheridan would certainly not have turned back. His desperately wounded, who could not be carried off, together with some wounded Confederates, who had fallen into his hands after the first day's fight, were left to the care of the Confederates.

GRANT ATTACKS PETERSBURG.

40. After Cold Harbor Grant found it necessary to give up for the present his attempt to take Richmond from the north side. He was convinced that it was useless to fight it out on that line, although the summer was not yet half gone. On the 13th of June Grant began to make preparations to abandon his position and withdraw his army to another line of operations. First he sent W. F. Smith with the Eighteenth corps back to Bermuda Hundreds, on the

south side of the James, with directions to begin at
once an advance upon Petersburg.   He intended to
follow with his own army, and his hope was to take
Petersburg before Lee could go to its rescue.

41. By the afternoon of the 14th Smith reached Bermuda Hundred, and by the next morning began his
attack upon Petersburg.   The four days of battle which
followed are remarkable on account of the obstinate
and successful defence made by Beauregard and his
gallant command against immense odds.   Lee's position at this time was a very trying one.   If he sent too
many of his men across the James, Grant might by a
sudden rush seize Richmond; and if he failed to reinforce Beauregard in time, Petersburg would fall, and
with that city in Grant's hands Richmond could not
long be held.

42. The Confederate forces opposed to Smith's corps
on the 15th of June consisted of the Twenty-sixth,
Thirty-fourth, and Forty-sixth Virginia regiments, the
Sixty-fourth Georgia, the Twenty-third South Carolina,
Archer's militia, Battle's and Wood's battalions, Sturdivant's battery, Dearing's small command of cavalry,
and some other transient forces, having a real effective
for duty of 2,200 only.[1]   General Henry A. Wise was
in immediate command of these forces, while Beauregard superintended all the necessary movements of
troops and the placing of reinforcements as they might
arrive.   Wise's brave troops resisted all day the attack
of 18,000 men.   Even the militia, who had hardly
been under fire before, rivalled the valor of the veter-

[1] G. T. Beauregard, in "Battles and Leaders of the Civil War." Vol.
iv., page 540.

ans by whose side they fought. Late in the evening, just as they were about to be driven from their position, there came "advancing at double quick Hagood's gallant South Carolina brigade, followed soon after by Colquitt's, Clingman's, and in fact by the whole of Hoke's division,"[1] just from Lee's army.

43. Hancock had now joined Smith, raising the Federal force to 38,000 men. Beauregard ordered Bush-

THE BATTLE-FIELD OF MALVERN HILL.

rod Johnson to evacuate the lines at Bermuda Hundred and march at once to Petersburg. Fortunately the attack was not renewed until the afternoon of the 16th. Burnside's corps had by this time joined Hancock and Smith. The Federals, 53,000 strong, attacked the works, now held by 10,000 men. Night closed the conflict with the line still firmly held. Warren had by this time come up, swelling the Federal force to 67,000 men.

44. Early on the 17th the fighting began. No farther reinforcements had yet come to Beauregard's

[1] G. T. Beauregard, in "Battles and Leaders Of the Civil War." Vol. IV, page 540.

hard-pressed men. Assault after assault was made
only to be repulsed, until just at dusk, when a part of
the Confederate line was pierced. But just then Gracie's brigade, fresh from Chaffin's Bluff, came up and
charged into the gap, retaking the line and capturing
more than 1,000 prisoners. On that same day Lee's
forces were approaching Petersburg, and he superintended in person the recapture of the Bermuda Hundred line, which had been seized by Butler when
Bushrod Johnson left it to reinforce Beauregard.
Pickett's and Field's divisions had been ordered to
retake this line; but finding that a new line could be
occupied without the loss of life that might result
from its recapture the order was revoked. Field's
division had been notified of this change; but Pickett's men, who had not yet heard of it, "began the
assault under the first order. The men of Field's
division, hearing the firing and seeing Pickett's men
engaged, leaped from their trenches—first the men,
then the officers and flag-bearers—rushed forward
and were soon in the formidable trenches, which
were found to be held by a very small force." [1]

45. Grant's whole army was now in front of the
lines of Petersburg, and an assault was ordered for 4
A. M. of the 18th. But Beauregard had caused a new
line to be fortified just in rear of the one that had
been so stubbornly held, and after midnight the troops
had been withdrawn to this new line. When in the
morning the assaulting column reached the old line
and found it abandoned the Federal generals halted
to reconnoiter before making an attack. Kershaw's

[1] Colonel C. S. Venable in " Battles and Leaders of the Civil War,"
Vol. IV., page 245.

A. P. HILL ORDERING LEE AND DAVIS TO THE REAR.

division of Lee's army reached Petersburg early on that morning, and two hours later came Field's division. Before it had been assigned to its place on the line Lee in person arrived. There were now about 20,000 Confederates in the works at Petersburg. At noon came the grand attack, which was promptly repulsed. At 4 in the afternoon the Federals tried it again, but their effort met with signal defeat. Beauregard says that their loss exceeded that of the Confederates in the proportion of nine to one. General Humphreys of the Union army in his " Virginia Campaign, 1864 and 1865," states that the Union losses in these assaults were 9,964 killed, wounded and missing.

46. A few days later (June 24th) Meade tried by a flank march to seize the Weldon road, but was defeated by A. P. Hill, with a loss of 4,000 men, mostly prisoners. About the same time Wilson and Kautz were sent with 8,000 cavalry to tear up the railroads to the south and west of Petersburg and inflict all possible damage. They did considerable damage to the railroads, but were attacked by Hampton's cavalry and on their retreat by the infantry of Mahone and Finegan. They were disastrously defeated, with the loss of many in killed and wounded, 1,000 prisoners, and sixteen cannon.[1]

EARLY'S MARCH ON WASHINGTON.

47. The retreat of Hunter into West Virginia had not only left the Shenandoah Valley open to the Confed-

---

[1] Three of the guns were destroyed and thirteen were captured by the Confederates.

erates, but had also uncovered Washington. Early was quick to see his advantage and prompt to improve his opportunity. By June 27th his army reached Staunton ; half the men were barefoot. Early ordered shoes to be sent on to them, and continued the march. Imboden was sent to destroy the railroad bridge over the South Branch of the Potomac and all the bridges on the Baltimore and Ohio railroad from that point to Martinsburg. By the 2d of July the Confederates entered Winchester. Advancing from this point, Early drove Sigel across the Potomac, and on the 6th led his army across that river into Maryland. On the next night the expected shoes arrived and were distributed.

GENERAL WADE HAMPTON.

48. Early's rapid march through the Valley greatly alarmed the North for the safety of Washington. And well might the North be alarmed, for there was no period of the war during which that city was in greater danger of capture. General Lew Wallace gathering as many troops as possible, set out from Baltimore to

oppose Early's advance. Most of Wallace's men were raw troops, but General Grant, realizing the danger that threatened the capital of the United States, had sent Rickett's veteran division to his help. These troops overtook Wallace at the Monocacy River ; here they formed line of battle and awaited the advance of the Confederates.

49. Early's men after marching fourteen miles on the 9th, discovered this force strongly posted on the eastern bank of the stream, and prepared at once to storm the position. McCausland with his cavalry moved against the left flank of the Federals. Breckinridge was ordered to send Gordon's division to the help of McCausland. Then, while Ramseur skirmished with the force in his front, Gordon charged in gallant style, assisted by the fire of King's and Nelson's artillery. Before Gordon's resistless advance the Federals were thrown into confusion and forced from their position. In this desperate charge General C. A. Evans, whose brigade led the attack, fell from his horse severely wounded through the body. Ramseur crossed on the railroad bridge and pressed the pursuit, in which Rodes also joined.[1] While these operations had been going on a contribution of $200,000 was levied on the city of Frederick and some much needed supplies were obtained.

50. After this brilliant victory Early continued his march on Washington and arrived in front of Fort Stevens early in the afternoon of the 11th. Rodes's division, which was in front, was ordered to deploy

[1] The Union army numbered 6,000 men and lost 1,880, of whom 1,100 were captured or missing. The Confederates engaged numbered 10,000, and they lost about 700.

into line and occupy the fort. Before this could be done a column of Federals filed into the works and threw out skirmishers. Early reconnoitered the position and ordered an attack for the next morning. But that night he learned by a dispatch from General Bradley T. Johnson that two corps from Grant's army had arrived.[1] Next morning, riding to the front, Early saw the parapet lined with troops. He had to give up the idea of capturing Washington, after he had arrived in sight of the dome of the capitol and given the whole North a terrible fright. If he had been just a day sooner he would have taken the city. On the night of the 12th Early retired, and on the morning of the 14th recrossed the Potomac, carrying with him the

GENERAL BRADLEY T. JOHNSON.

prisoners captured at the Monocacy, and a large number of beef-cattle and horses.

Early's Pennsylvania Raid.

51. For two months after Early's return from Washington he remained in the lower Valley,[2] keeping the

---

[1] Grant had sent the rest of Wright's corps to Washington and also the Nineteenth corps, which had just arrived from Louisiana

[2] The lower Valley is the northern part of it.

Baltimore and Ohio railroad and the Chesapeake and Ohio canal obstructed, and threatening Maryland and Pennsylvania. During this time some important events occurred. The troops that had saved Washington, instead of pursuing Early, returned to that city, under the impression that Early was returning to Richmond.

52. But Early had no notion of doing any such thing. Instead he advanced again, and defeated Crook and Averill at Kernstown (July 24th). The Federals were chased beyond Martinsburg, with the loss of 1,200 men, including General Mulligan, who was killed. Crook did not cease his retreat until he had crossed into Maryland, "leaving Early undisturbed master of the south side of the Potomac from Shepherdstown to Williamsport." [1] Maryland and Southern Pennsylvania were in utter panic.

53. Early now sent a cavalry expedition into Pennsylvania, which routed a small Federal force at Carlisle and then pushed on and captured Chambersburg. Here McCausland demanded a contribution of $100,-000 in gold. As the money was not raised, acting under Early's orders, he fired the town and destroyed two-thirds of it. Early says that he did this in retaliation for the partial burning of Lexington and of private residences in the Valley by the orders of Hunter. However this act of retaliation may be viewed, it would never have been allowed by General Lee, who did not believe in thus returning evil for evil, especially when by so doing the innocent would suffer for the crime of the guilty.

[1] Greeley's "American Conflict." Vol. II, page 606.

THE PETERSBURG MINE.

54. On the same day that Chambersburg was burned Grant suffered a terrible defeat at Petersburg. Having failed in other efforts to take this city, he decided to have a mine dug under one of the Confederate forts. Four tons of gun-powder were placed in it. In order to distract the attention of the Confederates Grant sent forces north of the James to threaten Richmond. This caused Lee to send some of his troops to meet this move of Grant's; but, as the event proved, Lee had retained enough for the defense of Petersburg. On the morning of July 30th the mine was exploded, making a crater 20 feet deep and 100 feet long. Instantly 110 cannon and 50 mortars, placed in commanding positions, commenced playing upon the ground to the right and left of where the Federal troops were expected to enter.

55. Ledlie's division of Burnside's corps moved forward and entered the crater, but did not get beyond. Other Federal divisions, among them Ferrero's colored troops, moved forward, most of them becoming crowded together in the crater. The Confederates, who had now rallied from their surprise, poured in a most destructive fire, and the crater became a perfect slaughter pen. Finally General Mahone led the Confederates in a charge which retook the whole line and captured more than 1,000 prisoners. The **Battle of the Crater** had proved for the Union army, as Grant himself says, "a stupendous failure." The Federals had lost 4,000 men and the Confederates about 1000.[1]

---

[1] George I. Kilmer, of the Union army, says: "It has been positively asserted that white men (Union soldiers) bayoneted blacks who fell back into the crater. This was in order to preserve the whites from Confed-

56. Grant now gave orders for a corps of infantry and a large body of cavalry to destroy fifteen or twenty miles of the Weldon railroad before Lee could get forces there to defend it. But getting news just at this time of Early's invasion of Pennsylvania, he revoked his order and directed that additional troops be embarked for Washington.

erate vengeance." Mr. Kilmer also says that there was a feeling among the Union soldiers that "they had been pushed into slaughter pens from the Wilderness down." He also says that "there was a determination to rebel against further slapdash assaults." These statements are made by Mr. Kilmer in an article entitled "The Dash into the Crater," which appeared in the Century Magazine of September, 1887.

BATTLE OF THE CRATER.

CHAPTER III.

FROM THE OPENING OF THE GEORGIA CAMPAIGN TO THE
FIRST PART OF AUGUST, 1864—EVENTS IN MISSISSIPPI—
DISCOURAGEMENT AT THE NORTH.

ET us now see what had been going on in
Georgia during the time in which the events
recorded in the last chapter were occurring.
On the same day that Grant crossed the Rapidan
Sherman by his direction began to advance against
Dalton. The army
under Sherman
numbered 100,000,
and he had author-
ity to call for more
as they were need-
ed. At Dalton Gen-
eral Joseph E.
Johnston had near
45,000 men, which
were increased by
reinforcements
soon after the cam-
paign opened to
about sixty-five
thousand. Sher-
man's army was
also increased to one hundred and twelve thousand.

GENERAL LEONIDAS POLK.

2. Sherman's plan was, by a series of flanking
movements, to compel Johnston's retreat from the
successive positions which he occupied. Johnston's

plan was to avoid a general engagement, unless the advantage of position was on his side, and at the same time to delay Sherman's march as much as possible. On May 7th the Union army was drawn up in line in front of the Confederate position. Next day Geary's division of Hooker's corps assailed the Confederates in Dug Gap, but met with a decided repulse by two regiments of Reynolds's Arkansas brigade and Grigsby's Kentuckians. On the 9th Newton's division of Howard's (Fourth) corps, supported by Judah's division of the Army of the Ohio, made five assaults upon the crest of Rocky Face Ridge, each of which was repulsed. Similar assaults were made upon Stewart's and Bates's divisions in Mill Creek Gap, but the Confederates held their ground.

3. On the same day (May 9th) at Resaca Major-General McPherson, who had made a flank movement through Snake Creek Gap for the purpose of capturing the town and railroad bridge in Johnston's rear, attacked, but failed to carry the position held by two Confederate brigades under General Canty. During that night General Johnston sent down General Hood with the divisions of Hindman, Cleburne and Walker to the assistance of Canty. McPherson then retreated to Snake Creek Gap and intrenched. Johnston having ascertained that the whole Federal army was moving towards Resaca, abandoned Dalton and concentrated his forces in Sherman's front. During May 14th and 15th there was heavy fighting at **Resaca.** The Federal assaults upon Hindman's positions were repulsed, and Hood, with Stewart's and Stevenson's divisions, drove the Federal left from its ground. McPherson, however, drove **Polk's (Confederate) skirmishers from**

the hill in front of his left, which commanded the Western and Atlantic railroad bridge over the Oostenaula.

4. While the fighting was going on at Resaca a Union force under General Sweeny was sent across the Oostenaula. John K. Jackson's brigade, of Walker's division, failed in an effort to drive back this force. Since a strong force was now threatening Johnston's rear, the Confederate army abandoned Resaca and retired toward Kingston.

5. On the 19th of May Johnston took position near Cassville, where he hoped to fight a decisive battle. There was heavy skirmishing during the day, and the Confederate soldiers were eager to decide at once the issue of the campaign. But the judgment of Hood and Polk was against fighting a defensive battle at that point. So the Confederates fell back to the Etowah River and crossed it the next day.

6. A few days later it was ascertained that Sherman's forces had crossed the Etowah far to the Confederate left. Johnston marched promptly to meet them, and took up a position extending from Dallas to the railroad. There now occurred a series of engagements between portions of the two armies, which Johnston and Sherman in their respective narratives of this campaign agree in calling the **Battle of New Hope Church**. The first of these occurred on the 25th of May, when the head of Hooker's column, driving in the Confederate skirmishers, came upon Stewart's division (of Hood's corps) near a little meeting-house, known as New Hope Church. Hooker formed his division in parallel lines and promptly attacked, but his vigorous assaults resulted in "a succession of bloody

repulses."[1] A heavy shower, accompanied with light-
ning and thunder, was going on during " these awful
charges."[1] Two days later Sherman sent Howard,
with two divisions, to turn Johnston's right. At
Pickett's Mill, thinking he had reached the extreme of
the Confederate line, Howard ordered an assault. It
fell upon Kelly's cavalry, deployed on foot as skirmishers, to whose assistance speedily came Granberry's
Texas brigade, of Cleburne's division. These checked
the Federals, who, however, renewed the assault. But
by this time Colonel Bancum, with two Arkansas regiments of Govan's brigade, had come up, and Cleburne
had hurried to his threatened right Lowrey's brigade
of Alabamians and Mississippians. The vigorous
charges of the Federals were all repulsed, as Howard
himself says, with much loss. The Confederates gathered up as trophies 1,200 small small arms. The
acknowledged loss in Howard's corps in this combat
at Pickett's Mill was 1,500 men. Cleburne's loss was
400. The next day McPherson tried to withdraw from
Dallas, so as to pass beyond Howard's left. But Bate's
division, of Hardee's corps, quickly assailed him,
meeting with a repulse, in which they lost about 700
men.[2]

7. On the 4th of June the Federal army extended
so far beyond the Confederate position that Johnston drew his army back to a new line. Sherman
says: " With the drawn battle of New Hope Church

---

[1] General O. O. Howard (Federal), in the Century Magazine for July,
1887. Page 452.

[2] Bate's division consisted of Kentuckians, Tennesseeans, Georgians,
and Floridians. They attacked on this occasion Logan's corps, consisting
of three divisions.

GENERAL GEORGE H. THOMAS.

and our occupation of Allatoona terminated the month of May and the first stage of the campaign."

8. For several weeks now there was constant skirmishing between the two armies. All this time the Federals kept shifting position, first in one direction and then in another, in the effort to turn the flanks of the Confederates, all of which movements were skillfully met by General Johnston. Constant rains added greatly to the discomfort of the soldiers. On the 14th of June Lieutenant-General Polk, who had been distinguished in every engagement of the Confederate army of the Tennessee, was killed by a cannon ball while on Pine Mountain reconnoitering the position of the Federals.

9. On the 19th of June the Confederate force was placed in a new position, the key of which was Kennesaw Mountain. On the 22d of June Schofield's and Hooker's troops attacked Hood's corps, but were repulsed. The Confederates then tried to carry the Federal position, but after seizing a line of breastworks were themselves repulsed, with the loss of about 1,000 men. This is known as the battle of **Kulp's** (or, more properly, **Kolb's**) Farm.

BATTLE OF KENNESAW MOUNTAIN.

10. Part of Johnston's line was on Kennesaw and part of it along the hills to the southwest, the extreme left extending down into the more level country. Sherman hoped that by a general assault he might penetrate some weak point of Johnston's long front. The assault was ordered for the morning of June 27th. It was preceded by a furious cannonade. Then the bugles sounded the charge, and the assaulting column moved

forward. Logan, supported by Blair and Dodge, moved against the Confederate right, east of the mountain and against the mountain itself. Logan's losses were heavy. Seven regimental commanders fell killed or wounded, so deadly was the fire from Featherstone's men. A furious charge upon French's division, especially upon Cockrell's Missouri brigade, though determined and impetuous, was also repulsed with heavy loss. The assailing columns broke through the skirmishers on Walker's right, attacking them in front and on the right and left. Lieutenant-Colonel Robert A. Fulton of the Fifty-third Ohio infantry says that the skirmishers encountered by his regiment were from the Sixty-third Georgia, and that they "fought with a desperation worthy of a better cause." He also tells how his command had with them "a hand-to-hand fight in which bayonets and butts of muskets were used." About eighty of Walker's skirmishers (mostly from the Sixty-third Georgia) were killed, wounded or captured.[1] Major J. V. H. Allen, who commanded them, rallied the remnant on the crest of a little hill, and aided by French's guns from Little Kennesaw drove back the Federals before they encountered Walker's line of battle. But the most determined assault was made by Palmer's corps, with Hooker in reserve, upon the "intrenchments held by Cheatham's and Cleburne's divisions, which extended through the rolling country south of the mountain."[2] By Cleburne's troops they were permitted to come

---

[1] One Company of the Sixty-third Georgia, known as the "Oglethorpes," lost two-thirds of their men that had been carried out upon the skirmish line.

[2] From Joseph M. Brown's Mountain Campaigns in Georgia.

within twenty paces before a gun was fired. On this part of the line especially the loss among the Federals was very severe. Sherman in his Memoirs says: "By 11:30 the assault was in fact over and had failed." In another account of this battle General Sherman says: "We failed, losing 3,000 men to the Confederate loss of 630." General Howard of his army also says: "Our losses in this assault were heavy indeed, and our gain was nothing."

11. Sherman now concluded to try another flank movement. So he sent a strong column, under Schofield and McPherson, down the valley of Olley's creek toward the Chattahoochee. Johnston seeing that this movement toward the south would break his communications with Atlanta, evacuated Kennesaw Mountain on the night of July 2d. He carried off everything—even the guns on Kennesaw being skillfully removed. Sherman had expected to take Johnston's army at a disadvantage on his retreat; but he was disappointed, for Johnston (as Sherman himself says) had prepared the way too well. He had done this by means of carefully-prepared lines of intrenchments all the way back to the Chattahoochee.

12. On the 10th Johnston crossed that river, "covered and protected," says Sherman, "by the best line of field intrenchments I have ever seen, prepared long in advance." Johnston had shown wonderful skill in manœuvring his army, and every retreat had been conducted in a masterly manner and without the loss of a gun or a wagon. His chief aim had been to keep between Sherman and Atlanta, which place he had thoroughly fortified, and which he believed he could hold with part of his army, while he used the rest

for more active operations.   But his "Fabian" policy
had dissatisfied many of the Southern people, and the
Richmond Government was very much displeased
with it.   He had handled his army well, but in carrying out his plan he had abandoned much territory.   Mr.

Davis did not
believe that
Johnston would
be able to hold
Atlanta any bet-
ter than other
strong positions
which he had
abandoned.   So
he removed
him from
command (July
18th) and ap-
pointed General
John B. Hood in
his place. John-
ston and his
friends have
always claimed
that he did in
Georgia just
what Lee did in

GENERAL JOHN B. HOOD.   Virginia. There

was this difference, however: Lee in carrying out
his plan had lost no territory. But Johnston's admirers claim that this was due to the difference in
the configuration of the country in Virginia and
Georgia.

13. Hood's idea was that whenever Sherman attempted a flanking movement, the Confederates should assail them. The passive defensive policy did not suit him at all. He did not believe in yielding any territory without first making a desperate fight to retain it. Though disabled in one arm at Gettysburg he was back in service in time to act an illustrious part in the battle of Chickamauga, in which he lost a leg close up to the hip-joint. Notwithstanding this great disability, he was in the field at the opening of the campaign of 1864. He wore a cork leg, and yet " could ride nearly as well as most men who have two legs and two arms."[1] An army consisting of men filled with his heroic spirit could never have been defeated except by annihilation.

The Battles of Atlanta.

14. On July 20th, while Thomas's wing of Sherman's army was crossing **Peach Tree Creek,** Hood sent the corps of Stewart and Hardee to attack him. Through bad management the attack was not made as promptly as Hood desired, nor with as good results as he had hoped; for the Confederates were repulsed with heavy loss.

15. McPherson with Sherman's left wing had already seized the Augusta railroad, and was preparing to continue his movement until he reached the Macon road, which was the main line of supply for the Confederate army. It was necessary to check this movement or Atlanta was in danger of speedy capture. Hardee was directed to move with his corps

[1] "The Georgia Militia about Atlanta," by General Gustavus W. Smith, in "Battles and Leaders of the Civil War," Vol. IV., page 335.

to the extreme left and rear of the Federal army and attack at daylight, or as near thereafter as possible. General Wheeler with his cavalry was to accompany Hardee. As soon as Hardee became fully engaged, Cheatham was to take up the movement from his right, and General G. W. Smith with the Georgia State troops was then to join in the attack. General

MAP SHOWING ATLANTA AND VICINITY.

Stewart, on Hood's left, was not only to watch Thomas and prevent his going to the aid of Schofield and Mc-Pherson, but also to join in the battle the instant that the movement became general. The movements thus planned by Hood brought on the severest battle of the Atlanta campaign (July 22d). The attack was made with great gallantry, but was only partially successful, because Hardee had not gone entirely to the rear of the Federals before beginning the attack. The fighting was fierce, and great determination was shown on both sides. At the close of the day the Confederate right held part of the ground previously occupied by the Federal left. Hardee bore off as trophies eight guns and thirteen stands of colors, while Cheatham captured five guns and five stands of colors. Both Hood and Sherman claimed the victory. But the fact that Sherman's flanking movement to the Confederate right was completely checked by this battle proves that it was more of a success to Hood than to Sherman, although the Confederates being the attack· ing party sustained the greater loss. General McPherson on the Federal and General William H. T. Walker on the Confederate side were killed in this engagement, generally known as the **Battle of Atlanta.**

16. Six days after this an attempt upon Sherman's part to turn the Confederate left brought on the battle of **Ezra Church.** This battle was fought by Lieutenant-General Stephen D. Lee, now in command of Hood's old corps, against Sherman's right, commanded on this occasion by General Howard. The Confederates were repulsed in their effort to capture the position of the Federals, who in their turn failed to take the position occupied by the Confederates.

17. Two great cavalry expeditions had been sent out by Sherman about this time. One column of 5,000 men, under Stoneman, was sent around the Confederate right, and another of 4,000, under McCook, around their left, with instructions to meet at Lovejoy Station, on the Macon road, and destroy the Confederate communications; then to push on to Anderson-

ville, if possible, and release 34,000 Union prisoners confined at that place. But General Wheeler defeated McCook at Newnan, inflicting heavy losses in killed and wounded, and capturing 950 prisoners, two cannon, and 1,200 horses with equipments. About the same time Generals Cobb and Iverson defeated Stoneman at Macon. Iverson pursued Stoneman, who surrendered with 500 of his men. Their horses and two cannon were also the trophies of the Confederates, and many more of Stoneman's routed troops were captured as they fled towards Eatonton.

EVENTS IN MISSISSIPPI.

18. While the campaign in Georgia was in progress important events were occurring in Northern Mississippi. When Sherman began his Georgia campaign he ordered out an expedition from Memphis to defeat the cavalry of Forrest, then in North Mississippi, and prevent its descent upon his line of communication. The expedition consisted of three brigades of infantry and two of cavalry, a good train of artillery, and 250 wagons, exclusive of ambulances and medical wagons. The whole force numbered about 9,000 effectives, and was commanded by General Samuel E. Sturgis. General B. H. Grierson commanded the cavalry. Forrest, with less than 4,000 men, encountered this force on Tishamingo creek at Brice's Cross-roads, near Guntown, June 10th. Making a fierce onset, he utterly overwhelmed the Federal force, capturing all their artillery (fourteen guns) and wagons and over 1,600 prisoners. The total Federal loss was 2,200. They did not cease their flight until they were safe in Memphis.

19. Ashamed of this defeat, the Federals organized a new expedition, consisting of two divisions of infantry and one of cavalry, besides a brigade of colored troops—14,000 in all, with twenty cannon. The whole force was commanded by General A. J. Smith, who had been with Banks in his ill-fated Red River expedition. To meet this force General Stephen D. Lee, who at that time commanded in Northern Mississippi, stated in a dispatch to Mr. Davis that he had only 7,000 men, including the commands of Forrest and Roddy. Near Tupelo the opposing forces met (July 14th), and Forrest made attack after attack upon the greatly superior Federal force. Smith claimed to have defeated Forrest in this engagement. But he retreated next day, harassed by Forrest's cavalry. On the 23d of July Smith was back in Memphis. Forrest still held control of the open country and considered himself the victor.

DISCOURAGEMENT AT THE NORTH.

20. The summer of 1864 was rapidly drawing to a close. After the most determined efforts and the most desperate fighting of the war, the Union armies seemed to be as far as ever from effecting the conquest of the South. The Virginia campaign had been to the North a dismal failure. Sherman had by his flanking movements penetrated far into Georgia, but he had been repulsed in several battles and had gained no decisive victory at any point. In Northern Mississippi and Western Tennessee the Confederate forces under Stephen D. Lee and Forrest held a sway which was only for a short time interrupted by the carefully-prepared and well-equipped expedition of A. J. Smith. In fact,

BEAUVOIR, MISS., THE HOME OF JEFFERSON DAVIS.

Forrest held such control of the country outside of the Union headquarters at Memphis that the Confederate legislature held its sessions in Jackson, Tennessee.

21. Of this period of the war the Northern historian, Horace Greeley, in his "American Conflict," says: "Cold Harbor was an exceedingly expensive and damaging failure—damaging not merely in the magnitude of our loss, but in its effect on the morale and efficiency of our chief army. It had extinguished the last hope of crushing Lee north of the James and of interposing that army between him and the Confederate capital.[1] The failure to seize Petersburg when it would easily have fallen, and the repeated and costly failures to carry its defences by assault, or even to flank them on the south; the luckless conclusion of Wilson's and Kautz's raid to Staunton River; Sheridan's failure to unite with Hunter in Lee's rear; Sturgis's disastrous defeat by Forrest near Guntown; Hunter's failure to carry Lynchburg and eccentric line of retreat; Sherman's bloody repulse at Kennesaw, and the compelled slowness of his advance on Atlanta; Early's unresisted swoop down the Valley into Maryland, his defeat of Wallace at the Monocacy, and his unpunished demonstration against the defences of Washington itself; the raids of his troopers up to the suburbs of Baltimore, on the Philadelphia railroad, and even up into Pennsylvania, burning Chambersburg and alarming even Pittsburg; and finally the bloody, wretched fiasco of the Mine explosion before Petersburg; these and other

[1] Swinton says that after the battle of Cold Harbor Grant's army, "shaken in its structure, its valor quenched in blood and thousands of its ablest officers killed or wounded, was the Army of the Potomac no more."

GENERAL GEORGE B. McCLELLAN.

reverses relieved by a few and unimpressive triumphs, rendered the mid-summer of 1864 one of the gloomiest seasons of our great struggle for the upholders of the national cause." Speaking about the financial condition during this period, when it took nearly three dollars of currency to purchase one of gold, the same writer says: "By the pecuniary gauge thus afforded, it appears that the very darkest hours of our contest—those in which our loyal people most profoundly despaired of a successful issue—were those of July and August, 1864; following Grant's repulse from Cold Harbor, the Mine explosion before Petersburg, and during Early's unpunished incursion into Maryland, and his cavalry raids up to Chambersburg and McConnellsburg."

22. The convention of the Democratic party that assembled in Chicago August 29th and nominated McClellan for the presidency pronounced the war a failure, and expressed a desire for an immediate cessation of hostilities, in order to try peaceable means for restoring the Union.

CHAPTER IV.

THE TIDE TURNS—MOBILE BAY—FALL OF ATLANTA—
SHERIDAN AND EARLY IN THE SHENANDOAH—HOOD'S
TENNESSEE CAMPAIGN—SHERMAN'S MARCH THROUGH
GEORGIA—CONFEDERATE SUCCESSES AROUND RICHMOND
AND PETERSBURG.

THE reader has now learned the wonderful record of Confederate achievements from the beginning of 1864 to almost the end of the summer of that year and their effect upon the feelings of the Northern people. But skill and valor cannot always supply the lack of numbers and resources, and even victories won at the cost of men that can never be replaced must end in defeat at last.

MOBILE BAY.

2. Ever since the capture of Vicksburg Grant had been anxious that a formidable expedition should be sent against Mobile. In the early part of 1864 he wanted to employ the southwestern Union forces in that way, but he was overruled, and the ill-starred Red River expedition was the result. In July a fleet of twenty-eight vessels under Admiral Farragut and a land force under General Gordon Granger was sent against Mobile. On the 5th of August Admiral Farragut with eighteen vessels, four of which were iron-clad monitors, attacked the Confederate fleet, consisting of the iron-clad ram *Tennessee* and three side-wheel gunboats. The Union fleet carried 159 guns and thirty-three howitzers, and the officers and crew

numbered 3,000 men. The Confederate fleet, commanded by Admiral Franklin Buchanan, carried twenty-two guns and only 470 officers and men. The guns of the Union fleet were also of heavier caliber than those of the Confederate vessels.

NAVAL BATTLE IN MOBILE BAY.

3. As the fleets approached each other for the battle Admiral Farragut, in order to have a better view of the movements of his ships, climbed the rigging of his flagship, the *Hartford*. Captain Drayton, fearful that even a slight wound might throw the Admiral to the deck, sent the signal quartermaster aloft with a small rope to secure him to the rigging. This was quickly done and through the hot fight which followed the Admiral occupied his dangerous post. The

little Confederate fleet made a gallant fight, in which
one of the gunboats was captured, one was run ashore
and afterward burned by her own crew, and one, the
Morgan, escaped through the hostile fleet up to the
city, in defense of which she afterwards did good service.   The *Tennessee*, after a battle with the whole
fleet, in which Admiral Buchanan was severely
wounded, became so disabled that her commander,
Captain James D. Johnston, found it necessary to
surrender.

4. On that same day Fort Powell was blown up by its
garrison, and two days later Granger took possession
of Fort Gaines.   He then began a siege of Fort Morgan.   On the 23d of August the fort had become untenable and was surrendered by her brave commander,
Brigadier-General R. L. Page.   In these operations
Granger had 5,600 men.   He captured with the forts
their garrisons, numbering 1,400 men, and their armament of 104 guns; but the Confederates had a strong
line of defences, and continued to hold Mobile until
just before the close of the war, though they could no
longer use it as a port.

The Fall of Atlanta.

5. But the taking of the outer defences of Mobile
would not have done much toward allaying the discouragement at the North, if greater successes for the
Federals had not come in other quarters.   After the
brilliant victories of Wheeler and Iverson over the
Federal cavalry, Hood sent Wheeler to the rear of
Sherman's army to tear up the railroad to Chattanooga, over which the supplies for that army were

hauled. Wheeler burned the bridge over the Etowah, captured Dalton and Resaca, and destroyed thirty-five miles of railroad in that vicinity; then going into Tennessee, he and Forrest did much damage to the Federal lines of supply in that State. But it was soon made clear that cavalry raids could not cripple Sherman's roads enough to make him retreat.

6. The Federal commander continued to extend his lines westward and southward. In one of these movements General Schofield's corps assaulted a part of the Confederate line near **Utoy Creek**, held by Bate's division.[1] Twice Schofield's troops assaulted, but each time were driven back with heavy loss. (August 6th.)

7. Taking advantage of the absence of Wheeler's cavalry, Sherman sent a force under Kilpatrick against the Macon road, but his expedition was defeated by General William H. Jackson's Confederate cavalry, and a raid along the Augusta road about the same time (August 22d) was likewise repelled.

8. During the greater part of this month the Federals kept up a bombardment of Atlanta. The 9th of August was made memorable by the most furious cannonade sustained by the city during the siege. General Hood, in his interesting work, " Advance and Retreat," says: " Women and children fled into cellars and were forced to seek shelter a greater length of time than at any period of the bombardment. The bombardment of the city continued until the 25th of August. It was

---

[1] This division consisted of Lewis's Kentucky brigade, Tyler's (or Smith's) brigade of Tennesseeans and Georgians, and Finlay's Florida brigade.

painful, yet strange to mark how expert grew the old men, women and children in building their little underground forts, into which to fly for safety during the storm of shell and shot. Often 'mid the darkness of night were they constrained to seek refuge in these dungeons beneath the earth. Albeit, I can not recall one word from their lips expressive of dissatisfaction or willingness to surrender."

9. On the night of the 25th, the very day that the Confederates in Virginia gained the brilliant victory of Reams's Station, Sherman disappeared from the

Confederate front and began a flank march to the west and south of Atlanta. He sent his sick and wounded back to his entrenched camp on the Chattahoochee, where he left Slocum with one corps. With the other five corps he moved to Fairburn on the West Point road and then turned southward towards Jonesboro (August 30th).

GENERAL WM. J. HARDEE.

10. Hood sent Hardee with his corps and that of Stephen D. Lee to attack the Federals and drive them back. In case of failure Hardee was to send back Lee's corps towards Atlanta, so as to protect Hood's line of retreat. Hardee made the attack (August 31), but the Federal force was already intrenched and **Hardee was repulsed.** Then according to **orders he**

sent Lee's corps back towards Atlanta. On the next day about noon a furious attack was was made upon Hardee's single corps which had before it the difficult task of holding its position in the face of five corps of the Federal army. Fortunately the attacks were not simultaneous all along his line, and Hardee was able to shift troops to the threatened points in time to repel the assaults. About the middle of the afternoon an angle held by Govan's Arkansas brigade and Lewis's Kentucky brigade was assailed by an overwhelming force. These two brigades, consisting of soldiers who had not their superiors in Hood's army, held to their line until the dense masses of Federal troops poured over the works and by weight of numbers forced back the brave defenders. The greater part of Govan's brigade and eight cannon were captured, but Granberry's Texans and Gordons's Tennessee brigade charging forward formed a new line in rear of the lost angle. By hard fighting Hardee's line thus rectified was held until night, and Hood's safe retreat from Atlanta[1] was secured. There was no more gallant fight of the war than the brave stand made by Hardee's men in this **battle of Jonesboro.** Hood left Atlanta on the evening of September 1st.

11. Next day Hood united his divided army at Lovejoy Station. Sherman took possesion of his

---

[1] In the Atlanta campaign the greatest strength of the Union army was 113,000 men. The greatest strength of the Confederate army is variously estimated. Some put it at 65,000, others as high as 84,000. Probably 70,000 is a correct estimate. The Union losses were reported to be 4,423 killed, 22,822 wounded, and 4,442 captured or missing—31,687. The Confederate losses were 3,044 killed, 18,952 wounded and 12,983 captured or missing—34,979. Major Dawes of Cincinnati estimates that each army lost 40,000. All these figures embrace the whole campaign from Dalton to the fall of Atlanta.

prize on September 2d and telegraphed to Mr. Lincoln, "Atlanta is ours and fairly won !" This dispatch electrified the North, and raised its drooping spirits. The fall of Atlanta was felt by the Southern people to be a disastrous blow. It was the first great victory won by the Union armies in 1864. Other events soon after occurred which raised still higher the spirits of the North, and increased the despondency of the South.

SHERIDAN AND EARLY IN THE SHENANDOAH.

12. We left Early master of the situation in all the country along the upper Potomac. Grant, feeling that he must put a check upon Early's movements, sent large reinforcements to the Union army in that quarter, and put General Philip Sheridan in command of the whole force (August 7th). Upon the advance of this greatly superior force Early fell back to Fisher's Hill. Soon afterwards Early received reinforcements, whereupon Sheridan, though still having much the larger army, retired to Halltown, near Harper's Ferry. Early then advanced to Winchester and beyond, and during the whole month from August 17th to September 17th remained in the lower Valley, keeping the Baltimore railroad and the canal obstructed and threatening Maryland and Pennsylvania. During this time there were several cavalry engagements, in which sometimes one party and sometimes the other was successful.

13. Finally Sheridan learned that Early's reinforcements had left him and were going back to Petersburg. He determined to make the best of his opportunity. Sheridan advanced against Early with 43,000 men of whom 10,000 were splendidly equipped cavalry under

Torbert, Merritt, and other distinguished leaders. Early's army was in position along the **Opequon,** near **Winchester,** and numbered but little over 13,000. Of this number about 3,000 were cavalry. Sheridan's magnificent body of cavalry, operating in an open

GENERAL PHILIP SHERIDAN.

country like the Shenandoah Valley, gave to the Union general a tremendous advantage. Early's men, who had been used to victory, met with determination the attack of Sheridan, which began on the morning of September 19th. As both sides fought without cover the losses were very great. At about noon the Union army had been repulsed all along the line. General Russell of the Union army and Generals Rodes and Godwin of the Confederate had been killed. The stress of battle compelled Sheridan to bring up his reserves, and late in the afternoon the Federal cavalry got into the rear of Early's left. There was now nothing left for the Confederates but to retreat. This they did under cover of the darkness which had come just as Early's lines were broken. Early continued his retreat to Fisher's Hill, where he had an intrenched camp.

14. Sheridan followed and on the 21st appeared in Early's front. During that day and the next he prepared to assail the lines at Fisher's Hill. Early, feeling sure that his army was not strong enough to encounter Sheridan, had given orders for retreating that night. But just before sundown Crook's infantry, whose movement had not been discovered, struck so suddenly Early's left and rear that his whole army was driven in confusion from its position. [1] Early retired to Mount Jackson and thence to New Market, where he turned off to the east toward Port Republic; he took this direction in order to meet reinforcements; for Kershaw, who had gone as far as Culpeper on his march to join Lee, was now ordered back to Early.

15. Torbert, with Sheridan's cavalry, went up the Valley as far as Staunton, where he destroyed great quantities of army stores; he also did considerable damage to the Virginia Central railroad. When Sheridan began his return march, the cavalry was deployed across the Valley, burning, destroying or taking away

---

[1] In the two battles of Winchester and Fisher's Hill Sheridan had taken twenty-one cannon.

every thing that was supposed to be of any value to the Confederates. So complete was the devastation of this lovely Valley that Sheridan telegraphed Grant that a crow in flying over it would have to carry his rations.

16. Early, whom defeats had not appalled, followed Sheridan as he retired down the Valley; his reinforcements had about supplied his losses at Fisher's Hill. Sheridan halted beyond Strasburg and went into camp at **Cedar Creek**. Early went into camp again at Fisher's Hill; he formed the bold plan of attacking Sheridan in his camp; he knew that the odds against him were great, but he felt that a victory was necessary, and that it could not be gained without fighting for it. General John B. Gordon, with General C. A. Evans and Captain Jed. Hotchkiss, took observations from the end of Massanutton Mountain, and reported that an attack could be successfully made upon the Federal left and rear, and that the approach to that part of the Union line was practicable for infantry but not for artillery. Early gave orders that the divisions of Gordon, Ramseur, and Pegram, under the command of Gordon, should take the road to the Federal rear, while he himself, with Kershaw's and Wharton's divisions and all the artillery, should move along the pike through Strasburg and attack the Union front and flank. The plan was a great success. At early dawn of October 19th the charging Confederates broke over the Federal works and rushed into their camp, capturing prisoners and guns, which they turned upon the routed troops. The corps of Crook and Emory left their camp in utter confusion. Officers and men were driven from their beds, hurrying into their clothes as they fled in terror. Wright's corps, which was

PEGRAM'S DEATH.

farthest from the point of attack, retired in tolerable order, but offered only a feeble resistance. The cavalry on the extreme right of the Union line was unbroken and retired in order, delaying the Confederate advance. The pursuit slackened, and just beyond Middletown the retreating Federals halted. The cavalry and Wright's corps considerably outnumbered the victors of that morning's battle. The Confederates had halted and many of the men had left their ranks and were plundering the captured camp. General Wright, assisted by Torbert, took up a new position, and many of the routed Federal troops were rallied and brought again into line.

17. Sheridan, who had been to Washington and had stopped at Winchester during the night of the 18th, heard the noise of the battle on the morning of the 19th, and mounting his horse hurried to the field, which he reached at about half-past 10. On the road he met stragglers, who turned and followed him as he shouted to them: "Come, boys! we are going back." He found his army already reformed. Many of those who had fled in the morning had now returned and were ready to fight again. Sheridan made the necessary dispositions to renew the battle. Before ordering an advance he rode down the whole front of his infantry line and was greeted with hearty cheers. This was after mid-day, as Sheridan himself tells us. Late in the afternoon his whole line advanced. Before the impetuous onset the Confederates were forced to give way. Around their flanks poured Torbert's cavalry, which alone outnumbered their whole infantry force. Their officers tried to rally them, but in vain. The gallant Ramseur, while bravely stemming the tide, fell

mortally wounded. Sheridan pressed on, recovering nis camp, taking 1,000 prisoners and twenty-three cannon, besides the twenty-four which had been captured from him in the morning. The Confederates halted for the night at Fisher's Hill, and next morning continued their retreat. The pursuit stopped at Mt. Jackson. The defeated army went into camp at New Market. They brought off with them from the battlefield 1,500 prisoners, who were sent to Richmond.

18. Notwithstanding these defeats Early afterwards advanced again, and for two days (November 11th and 12th) confronted Sheridan's whole force north of Cedar Creek without being attacked. He also sent out a cavalry expedition under General Rosser, which surprised and captured a fortified post at New Creek, on the Baltimore and Ohio railroad, bringing off 800 prisoners and four cannon.[1]

19. In December Lee called back to Richmond his Second corps, which was now placed under the command of General John B. Gordon. Grant also called to Petersburg his Sixth corps. Early remained in the Valley, moving back to Staunton with Wharton's division and a small force of cavalry and artillery. Sheri-

---

[1] According to the return of September 10th Sheridan's army numbered 43,000 men in the field and 7,000 in garrisons at Harper's Ferry, Martinsburg, and other points. His losses in the principal engagements were as follows: At Winchester, 697 killed, 3,983 wounded, and 338 captured or missing—5,018; at Fisher's Hill, 52 killed, 457 wounded, and 19 captured or missing—528; at Cedar Creek, 644 killed, 3,430 wounded, and 1,591 captured or missing—5,665; his total loss in all these battles, 11,211. Including all the cavalry fights and skirmishes Sheridan's total loss was 1,938 killed, 11,893 wounded, and 3,121 captured or missing—16,952. Early's maximum strength in the Valley was about 20,000 on August 15, 1864, but the departure of Kershaw's division left him 14,000 men. At Winchester he had 13,000 effectives. After the return of Kershaw's division he had just enough to make up his losses at Winchester

dan went into winter quarters at Kernstown. Toward
the last of December Torbert led two divisions of cavalry on a raid against the Virginia Central railroad,
but he was forced to retreat. Custer also moved up
the Valley to attack the cavalry of Early, but near
Harrisonburg he was surprised and defeated.

Hood's Tennessee Campaign.

20. Upon the fall of Atlanta General Hood felt that
any farther retreat would be attended with evil results
to the army commanded by him. The rapidity with
which Sherman was collecting supplies and recruits
from the North at Atlanta showed that the Federals
would not long remain idle. It was absolutely necessary to check the farther progress of the Federals,
recover what had been lost in Georgia, save the Gulf
States, and retain possession of the railroads on which
the Southern armies depended for supplies. On September 18th Hood moved westward, and on the 20th
fixed his headquarters at Palmetto, on the West Point
railroad. Here Mr. Davis visited the army, to which
he made an encouraging speech, and, in consultation
with General Hood, formed a plan by which it was
hoped that Sherman could be made to give up his con-
quests in Georgia.

and Fisher's Hill. So at Cedar Creek his numbers were about the same
as at Winchester. His loss at Winchester was 3,611 in the infantry and
artillery, and adding the cavalry, about 4,000. Over half of these were
prisoners. At Fisher's Hill he lost 30 killed, 210 wounded, and 995 missing. At Cedar Creek Early lost 1,860 in killed and wounded and a thousand captured or missing—2,860. In view of the official returns of Early's
and Sheridan's forces, how absurd is the statement made by Grant in
his memoirs that "Early had lost more men in killed, wounded and
captured in the Valley than Sheridan had commanded from first to last."

21. The plan was for Hood to move with his whole army to the rear of Sherman, tear up the single line of railroad over which the Federal supplies were carried, destroy by cavalry raids the great railroad bridge over the Tennessee, and completely cut off communication between Atlanta, Chattanooga and Nashville.

FEDERAL TROOPS FORAGING.

It was hoped that this would force Sherman to retreat towards Tennessee. Or, if he should start from Atlanta to march through Georgia to the Atlantic coast, the Confederate army having already cut his communications with the north, should fall upon his rear, while the cavalry and other forces placed in his front

should delay his march and prevent him from foraging upon the country. It was thought that by pursuing this course the army of Sherman could be overwhelmingly defeated. Mr. Davis never intended that
Hood should move his army beyond striking distance
of that of Sherman.

22. Hood crossed the Chattahoochee on the 1st
of October and moved to Dallas. From thence he
sent a strong force against the railroad above Marietta,
which destroyed it for fifteen miles. At Allatoona were
large supplies collected for the use of Sherman's army.
Major-General French was sent with his division to
capture this post. With valor unsurpassed French's
men attacked in the early morning of October 5th,
captured part of the Federal works, and drove them
into a little "star fort," which was bravely held by
Corse's gallant men until French received news that
Sherman was advancing against him. Fearing that
he might be cut off from the main army, French
retired. Could he have remained a short while longer
Corse would have been compelled to surrender.[1]

23. Hood's movements caused Sherman to leave
one corps in Atlanta and march northward with the
main body of his army. Hood continued the work of
destruction on the railroad, tearing it up from Resaca
to Tunnel Hill, and capturing the Federal posts at
Tilton, Dalton and Mill Creek Gap. Then, avoiding
battle, he marched to Gadsden, in Alabama, where he
had abundant supplies. Thence he moved in the
direction of Florence, on the Tennessee. Sherman

---

[1] In this battle 2,500 Confederates assaulted 2,100 Federals, who, besides being fortified, were greatly aided by the fact that some of them
were armed with repeating rifles, which the Confederates did not have.

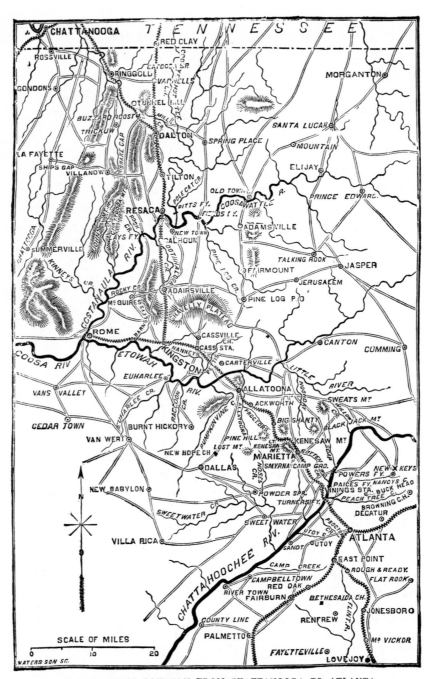

MAP SHOWING COUNTRY FROM CHATTANOOGA TO ATLANTA.

says that thus far Hood's movement against his communications had been rapid and skillful.

24. Sherman now sent by rail two of his six corps with General Schofield, to reinforce Thomas at Nashville, and with the rest of his army turned back toward Atlanta. Hood, instead of hanging on his rear, preventing him from repairing the railroad and harassing him in every way, after consulting with General Beauregard, who had been placed in command of the Western Department, decided to march into Tennessee. Hood gives as his reason for thus departing from the plan agreed upon between himself and Mr. Davis that to follow Sherman southward would be construed by his army into a retreat, and would therefore be discouraging and disastrous. He hoped by a rapid march into Tennessee to cut off and destroy Schofield's army before it could unite with Thomas at Nashville.

25. Before entering Tennessee Hood, by Beauregard's direction, sent back nearly all of his cavalry under Wheeler to watch and delay Sherman as much as possible. At the same time Beauregard directed Forrest, who was near Jackson, Tennessee, with a large cavalry force, to march eastward and unite with Hood. When the soldiers were informed that they were about to enter once more the State of Tennessee, there went up a hearty Confederate shout, so familiar to all who served in either army, and called by their enemies the "rebel yell."

26. On the 19th and 20th Hood crossed the Tennessee. He then pushed forward, with Forrest's cavalry in front, hoping by a rapid march to get in rear of Schofield's forces before they could reach Duck River. The Federals, however, took the alarm and reached

Duck River ahead of him. During the night (November 28th) Hood's pontoons were laid across Duck River by Colonel Presstman, and at early dawn the army again started by a forced march to intercept the Federals.

GENERAL FORREST AND HIS ROUGH RIDERS.

27. Near **Spring Hill** came the wished-for opportunity to not only shut out the Union army from the road to Nashville, but to also effectually bar the way in every other direction. "A single Confederate brigade like Adams's or Cockrell's or Maney's, veterans since Shiloh, planted squarely across the pike, either south or north of Spring Hill, would have effectually prevented Schofield's retreat, and daylight would have found his whole force cut off from every avenue of escape by more than twice its numbers, to assault whom would have been madness, and to avoid whom would have been impossible."[1] By a strange misunderstanding, the way was not barred, though Hood expected it to be, and though two corps of his army were not half a mile

[1] Colonel Henry Stone, of the staff of General Thomas, in "Battles and Leaders of the Civil War," Vol. iv., page 446.

away. "The afternoon and night of November 29th, 1864, may well be set down in the calendar of lost opportunities. The heroic valor of the same troops the next day, and their frightful losses as they attempted to retrieve their mistake, show what might have been."[1]

28. Although the Confederate forces marched in pursuit next day with all possible speed, the Federals reached Franklin in time to make a good fortification before the arrival of Hood's army. It was after 4 in the afternoon when the attack began. The onward rush of Cleburne's and Brown's divisions swept the Federals out of their first line of works and carried the Confederates into their main line with them; but Opdycke with his brigade, which had stood in reserve, rushed into the breach. Stanley and Cox led other troops to the rescue, and recovered their inner line. Charge after charge was made by the determined Southerners. More than one color-bearer was shot down on the parapet. Colonel Stone, who has been already twice quoted, says: "It is impossible to exaggerate the fierce energy with which the Confederate soldiers that short November afternoon threw themselves against the works, fighting with what seemed the madness of despair." In that fearful struggle fell hundreds of the bravest soldiers and several of the ablest generals of Hood's army. General John Adams, as he rode his horse over the works and tried to grasp the flag of the Sixty-fifth Illinois from the hands of the color-bearer, was killed and fell just outside the parapet, astride of which fell also his horse, killed at

[1] Colonel Henry Stone, in "Battles and Leaders of the Civil War,' Vol. iv., page 446.

the same instant. About fifty yards from the works fell Pat. Cleburne, the "Stonewall Jackson of the West." Near him lay Granberry, commander of the famous Texas brigade. Generals Strahl and Gist were also killed, and Cockrell, Quarles and Brown were severely wounded. General G. W. Gordon was captured inside the Federal works. The Federals claimed to have also captured thirty-three Confederate flags, taken from color-bearers shot down or captured inside their works. The fighting continued until late in the night. After midnight Schofield withdrew his forces, and, crossing the Harpeth, hastened on to Nashville, leaving his dead and wounded behind. Hood followed the retreating Federals, and appearing before Nashville threw up works and prepared to hold his ground. He admitted a loss at Franklin of 4,500 in killed, wounded and captured. The Federals, protected by their breastworks, and many of them armed with repeating rifles, had inflicted terrible losses upon their assailants and had lost 2,300 men, of whom 1,100 were captured. Of all the battles of the war there was not one more hotly contested than that of **Franklin.** A reunited country should cherish with pride the memory of the gallant men who attacked, and of the equally gallant men who held the works that terrible November afternoon.

29. Hood's army before Nashville was not the same in spirit and hope as before the great blunder at Spring Hill, and its fearful losses at Franklin, where every soldier felt that the very flower of the army had fallen. The absence of so many noble officers, the pride and glory of that army, on whose faces they should never look again, filled their hearts with gloom. They had hoped for brilliant results in Tennessee. Instead they

GENERAL GEORGE G. MEADE.

had met with disaster. Besides their losses in killed and wounded many were disabled by sickness, caused by the exposure to the rigors of an unusually severe winter. By the absence of Forrest's cavalry and two brigades of infantry their effective strength was reduced to 30,000 men. By the 15th of December Thomas was ready with near 60,000 splendidly equipped and well-fed troops to attack Hood's diminished force. Though bravely resisted, the Federals captured the infantry outposts and some artillery in the unfinished works. Next morning the battle was renewed. All along the line the Federals were repulsed until late in the afternoon. Then the Federals succeeded in piercing the Confederate line a little to the left of the centre. The line thus pierced gave way, and soon after broke at all points.[1] At Brentwood, a few miles in rear of the scene of disaster, order was in a measure restored among the routed troops through the promptness and gallantry of Clayton's division. Fifty-four cannon and thousands of prisoners fell into the hands of the Federals in this disastrous **Battle of Nashville.**

30. General S. D. Lee showed his usual energy and skill in handling his troops while protecting the rear of the army during the 17th. In the afternoon he was wounded, and General C. L. Stevenson took command of his corps and ably discharged his duties during the continuance of the retreat. Near Columbia General Walthall, one of the best commanders of the army, was ordered to form a rear guard of eight picked brigades (of which Mercer's had not been in

---

[1] It was at this time that Miss Mary Bradford of Tennessee rushed amid the routed troops and begged them to rally.

the rout at Nashville) and Forrest's cavalry. The rear guard thus formed did its duty bravely, and saved the army from farther disaster. The Federal cavalry under General Wilson pressed upon the Confederates, picking up stragglers and making frequent attacks upon the rear guard. Just before sundown on Christmas day Forrest made a stand on a thickly wooded ridge at the head of a ravine, and by a sudden charge forced back the Union cavalry and captured one of their cannon, which he carried off with him. Without farther serious molestation the army crossed the Tennessee and continued the retreat to Tupelo, in Mississippi, at which place Cheatham's corps, the last in the line of march, went into camp on the 10th of January, 1865. The army, when it reached Tupelo, numbered about 21,000 of all arms. Here, at his own request, General Hood was relieved of the command.[1]

[1] The Union forces during Hood's Tennessee campaign amounted to 71,000 men. Of these 25,000 were in the battle of Franklin and 55,000 were at the battle of Nashville. General Thomas reports his total loss during the campaign at 10,000. Hood's strength on November 6th was about 45,000. The arrival of Forrest's cavalry would have increased it to over 53,000; but the sending back of Wheeler's cavalry to Georgia left his strength about the same as on the 6th. At the battle of Franklin Hood had probably 35,000 men engaged. At the battle of Nashville, with Forrest's cavalry and two infantry brigades absent, his force was rather under than over 30,000. Hood stated that his losses during the whole campaign did not exceed 10,000, including prisoners. Thomas claims to have taken during the campaign 13,189 prisoners. But this includes captures in East Tennessee and Southwest Virginia—in fact, throughout the whole Department of Tennessee from September 5th, 1864, to January 20th, 1865. Thomas says that during the same period over 2,000 deserters were received. As these prisoners and deserters were from other commands besides Hood's, it is probable that Hood's entire loss was not over 12,000 all told.

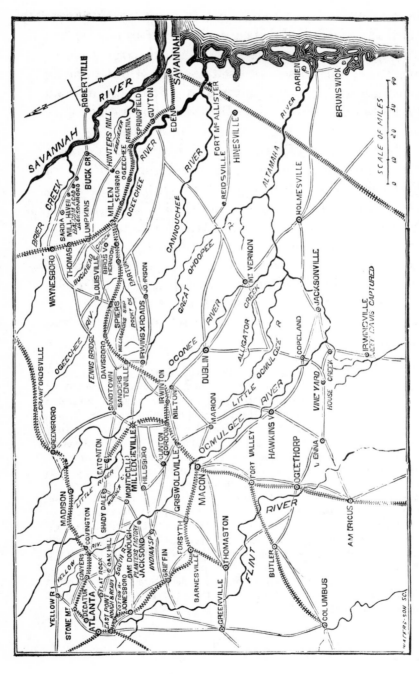

SECTION TRAVERSED BY SHERMAN IN HIS MARCH TO THE SEA.

Sherman's March to the Sea.

31. When Hood turned off toward Florence to march into Tennessee Sherman, after sending Thomas and Schofield, with two corps from his army, to reinforce the Union troops already in that State, turned back into Georgia. He repaired his railroad until he had collected abundant supplies in Atlanta; then destroyed it from Dalton to Atlanta, and burned the foundries and mills at Rome and other places. He had driven the inhabitants out of Atlanta soon after its capture by him. Now, with 63,000 infantry and artillery and 5,000 cavalry, he made ready to march to the sea.

32. He first utterly destroyed the city of Atlanta by fire. Not a single house was spared—not even a church. Captain Daniel Oakey, of the Second Massachusetts volunteers, says: "Sixty thousand of us witnessed the destruction of Atlanta, while our post band and that of the Thirty-third Massachusetts played martial airs and operatic selections." On November 15th the Federals left their intrenchments around Atlanta. Sherman accompanied Slocum's column of 30,000 men, which marched first by the Augusta road and then turned off and passed through Milledgeville. Howard marched by the Macon road at the head of 33,000 infantry and artillery. With him for several days went Kilpatrick with 5,000 cavalry.

33. There was no force to oppose Sherman's march except 3,000 Georgia State troops, under General Gustavus W. Smith, and Wheeler's cavalry. Smith, by presenting a bold front at Griffin, Forsythe and Macon successively, caused Howard to pass those places unmolested. At Griswoldville the State troops, contrary

to Smith's orders, made an attack upon an intrenched Federal division and were repulsed with a loss of fifty-one killed and four hundred and seventy-two wounded. Yet they remained close to the Federal line until dark. Then they were withdrawn to Macon and sent by rail to Thomasville, and from that point to Savannah.

ALL THE LIVE STOCK LEFT ON McGILL S FARM.

Wheeler with his cavalry harrassed the Federals as much as possible, defeating exposed detachments, preventing their foragers from venturing far from the main body, defending cities and towns along the railroad lines, and saving in some instances depots of supplies and arsenals.

34. Along the line of march of Sherman's army his "Bummers" entered private houses, took from them everything that was valuable, burned what they could not carry off, and sometimes set fire to the house itself. Rings were taken from the fingers of ladies, and old men were hung up to make them tell where their treasures were concealed.

35. Beauregard was unable to assemble troops enough to do more than delay for a little the march of Sherman's army, which appeared near Savannah about December 10th. This place was held by Hardee with about 18,000 men. On the 13th Hazen's division, nearly four thousand strong, stormed and captured Fort McAllister, which was defended by two hundred and thirty men. These fought the assailants until they were individually overpowered. Now Sherman's army opened communications with the fleet. Slocum crossed the Savannah, and Hardee evacuated the city to save his little army from capture. Sherman entered the city December 23d, and sent the following dispatch to Mr. Lincoln: "I beg to present to you as a Christmas gift the city of Savannah with one hundred and fifty heavy guns and plenty of ammunition, and also about 25,000 bales of cotton." In Sherman's official report he states that he had carried away with him 10,000 horses and mules and a countless number of slaves. He estimated the damage done to Georgia and its military resources at \$100,000,000, at least \$20,000,000 of which inured to the advantage of the Federal army and government.

36. While Sherman was on his march through Georgia the Federal General Hatch, with 5,500 men, marched to destroy the railroad between Charleston and Savannah. At **Honey Hill** he was met by General G. W. Smith, with less than 2,000 men (Georgia State troops, the Forty-seventh Georgia, and a battery of South Carolina artillery). Hatch was repulsed, with the loss of 754 men. A remarkable feature of this battle was the presence among the Confederates of some boy volunteers, even under the age subject to

conscription. Soldiers who were present in that battle say that some of these boys were not tall enough to shoot over the parapet. So they resorted to the following device: A boy would get upon his hands and knees, another would stand upon his back, deliver his fire, and then change places with his friend, so that he might get a shot at the "Yanks."

OTHER CONFEDERATE REVERSES.

37. In the months of September and October General Price, of the Trans-Mississippi Department, advanced far into the interior of Missouri, driving for a while every thing that opposed him. At last he was attacked and defeated by General Rosecrans on the Big Blue (October 23d). Price then retreated into Arkansas.

38. Plymouth, North Carolina, since its capture by the Confederates in the spring of 1864, had been held by a small force, assisted by the ram *Albemarle*. On the night of October 27th Lieutenant W. B. Cushing, of the United States navy, went with a few men in a small boat and succeeded in approaching near enough to the *Albemarle* to explode a torpedo under that vessel. Then, under a terrific fire of grape that sank his boat, he sprang into the river, and in the darkness succeeded in swimming to the Union fleet. By this daring act the *Albemarle* was destroyed and the Confederates could no longer hold the town.

39. On the ocean also the Confederate cruisers met with disaster. After a wonderful career, in which they had inflicted great damage on the Northern commerce, the *Alabama* was sunk by the *Kearsarge* on the

19th of June, and the *Florida* was captured by the *Wachusett* on the 7th of October.

SOME CONFEDERATE SUCCESSES.

40. There was a slight silver lining to the cloud that hung so darkly over the Confederacy as the year 1864 drew to a close. In Northern Virginia Mosby and his daring men performed many wonderful exploits, making important captures and keeping the Confederate authorities informed of the movements of the Federals. All Federal attempts to capture Charleston and Fort Sumter failed throughout the year. An expedition against Fort Fisher, at the entrance of Cape Fear river, consisting of a land force under General Butler and a fleet of seventy vessels under Commodore Porter, was repulsed on the 24th and 25th of December.

41. Around Richmond and Petersburg Lee and his noble army still baffled all Grant's efforts. On August 18th General Warren advanced with a strong body of Federals, and placing them across the Weldon railroad at Globe Tavern fortified his position. He was preparing for a farther extension of his lines when he was attacked by A. P. Hill (August 19th and 20th). Warren's position was so strong that he could not be driven from it, but he was prevented from advancing his line farther. In these battles at **Globe Tavern** the Federals lost 4,000 men, of whom 2,500 were prisoners. The Confederate loss was about 2,000. They continued to use the railroad.

42. Hancock now moved out with another force and took position at **Ream's Station,** farther south. Here he was attacked by A. P. Hill (August 25th) and defeated,

with a loss of 2,700 men and five cannon. The Confederates captured 2,000 prisoners. Their loss was 700 in all. They continued the rest of the year to

A CABIN HOME BEFORE THE WAR

use the Weldon railroad for bringing supplies from North Carolina, running the trains to the point which they held close up to the Federal lines. The part of the road above Globe Tavern was held by the Federals.

43. Hampton's "Beef Raid" was to Lee's men one of the most grateful enterprises ever performed by the cavalry of that army. On the 16th of September General Wade Hampton got into Grant's rear at City Point and brought off 400 prisoners and 2,500 beeves. This joke at the expense of the "Yanks" was well relished by Lee's half-starved soldiers. They had secured enough meat for rations for 50,000 men for forty days.

44. In the latter part of October Grant made attempts to push forward his lines both on the north and south sides of the James. These movements were attended by partial engagements, with success sometimes to one party and sometimes to the other. But the final outcome was that the Federals were thwarted in their plan and returned to their former lines without accomplishing that which they had undertaken. This closed active operations around Richmond and Petersburg for the winter.

45. By the table in chapter second of this section it is seen that the losses of the Union armies of the Potomac and the James in the campaign against Richmond and Petersburg from May 5th to June 15th were, according to the official records published by the United States Government, 61,144 in killed, wounded, and captured or missing. From June 15th to December 31st the losses of these armies were, according to the same authorities, 47,554—making the appalling aggregate of 108,698 in killed, wounded and captured in the armies operating under Grant directly against Petersburg and Richmond. This is exclusive of losses in the Shenandoah Valley. The Confederate losses during the same period were about 40,000.

THE SITUATION AT THE CLOSE OF 1864.

46. By the close of 1864 the Confederate power in the West had been almost annihilated. The Confederates had also met defeat in the Shenandoah Valley, where hitherto they had known only victory. Charleston and Wilmington still held out. Lee's army, though suffering great hardships and compelled to be ever on the watch, still barred the way to Petersburg and Richmond. Had Lee been made commander-in-chief of all the Southern armies in the spring of 1864 his admirers believe that the Confederate disasters in the West would have been avoided, and that the year 1864 would have closed with bright prospects for the South.

PART III.

The War Between the States and its Results.

Section V.—The Final Campaigns—Reconstruction.

CHAPTER I.

PRISONERS OF WAR—THE FINAL CAMPAIGN.

BEFORE giving an account of the closing struggle, let us consider for a short while the subject of the exchange and treatment of prisoners. At first the United States authorities would not recognize the belligerent rights of the Confederates, and hence would enter into no exchange with them. They even declared their intention to treat Confederate privateers captured by them as pirates. But the many victories of the Confederates, and the large number of prisoners that fell into their hands, caused the Federal Government to recede from this position. In the summer of 1862 an exchange was agreed upon by commissioners appointed by the two governments, and it was also agreed that Confederate privateers should be treated like any other prisoners of war.

2. In 1864 Grant adopted as part of his plan no exchange of prisoners, on the ground that so long as prisoners were exchanged the Southern ranks could be kept full, and the South be enabled to continue the war. In order to prevent any exchange General Grant ordered General Butler, in whose hands the matter had been placed by him, to demand as a condition of exchange that the Confederate Government should treat negro soldiers in the same way as the white men. The Confederates were willing to do this, except in cases where negro soldiers were slaves who had run away from their masters and enlisted in the Union armies. These they regarded as deserters. General

Butler himself says that he put forth the Federal claim to captured slaves enlisted in their armies in the most offensive form possible for the purpose of carrying out the wishes of the Lieutenant-General "that no prisoners should be exchanged."

AN OLD PLANTATION HOME.

3. The laying waste of the fields of the South, the tearing up of railroads, and the destruction of the means of transportation brought great suffering on the Southern people and soldiers, in which, of course, prisoners of war also shared. Medicines for the sick were exhausted and could not be procured. The Confederate commissioner, Mr. Ould, had proposed as early

as 1863 "that all prisoners on each side should be attended by a proper number of their own surgeons, who under rules to be established, should be permitted to take charge of their health and comfort. It was also proposed that these surgeons should act as commissaries, with power to receive and distribute such contributions of money, food, clothing and medicines as might be forwarded for the relief of the prisoners. It was further proposed that these surgeons should be selected by their own Government, and that they should have full liberty at any and all times, through the agents of exchange, to make reports, not only of their own acts, but of any matters relating to the welfare of the prisoners. "To this communication no reply of any kind was ever made." [1]

4. When it was at last found (in 1864) that no exchange of prisoners would be made, the Confederate Government offered to the United States authorities to send them their sick and wounded without requiring any equivalents. They offered to deliver from 10,000 to 15,000 at the mouth of the Savannah River, and added that if the number for which transportation might be sent could not be made up from sick and wounded the difference would be supplied with well men. Although this offer was made in the summer, transportation did not arrive until November. As at that time the prisoners had most of them been removed fom Georgia, and enough sick and wounded could not be brought to Savannah in time, 5,000 well men were substituted.

[1] "Rise and Fall of the Confederate Government," by Jefferson Davis, Vol. ii., page 598.

RUINS OF RICHMOND AFTER THE WAR.

5. On two occasions the Confederate authorities were requested to send the very worst cases that they had. This was done, and on their being delivered they were taken to Annapolis, Maryland, and there photographed as specimen prisoners. This was done to make the people of the North believe that the Southern people had purposely mistreated their prisoners; and yet Mr. Ould had in the summer of 1864 proposed to purchase medicines from the United States authorities to be used exclusively for the relief of Union prisoners. It was moreover proposed by Mr. Ould that United States surgeons should be allowed to go within the Confederate lines and dispense these medicines themselves. Mr. Davis, the Confederate President, says: "Incredible as it may appear, it is nevertheless strictly true that no reply was ever received to this offer."

6. The Northern people were made to believe that their prisoners were willfully starved and mistreated in Southern prisons. Those who had charge of Northern prison camps, believing this, were often cruel in their treatment of Southern prisoners. The United States Secretary of War, E. M. Stanton, a bitter enemy of the South, in his report made on July 19th, 1866, says that of all the Federal soldiers confined in Southern prisons 22,576 died, while of all Confederate soldiers confined in Northern prisons 26,246 died. Surgeon-General Barnes of the United States army says that the number of Confederate prisoners in their hands from first to last was 220,000, and that the number of Union prisoners in the hands of the Confederates was from first to last 270,000. These figures speak for themselves.

THE FINAL CAMPAIGNS.

7. **A Second Attack on Fort Fisher** was made in January by the Union fleet under Commodore Porter and a land force under General Terry. This attack was successful. The fort was taken, together with the garrison of 2,000 men and 169 heavy guns (January 15th, 1865). The heroic General Whiting was mortally wounded, and Colonel Lamb, the gallant commander of the fort, was seriously wounded. Both fell into the hands of the Federals. Soon after this Wilmington also fell.

8. An attempt at negotiations for peace was made early in February. Alexander H. Stephens, Vice-President of the Confederacy, with R. M. T. Hunter and John A. Campbell as commissioners on the part of the Confederate Government, met President Lincoln and Secretary Seward to discuss terms of peace. The meeting took place at Hampton Roads. General Grant in his "Memoirs" says that Mr. Lincoln told him that he had said to the commissioners "that there would be no use in entering into any negotiations unless they would recognize—first, that the Union as a whole must be forever preserved; and second, that slavery must be abolished. If they were willing to concede these two points then he was ready to enter into negotiations, and was almost willing to hand them a blank sheet of paper with his signature attached for them to fill in the terms upon which they were willing to live with us in the Union and be one people." The commissioners had no authority to treat upon any terms not recognizing the Confederate States. Hence this effort at negotiation came to noth-

ALEXANDER H STEPHENS.

ing. If the terms were as liberal as Grant would have us to infer, although they required the absolute yielding of the right of secession and the abolition of slavery, in view of the prospects of the Confederacy at that time, they ought to have been accepted. Mr. Davis, however, was in a trying position. He did not believe that the people whom he represented would think him justifiable in thus accepting what they would regard as absolute submission.

HON. JOSEPH BROWN, WAR GOVERNOR OF GEORGIA.

9. Sherman's march northward from Savannah began early in February. His army moved in two columns, one threatening Augusta and the other Charleston, each of which cities the Confederates tried to defend. Mr. Davis admits in his history of these events that instead of pursuing such a policy all

the Confederate forces in the Carolinas and Georgia ought to have been concentrated in Sherman's front. General Hampton also tells us that such was the opinion of General Beauregard, but does not know why it was not done.

10. As Sherman marched through South Carolina he sent Kilpatrick against Augusta; but Kilpatrick was defeated at Aiken (February 11th) by General Wheeler. Thus Augusta was saved. But Columbia, the beautiful capital of South Carolina, did not thus escape. As Sherman approached this city the Confederate force of only 5,000 men retired. The Mayor met the advancing Federals and surrendered the city, "with the hope that, as no resistance had been offered, it would be protected from pillage and destruction." During that night the greater part of Columbia was burned. The city was full of helpless women and children and invalids, many of whom were driven from their dwellings, to which the torch was applied An effort was made by Sherman to shift the blame upon Hampton by declaring that by that General's orders the cotton in the city was fired, and that the burning cotton was the cause of the conflagration. But General Hampton denied most positively that any cotton was fired by his orders. He also denied that the citizens set fire to bales of cotton, and also that any cotton was on fire when the Federals entered the city. The people of Columbia, both white and black, have borne abundant testimony to the fact that Columbia was burned by the Federal soldiers. General Slocum admits as much when he says: "I believe the immediate cause of the disaster was a free use of whiskey (which was supplied to the soldiers by citi-

zens with great liberality).   A drunken soldier, with a
musket in one hand and a match in the other, is not
a pleasant visitor to have about the house on a dark,
windy night." He says, however, that he does not
believe it was done by Sherman's orders.   Sherman
in his memoirs says: "The army having totally ruined
Columbia, moved on toward Winnsboro." There is

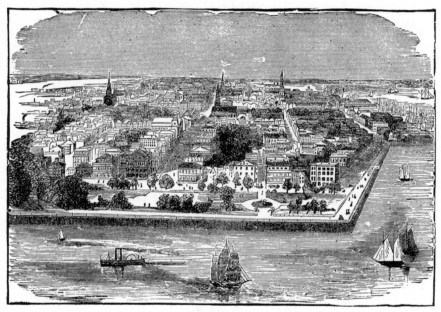

CHARLESTON, S. C.

no doubt that the Federal soldiers burned the city, and
that they were never punished for it, whether Sherman
ordered it or not.

11. On the same day that Sherman entered Columbia the Confederates under Hardee evacuated Charleston and moved toward North Carolina, into which
State various other Confederate commands were marching.   General Lee, who had at this late day been made
commander-in-chief of all the armies of the Confed-

eracy, now called upon General Joseph E. Johnston to
take command of all the forces in Carolina, concentrate them, and drive back Sherman.

12. Johnston at once took vigorous measures to perform the part assigned him. He rapidly brought
together Hardee's command from the Charleston garrison, Stevenson's and Cheatham's divisions from the
Army of Tennessee, also Hampton's and Wheeler's
cavalry, who had been skirmishing with the Federals
as they advanced. Hoke's veteran division from the
Army of Northern Virginia, which had been operating
under Bragg, also joined him. Before the concentration had been effected Bragg had gained a partial success
over the Federal General Cox at Kinston (March
8th), and Hardee had fought an indecisive battle at
Averysboro (March 16th).

13. As Johnston wished to attack the Federals
before all their forces could be united he decided not to
await the arrival of all Cheatham's troops,[1] but to press
on with what force he had. Sending Hampton ahead
with Butler's division of cavalry to occupy a strong
position and hold it until the infantry and artillery
could come up, Johnston hurried forward. At **Bentonville** he struck the Federals (March 19th). Bragg and
Hoke on the left repulsed them, and Hardee on the
right led a charge, which forced them back for some
distance. In this charge Hardee on horseback dashed
over the Union breastworks in front of his men.
That night Sherman's whole army was united in Johnston's front. For two days Johnston held in check
Sherman's 70,000 men with not more than 20,000 of

---

[1] Major-General Bate commanded the troops of Cheatham, who were
present at Bentonville.

all arms. In a successful charge on the 21st led by Hardee that general's son, a noble lad of sixteen, fell mortally wounded. Finding the Federals in overwhelming force concentrated on three sides of him, Johnston withdrew that night toward Raleigh.

14. Lee's noble army, the last hope of the Confederacy, saw the toils fast closing around it. For nine months it had been engaged in the difficult task of defending two cities twenty miles apart against a greatly superior force, whose lines were so strongly entrenched that they presented no vulnerable point. During a great part of that time one corps of the army had been absent in Northeastern Virginia under Early, who after three months' successful campaign was thrice defeated by Sheridan, and yet, even after the return of the Second corps to Petersburg, continued with a small force to hold the Upper Valley. Early even sent out an expedition under Rosser, which went as far as Beverly, in West Virginia, captured that place (January 11th) with 400 prisoners and much spoil in the shape of horses and military stores, and securing much needed supplies returned in safety to the Valley. The brave defenders of Richmond and Petersburg had also during the winter been cheered occasionally by some daring exploit of Mosby, who with a small force gave great trouble to the Federals, and had everything so much his own way in Eastern Virginia that the country in which he operated was called "Mosby's Confederacy." Lieutenant McNeill with a squad of Mosby's men actually crossed the Potomac, and dashing into Cumberland, Maryland, at 3 o'clock in the morning of February 21st captured Major-Gen-

erals Kelley and Crook in their beds, mounted them
on horses and hurried them off to Richmond

15. Early in February Grant renewed his efforts to
extend his lines around Lee's right. Warren[1] and Humphreys drove the Confederates across Hatcher's Run
and advanced to Dabney's Mill, the cavalry going as
far as Dinwiddie
Courthouse (Febru-
ary 5th). But A. P.
Hill now struck them
in front, while Gor-
don[2] assailed them in
flank and rear, and
forced them back to
Hatcher's Run. To
this point the Fed-
eral left was extended,
but their attempt to
advance beyond it had
been defeated. The
Weldon road could no
longer be used by the
Confederates as it had
been. Grant's aim
was now to get pos-

GENERAL JOHN B. GORDON.

session of the Southside railroad, Lee's last remaining line of supply.

16. Lee wished to retire from Richmond and Petersburg and have his army free for movements in the

---

[1] In December Warren had led an expedition which tore up the Weldon road as far south as Hicksford. But as far as that point the Confederates still used it.

[2] Gordon had now been promoted to the command of a corps and
Evans to the command of a division.

open country, but yielded his better judgment to the desire of Mr. Davis to hold on where he was as long as possible. There was some slight hope that Johnston might defeat Sherman in North Carolina and then hasten to Lee's help. But it was evident after Bentonville that Johnston could not with the force under him do more than delay the march of Sherman. Troops that ought to have been with Lee were obliged to remain in North Carolina.

17. The case of the Confederacy was indeed desperate. But Lee's veterans, though with diminished hope, yet with undaunted spirit, faced the hostile host. Faithful unto death,

> "For Dixie's Land they took their stand,
> To live or die for Dixie."

During March Lee transferred Gordon's corps from the extreme right of the Confederate army to the trenches in and around Petersburg, and, after consultation with Gordon, planned an attack upon **Fort Steadman**, near Grant's center, with the hope of being able to pierce the Union lines and throw into the gap thus made a force sufficient to destroy the left wing of Grant's army before he could concentrate his forces and come to its assistance. Gordon was to lead the assault, and a force of 20,000 men was to follow up and secure the ground that Gordon might seize. Gordon moved forward before daylight of March 25th, with the division of Evans in front, captured **Fort Steadman**, and turned its guns upon the other Union works. Several batteries to the right and left were thus cleared of their defenders and were occupied by Gordon's brave men. The supporting column did not get up in time to go promptly forward, so the Federals were enabled to con-

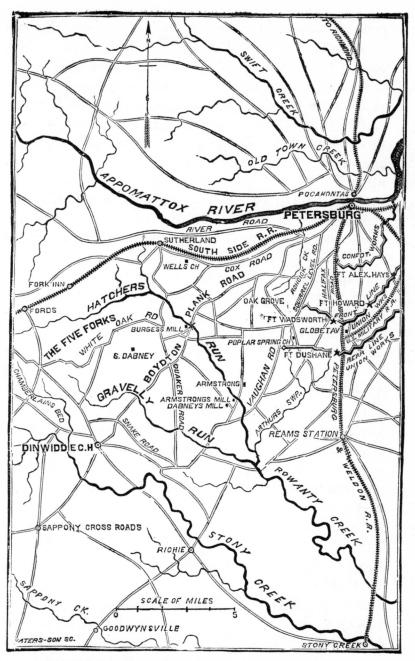

MAP SHOWING POSITION OF ARMIES NEAR PETERSBURG, VA.

centrate against Gordon in such force that he was obliged to fall back to his own lines with heavy loss.

18. Two days later Sheridan joined Grant with 10,000 cavalry. He had come down from the Shenandoah Valley, defeating near Waynesboro Early's small force of less than 2,000 men, and doing immense damage all along the line of his march. Grant now rapidly concentrated his principal force to the south and west of Petersburg with the purpose of assailing the Confederate right. This movement did not escape Lee's watchful eye. Leaving the works north of the James under Longstreet and those of Petersburg under Gordon weakly garrisoned, he moved with the rest of his force into the works along the White Oak road.

19. Without waiting to be attacked Lee fell upon the exposed flank of the Federals entangled in the swampy forest with so sudden and heavy a blow that the divisions thus struck gave way. Lee pursued until he came to a force too strongly posted to be assailed. So he drew his troops back to his own works. On the same day Sheridan advanced toward Five Forks, but he was assailed by the Confederate cavalry under Fitz Lee and the infantry under Pickett, and was driven back to **Dinwiddie Courthouse** (March 31st).

20. Next day (April 1st) Sheridan, being reinforced by two corps of infantry, attacked **Five Forks**. Late in the evening the Confederates, assailed on three sides by this overwhelming force, were after a desperate resistance driven from their position. Early next morning, before Longstreet could be brought over **from Richmond, the Federals attacked all along the**

line, and broke through at several points[1] where Lee's line was so separated that there was only one man to every seven yards. They then took possession of the Southside railroad, and followed the Confederates until checked by the guns from Forts Alexander and Gregg, which held them back until Longstreet came up and interposed his corps. The farther advance of the Federals was then arrested by the Confederates, who had retired to an inner line, which they held against several assaults. The two forts which had enabled the Confederates thus to rally were, however, captured by the Federals. The garrison of Fort Gregg consisted of only 250 men, who repulsed three assaults made by Gibbon's division. When at last the fort was captured only thirty of its brave defenders were still unhurt, and 500 Federals lay stretched upon the ground. Among the slain in the desperate fighting of this day was A. P. Hill, one of Lee's ablest generals, who had borne a conspicuous part in every battle of the Army of Northern Virginia.

21. Lee at once telegraphed to Mr. Davis that Richmond must be abandoned. That night he withdrew his forces from the lines of Petersburg and Richmond, which had been held so long and skillfully. On the next morning the Federals entered the two cities, at whose gates they had been hammering so long. The burning of some Confederate government buildings at Richmond caused a conflagration which the combined efforts of the citizens and troops could not arrest

---

[1] Lee's line was so long that many parts of it were almost bare of troops. He had to strip some parts to strengthen others. It was this that enabled the Federals to break through.

until nearly one-third of that beautiful city had been destroyed.

22. Lee's retreat was continued with his usual skill, but the failure to procure supplies at Amelia Courthouse caused a delay which was fatal to his plans. The devotion of the famished men to their noble leader in this trying hour was truly pathetic. As they trudged along, weary

GENERAL A. P. HILL.

and ready to faint, the sight of him would revive their flagging energies, and with such expressions as "God bless Uncle Robert," "Who wouldn't follow Marse Robert?" they would press on with renewed determination.

23. The pursuit was pressed with untiring energy. Attacks on flank and rear were repulsed, sometimes with heavy loss to the pursuers. But at Sailor's Creek Ewell's corps was cut off and captured (April 6th). On the morning of the 9th, near Appomattox Courthouse, Lee found his way barred by the Federal cavalry under Sheridan. Gordon, with his corps, assisted by Fitz. Lee's cavalry, charged this force and drove it aside, capturing 1,000 prisoners. But now he came upon

heavy masses of infantry, and halted. Longstreet was too busily engaged to send him any aid. It was now plain that nothing more could be done. It would be madness to prolong the struggle. Two days before Grant had addressed a note to Lee proposing to accept the surrender of the Army of Northern Virginia, and several notes had passed between the two generals. Lee now addressed one to Grant, agreeing to meet him to discuss the terms of surrender, which Grant had again proposed in a note written that morning. A truce was made until the meeting could take place. General C. A. Evans, whose division formed the left wing of Gordon's line of advance, was in front of his old brigade and had pushed out his skirmishers, under Captain Kaigler. [1] The notice of the surrender had not reached him. Suddenly a Federal force appeared advancing on his flank and a small battery opened fire. Immediately forwarding his skirmishers under Kaigler, Evans led a desperate charge, capturing the battery, with a number of prisoners, and driving his assailant from the field. At this moment General Custer came riding up to Evans on a magnificent horse. After saluting, he asked where General Lee could be found, and stated that a surrender had been agreed upon. A few minutes later Evans received official notice of the surrender, and slowly drew back his com-

---

[1] General Gordon says that after he had received notice of the surrender he and Sheridan were on the right of his line engaged in conversation, when the sudden and fierce firing on the Confederate left caused Sheridan to rise quickly and say: "General, what does that mean?" Gordon replied, "I do not know. Perhaps the notice of the surrender has not reached that part of the line. I have sent away all my staff and every courier on this duty." Sheridan proposed to lend him one of his own aides, and the notice was thus sent.

mand toward Appomattox. He and his gallant men, all unconscious of what was transpiring elsewhere, had gained one more victory for the falling Confederacy, and had shed a parting glory over the last hours of the Army of Northern Virginia.

24. A suitable room for the interview was selected in the house of Mr. McLean in the little village of Appomattox Courthouse. After some pleasant conversation, the terms were discussed and agreed upon. Then Grant wrote them out, and Lee wrote a reply accepting the terms offered. These were that the officers and men should give their parole not to take up arms

GENERAL CLEMENT A. EVANS.

against the United States until properly exchanged ;

.   .   .   .

that the arms and artillery and public property were to be parked and stacked and turned over to the officers appointed to receive them; that the officers should retain their side arms, private horses and baggage; and that officers and men should be allowed to return to their homes, not to be disturbed by the United States authorities so long as they observed their paroles and the laws in force where they might reside. Lee men·tioned to Grant that a great many of the men owned their own horses and mules. Grant replied that they might keep them, and that he would instruct his officers to let " all the men who claimed to own a horse

GENERAL LEE SIGNING THE TERMS OF SURRENDER.

or mule take the animals home with them to work their little farms."[1]

25. When Lee returned to his army his men greeted him with the old shout of welcome; then, remembering the occasion, became silent. Every hat was raised and tears rolled down the cheeks of the grim warriors who had faced death on many a bloody field. Filled with deep emotion Lee at length found words to say: "Men, we have fought through the war together. I have done the best that I could for you." Then he told them to return to their homes and prove themselves as worthy in peace as they had been in war. Such was the parting between Lee and that gallant band that had never yet known fear.

26. Horace Greeley in his "American Conflict" says: "Of the proud army which, dating its victories from Bull Run, had driven McClellan from before Richmond, and withstood his best effort at Antietam, and shattered Burnside's host at Fredericksburg, and worsted Hooker at Chancellorsville, and fought Meade so stoutly though unsuccessfully before Gettysburg, and baffled Grant's bounteous resources and desperate efforts in the Wilderness, at Spotsylvania, on the North Anna, at Cold Harbor, and before Petersburg and Richmond, a mere wreck remained. It is said that 27,000 were included in Lee's capitulation, but of these not more than 10,000 had been able to carry their arms thus far on their hopeless and almost foodless flight. The rebellion had failed and gone down;

[1] General Fitzhugh Lee, in his "Life of Robert E. Lee," says: "General Grant's behavior at Appomattox was marked by a desire to spare the feelings of his great opponent. There was no theatrical display; . . . 'he' promptly stopped salutes from being fired to mark the event, and the terms granted were liberal and generous."

but the rebel army of Virginia and its commander had *not* failed."

27. Swinton in his "Army of the Potomac" often pays high tribute to Lee's ability as a soldier, and on page 16 thus speaks of the Army of Northern Virginia: "Nor can there fail to arise the image of that other army that was the adversary of the Army of the Potomac, and which who can ever forget that once looked upon it? That array of tattered uniforms and bright muskets; that body of incomparable infantry, the Army of Northern Virginia, which for four years carried the revolt on its bayonets, opposing a constant front to the mighty concentration of power brought against it; which, receiving terrible blows, did not fail to give the like; and which, vital in all its parts, died only with its annihilation."[1]

28. A farther prosecution of the war was now hopeless. After an interview with Generals Johnston and Beauregard at Greensboro', North Carolina, Mr. Davis authorized General Johnston to make whatever terms he could for the termination of the war. On the 18th of April Johnston and Sherman met at the house of

[1] The total force at Grant's disposal on March 1st, 1865, was stated in the report of the Secretary of War to the Thirty-eighth Congress to be 162,000. According to the revised returns he began the Appomattox campaign on March 29th with 120,000 effectives. His losses during the campaign were 10,615 in killed, wounded and missing. According to the returns of February 28th Lee's total effective force was 55,000, and on March 29th Lee, according to his own statement, had 33,000 muskets from his left on the Chickahominy to his right at Dinwiddie Courthouse. This would indicate a total force of only 45,000 men to cover his long line. He began the retreat with 30,000 effectives. At Appomattox 28,000 men were paroled, including wagoners, extra-duty men, sick and broken-down men. His effective force numbered only 10,000, of whom about 8,000 were infantry. This force was hemmed in on every side by more than 100,000 men.

INTERVIEW BETWEEN SHERMAN AND JOHNSTON.

a **Mr. Bennett near Durham's Station**. The terms then agreed upon were that the troops should march to their respective States and deposit their arms in the State arsenals, each officer and man pledging himself to cease from acts of war and abide the action of State and Federal authority; the President of the United States to recognize the several State governments on their officers and legislatures taking the oath of allegiance to the United States, and all persons to be secured in person, property and political rights. This agreement was designed to immediately restore the Union and end the war. Sherman thought that the terms agreed with the views expressed by Mr. Lincoln.

JOHN WILKES BOOTH.

29. But Mr. Lincoln had been assassinated at Ford's Theatre, in Washington city, on the night of April 14th by John Wilkes Booth, an actor of considerable note. The Southern people were as much shocked by this horrible crime as were the people of the North. They had waged war like honorable men and did not **countenance** brutal and cowardly murder. The tem-

per of the Northern people was such after Mr. Lincoln's assassination that the liberal terms offered by Sherman were not acceptable to them. Andrew Johnson, a Unionist of Tennessee, who, in the preceding fall had been elected Vice-President, now by the terms of the Constitution became President. He refused to ratify the treaty between Sherman and Johnston.

30. The two generals then had a second meeting and agreed upon terms of capitulation similar to those given to Lee, with the additional provision that each brigade or separate body of troops was permitted to retain a number of arms equal to one-seventh of its effective strength, which, when the troops reached the capitals of their respective States, were to be disposed of as the general commanding the department might direct. This agreement embraced all the troops in Johnston's department, which included the States of North and South Carolina and Georgia. The date of this agreement, April 26th, 1865, is considered the close of the civil war. The surrender of Johnston was followed by that of all the other Confederate armies, who received the same terms as Lee and Johnston. Between the surrender of Lee and that of Johnston Mobile yielded to an attack by land and water, and General Wilson, with a cavalry expedition from Nashville, captured the cities of Selma, Montgomery, Columbus and Macon.

31. The last surrender was that of General E. Kirby Smith in Texas on the 26th of May. The last fight occurred near **Palmetto Ranche,** on the Rio Grande, in Texas, on the 13th of May, 1865. A Federal force under Colonel Barrett, which was plundering a Confederate camp, was attacked and defeated by some

CAPTURE OF JEFFERSON DAVIS.

Confederate cavalry led by General J. E. Slaughter and chased a distance of fifteen miles. Thus the last combat of the war, like the first, was a Confederate victory.

32. Some of the civil officers of the Confederacy left the country. Mr. Davis, the President, was captured and closely confined in Fortress Monroe, and Mr. Stephens, the Vice-President, was imprisoned in Fort Warren, in Boston Harbor. Mr. Stephens was soon released. Mr. Davis, though always anxious for a trial, remained a prisoner for nearly two years. Desperate efforts were made to have him hanged on some trumped-up charge. He was first accused of being an accomplice in the murder of Mr. Lincoln, but there was not the least evidence of such a thing. Even such bitter enemies as Secretary Stanton and Judge-Advocate Holt found it necessary to abandon this charge. Then they accused him of cruelty to prisoners. But in this they failed utterly to " make out a case." Then an effort was made to have him tried for " treason." But the authorities at Washington and Chief-Justice Chase himself decided, after full consideration and consultation with the best lawyers of the country, that the charge of treason could not be maintained. Mr. Davis was carried to the United States court-room in the Custom-House at Richmond and there admitted to bail. Horace Greeley, of New York, was the first to sign his bond, on which were also Gerritt Smith and Cornelius Vanderbilt. He passed out of the court-room to his carriage amid the cheers of the people. The negroes also united in the general rejoicing, many of them " climbing upon his carriage, shaking and kissing his hand " and calling out " God bless Marse

Davis." Mr. Davis was never brought to trial, but an "unwilling to prosecute" was entered in his case.[1] Mr. Davis survived the war many years. Twice he made a journey from his home at Beauvoir, Mississippi, through the States of Mississippi, Alabama and Georgia and received a perfect ovation all along the way. He died in the city of New Orleans December 6th, 1889, at the advanced age of eighty-one, sincerely mourned by the people whom he had once served so faithfully.

33. After the surrender at Appomattox General Lee went back to Richmond, riding on his iron-gray "Traveler," who had borne him through all the years of the war. All along the road to Richmond he received every evidence of admiration and respect from friends and former foes. On reaching Richmond he was riding toward his home in Franklin street when he was recognized, and the people rushed out from all directions to meet him, cheering and waving hats and handkerchiefs. Simply raising his hat in reply to these greetings, Lee hurried to his home. Secretary Stanton was determined to have Lee arrested, but General Grant opposed it so earnestly that the Government of the United States was saved the disgrace of violating the protection promised at Appomattox. Lee became president of Washington College at Lexington, Virginia, where he died on October 12th, 1870, beloved and mourned by the whole South and honored by the whole world. The college over which he presided has since his death been known as the Washington-Lee University.

---

[1] Abridged from an account by Rev. J. Wm. Jones, in his "Davis Memorial Volume."

WASHINGTON AND LEE UNIVERSITY.

He was sixty-three years old at the time of his death.

NOTE ON THE UNION AND CONFEDERATE ARMIES.—The total enlistments in the Union army and navy were 2,773,304. Of these 178,975 were colored troops. Of the white troops 282,619 were from the slave States, and 54,000 of that number were from the eleven seceding States. A liberal allowance for reinlistments would make the total number brought into the field on the Union side amount to 2,400,000. The number of deaths from all causes was 360,222.

The total number of enlistments in the Confederate army from first to last was 700,000. The naval force did not exceed 30,000. Considering that the militia embraced only those who were exempt from service in the army 100,000 would be an exceedingly liberal estimate for them. So the total number of men in the armies of the Confederacy, including militia and seamen, did not exceed 830,000. At the close of the war the North had in the field 1,000,000 men and the South 170,000. If, as claimed by Northern writers, the deaths in the Southern armies numbered 300,000, the war cost the lives of 660,000 men. It has been estimated that the loss on both sides, including those permanently disabled, amounted to more than 1,000,000 men.

CHAPTER II.

RECONSTRUCTION—THE UNION RESTORED—CLOSING RE-
MARKS.

ANDREW JOHNSON, the new President of the United States, on the 29th of May, 1865, issued a **Proclamation of Amnesty** to the great majority of those who had fought for the Confederate States in the late war. He was at first inclined to be very severe towards the Southern leaders, and excluded from the benefits of this amnesty all the higher civil and diplomatic officers and agents, and all officers of the Confederate service above the rank of colonel in the army and lieutenant in the navy, and all who had been educated at the United States military and naval academies. But Mr. Johnson's sentiments afterwards changed very much, and his feelings toward the Southern leaders were greatly softened. On the 7th of September, 1867, he reduced the exceptions to all Confederate officers above the rank of brigadier-general in the army and captain in the navy. Finally, on Christmas day, 1868, he issued another proclamation extending unconditional pardon, without the formality of any oath and without exception, to all who had in any way sided with the Confederacy during the war.

2. Upon the close of the war, the most important question was the terms on which the seceded States should be restored to their places in the Union. The President appointed provisional governors in all the States that had seceded, except Tennessee, which had been restored to the Union just before the close of the

ANDREW JOHNSON.

war. Those States were required to hold conventions which should form new State Constitutions, repeal their ordinances of secession, and ratify a **Thirteenth Amendment** to the Constitution of the United States providing for the complete abolition of slavery.[1] The President assured them that when this was done they should be at once restored to all their original rights in the Union. The seceded States complied with the required terms and elected senators and representatives to Congress.

3. But when Congress met in December, 1865, the Republican majority refused to admit the Southern members unless their States would ratify a **Fourteenth Amendment**, making citizens of the negroes and fixing political disabilities on every one who had ever held a State or a Federal office and afterwards sided with the Confederates. When the seceded States refused to ratify the fourteenth amendment the Republican majority in Congress passed an act declaring the States of Virginia, North Carolina, South Carolina, Georgia, Florida, Alabama, Mississippi, Arkansas, Louisiana and Texas to be in a state of rebellion. This act overturned the existing governments of these States and divided them into five military districts, each governed by an officer of the Federal army. It also provided for the calling of new conventions in all these States, disfranchised thousands of the whites and gave the right to vote to all male negroes above twenty-one years of age. The President vetoed these measures

[1] Before the close of the war, the Southern people had begun to look upon slavery as doomed, no matter which way the war might end. Cleburne, and afterwards Lee, Beauregard and others recommended the enlisting of negroes, and the giving of freedom to all who enlisted. Such enlistment had actually begun when the war ended.

as contrary to the Constitution, and he was right. If the seceded States were in the Union they had as much right to reject as to approve an amendment, and their rejection of it did not make them rebels. Every Southerner ought to be proud of the fact that the Southern people had the manhood to refuse to purchase their former privileges in the Union by placing a stigma on the men whom they had chosen to lead them in their struggle for what they deemed the right, and that the ratification of the fourteenth and fifteenth amendments to the Constitution was secured by stifling the voice of the white people of the South. Congress passed its favorite measure over the President's veto.

4. The rescue at this time of the **Great Seal of Georgia** from the hands of the usurper deserves to rank with the hiding of the charter of Connecticut in the old colonial days. When the Governor of the State, Charles J. Jenkins, was deposed and an officer of the United States army appointed in his place, he carried off the great seal of the State and refused to give it up or tell where he had placed it until a governor should be elected by the free voice of the people. This occurred in 1872, when James M. Smith was elected governor. Then Mr. Jenkins restored the seal, and received the thanks of the legislature for his fidelity to the honor of Georgia.

5. Under the reconstruction measures of Congress, elections were held for conventions in all the seceded States affected by the law. In some of these States the officers in charge of the election continued it for three days, so that the negroes might vote "early and often." By January 24th, 1868, the Republican plan had been

GENERAL LEE TAKING LEAVE OF HIS SOLDIERS.

carried out in Arkansas, Alabama, Florida, Louisiana, North Carolina, South Carolina, and Georgia, which States were then re-admitted to the Union. But Georgia's representatives were soon after excluded because the legislature of that State had refused to let negroes sit in that body. It was declared that Georgia should not be re-admitted until it should ratify the fifteenth amendment. In order to insure its ratification by Georgia, a man named Harris was appointed to purge the legislature until it had the kind of majority that was desired.

6. **The Fifteenth Amendment** declares that the right of citizens of the United States to vote shall not be denied or abridged by the United States or by any State on account of race, color, or previous condition of servitude. This amendment was carried through in the same manner as the fourteenth. In 1870, after the fifteenth amendment had been ratified, Virginia, Mississippi and Texas were re-admitted, and, last of all, Georgia was a second time re-admitted. Grant was President when reconstruction was thus completed.

7. The last year of Johnson's term an effort was made to remove him from office because he was too much in the way of the Republican majority in Congress. The pretext for this was his quarrel with Stanton, the Secretary of War. Mr. Johnson attempted to dismiss Mr. Stanton from his office. For this he was impeached by the House of Representatives on the 22d of February, 1868. He was tried by the Senate, Chief-Justice Chase presiding. The President was acquitted by one vote (May 26th).

8. **Test Oaths, Confiscation Laws, and Civil-Rights Bill.—** Among other laws unfriendly to the South, Congress

passed an act forbidding lawyers to practice in courts unless they would take an oath that they had never in any way aided the Confederacy. This practically excluded every southern lawyer from practice, since there was not one in a hundred of them who could truthfully take any such oath. Augustus H. Garland, of Arkansas, who was afterwards Attorney-General of the United States, contested this law in every court up to the Supreme Court of the United States. Most of the judges of this court were Republican and hence of the same party with the majority in Congress; but the court solemnly declared the law to be unconstitutional. The Supreme Court also declared that the laws passed by Congress confiscating the property of Confederates were contrary to the Constitution. Congress also passed a civil-rights bill, one of the purposes of which was to compel hotels to receive negro guests just as they did whites. The Supreme Court also decided this law to be contrary to the Constitution. Thus in this dark hour, when partisan hatred seemed about to make total wreck of individual as well as State rights, the Supreme Court stood as the bulwark of liberty, and earned the lasting gratitude of every lover of freedom.

9. **The Carpet-bag Governments.**—The State governments that had been established in the South under the reconstruction measures were notoriously corrupt. They had been organized by a few whites and all the negroes under the lead of Northern adventurers, whom the Southern people called carpet-baggers. The few Southern white men who joined in with the carpet-baggers were called "scalawags." In some of the States there were returning boards, who had power to revise election returns and throw out such votes as

LAST MEETING OF THE CONFEDERATE CABINET.

they might decide to be illegal.   In 1873, after Grant's election to a second term, the Louisiana returning board seated as governor a man who had not been elected.   The Southern white people at last resolved to put forth every effort to overthrow the so-called carpet-bag governments.

10. **Congressional Elections of 1874.**—The Democratic party favored the wishes of the white people of the South.   The Republicans backed up the carpet-bag governments.   On this issue mainly the two parties went before the country in the congressional elections of 1874, and the result was an overwhelming Democratic triumph.

11. **Trouble in Louisiana.**—Elections were also held in Louisiana for members of the State legislature, and the returning board gave certificates to men who had not been elected.   The elected men took possession of the State-house, but were driven out by United States troops.   But the Democrats of Louisiana were determined to contend for their rights, and serious trouble was feared.   The time had not yet come for the new Democratic Congress to assemble, and the Republican Congress was in session.   This body appointed a committee of investigation, headed by W. A. Wheeler of New York, afterwards Vice-President of the United States.   The committee condemned the outrage, and the elected Democrats were allowed to take their seats. A similar thing occurred in Arkansas, and with a like result.

12. **Presidential Election of 1876.**—When the time came to elect a successor to General Grant the Republicans nominated Rutherford B. Hayes of Ohio for President and William A. Wheeler of New York for Vice-Pres-

ident. The candidates of the Democrats were Samuel J. Tilden of New York for President and Thomas A. Hendricks of Indiana for Vice-President. The Democrats carried enough States to give them a good majority of the electoral vote. But the returning boards of Louisiana and Florida, which were made up of Republicans acting under the authority of the carpet-bag governments, threw out thousands of Dem-

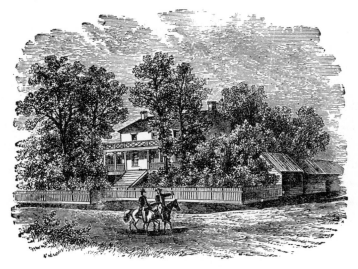

M'LEAN'S HOUSE, APPOMATTOX, C. H., WHERE LEE AND GRANT ARRANGED THE TERMS OF SURRENDER.

ocratic votes in each of those States, so as to give their electoral vote to Hayes and Wheeler. South Carolina also was in doubt, and one of the electors of Oregon was claimed by the Democrats.

13. There was intense excitement throughout the country. The Republicans contended that it was the duty of the President of the Senate to decide the dispute about the electoral vote in the contested States. The Democrats insisted that the dispute should be

settled under the joint rule controlling both houses. By a compromise between the House and Senate the matter was referred to an Electoral Commission consisting of five from each house and five judges of the Supreme Court. On this commission the Republicans had one majority, and on the plea that they could not go behind the official returns from a State the eight Republicans voted to give all the disputed votes to Hayes and Wheeler, which would elect them by one majority. The Democrats considered the decision unjust, but submitted to it for the sake of peace. There were some Republicans who agreed with the Democrats in their opinion about the decision of the " eight-by-seven commission."

14. **Troops at the State-Houses.**—In Louisiana and South Carolina the Republicans tried to hold on to the State governments, although everybody knew that the Democratic candidates had been elected. United States troops were stationed at the capitals of these two States, who forcibly prevented the entrance of Democratic members of the legislature and upheld the usurping governors. Such was the state of affairs at the close of Grant's administration.

15. **Removal of the Troops.**—One of the first acts of Mr. Hayes, the new President, was the removal of the United States troops from the capitals of Louisiana and South Carolina.[1] Immediately the Democratic State governments were peaceably established, and the reign of the carpet-bagger was ended. At once there began to prevail a better feeling between the North and the South.

---

[1] South Carolina owed her deliverance in a great measure to the untiring efforts and undaunted courage of the gallant Wade Hampton, to whom she owes a debt of gratitude that can never be paid.

Some of the Republicans were displeased at what Mr. Hayes had done, but the great mass of the people of both political parties approved it.   They were tired of strife, and longed for peace and for the Union of their fathers—not a Union one part of which was pinned to the other by bayonets, but a Union of co-equal States.

16. **A new era of good will** had begun.   Since that time so unmistakable has been the voice of the American people against any more legislation unfriendly to the South, that even in times when the Republican party has had full control again very little

HOUSE IN WHICH JOHNSTON AND SHERMAN MET.

such legislation has been attempted.   When it has been attempted, there have been found conservative Repubiicans who helped the Democrats to defeat it, and on the first opportunity the people have through the ballot-box rebuked even the attempt.   The people have twice elected a Democratic President.   Prominent ex-Confederates have held positions in the President's Cabinet and have been made judges of the Supreme Court.   There have been friendly re-unions of Union and Confederate veterans on the old battle-fields of the war.   One of the most notable of these was on the battle-field of Gettysburg, where the survivors of Pickett's division again moved up the slope of Cemetery Hill, and were met by some of their former foes with hearty clasp of the hand and cordial greetings.

17. **The Sentiment of the South.**—In 1861 the majority of the Southern people believed that there was no security for the South in the Union. Therefore they desired peaceable separation. This was not allowed, but coercion was the policy adopted by the Government. This the South resisted with all its power. The Confederate soldier never thought that he was fighting to destroy the Government of the United States. He fought only for home and loved ones and the liberty of the South. No truer patriots ever mustered for battle than those who marched under the Starry Cross of the Confederacy. When the sun of the Confederacy went down at Appomattox they who had followed Lee in war continued to follow him in peace. They tried to imitate their peerless leader, as he followed Christ, in casting from him every vindictive sentiment. With no feeling of shame, but with a consciousness of duty well performed in their brave defense of what they deemed the right, they accepted in good faith the results of the war, abandoned secession, and without mental reservation agreed to the abolition of slavery. In the same good faith they renewed their allegiance to the Union, and are ready to defend it against any and all foes. They build monuments to their hero dead and tell of their valorous deeds to their children's children. They cherish as a sweet memory the Southern Cross, under whose folds their half-starved, ragged veterans performed such mighty deeds of valor, but at the **same time** they hail the Stars and Stripes as

DISTRIBUTING TRACTS IN THE TRENCHES.

the banner under which the great Southern General Washington led their fathers to victory and independence, and look upon it as the symbol of sovereign, co-equal States joined together in an indestructible Union.

18. The lesson of the war and of events since its close is that there is a stronger defense for the rights of the States in one majority in either house of Congress or in the Supreme Court of the United States than in hundreds of thousands of armed warriors, and that the liberties of States and individuals are best secured in the Union and under the broad ægis of the Constitution. "God bless our whole country and make ours a union of hearts and of hands" is the prayer of every true patriot North and South.

NOTE.—The wonderful revivals of religion that occurred in the Southern camps is a subject worthy of an entire volume. The great work that was done among the officers and soldiers of the Army of Northern Virginia has been well told in that excellent work of Rev. J. William Jones entitled "Christ in the Camp." There was throughout the Southern army a strong religious sentiment, and many of the officers and men were deeply pious. It was the firm belief in the overruling providence of God, who doeth all things well, that prepared Lee and other prominent leaders to accept the result as an expression of the Divine will, and to set an example of quiet submission to the inevitable, which was followed by those who had been in the habit of looking to them for counsel and direction. Firmly believing that God gave to them all the brilliant victories that shed such lustre on their arms, they also believed that God in his wisdom had given to them final defeat. It is this feeling that has caused the Southern people, without any consciousness of guilt or shame, to accept in perfect good faith the result of the war and the changed order of things, and at the same time to use every constitutional method to maintain the rights of their States as co-equal members of the Union.

NOTES.

The fidelity of the great mass of the slave population during the war has already been spoken of. Perhaps it may be well to give two incidents of individual devotion and heroism on the part of slaves—one of which came under the writer's own observation, while the other is related in General Dick Taylor's "Destruction and Reconstruction."

At the battle of Greenbrier River (October 3, 1861,) Dr. Frank Rudersill, whose heroic spirit had impelled him to go to the field notwithstanding a very painful physical disability, was acting as assistant surgeon of the First Georgia Regiment. While busily employed with the wounded, he remembered that a case of surgical instruments, which he very much needed, was in a house exposed to the hottest fire of the Union artillery. A young colored man, his slave, volunteered to go for the case of instruments, and at the imminent peril of his life brought it to his master.

The other incident is best told in General Taylor's own words: "I used to fancy that there was a mute sympathy between General Jackson and Tom, as they sat silent by a camp fire, the latter respectfully withdrawn; and an incident here at Strasburg cemented this friendship. When my command was called into action, I left Tom on a hill where all was quiet. Thereafter, from a change in the enemy's dispositions, the place became rather hot, and Jackson passing by advised Tom to move; but he replied, if the General pleased, his master told him to stay there and would know where to find him, and he did not believe shells would trouble him. Two or three nights later Jackson was at my fire when Tom came to give me some coffee; whereupon Jackson rose and gravely shook him by the hand, and then told me the above."

General Taylor adds: "After the war was closed, Tom returned with me to New Orleans, found his wife and children all right, and is now prosperous."

Reunions of the "Blue and Gray" on the old battle-fields of the war have of late years been quite frequent. In August, 1890, the Congress of the United States passed a bill, which was approved by the President, to establish a National Military Park on the battle-field of Chickamauga. The commission appointed to superintend this work consists of one member from the Union volunteer army, one from the regular army, and one from the Confederate army. In the battle of Chickamauga four brigade commanders on each side were either killed or mortally wounded. The names of the four on the Southern side were Helm of Kentucky, Peyton Colquitt of Georgia, Deshler of Arkansas, and Preston Smith of Tennessee; the four on the Northern side were King, Baldwin, Hegg, and Lyttle, the latter being the Cincinnati poet. The government has erected monuments to these officers on the spot where each one fell, and without making any distinction between those who fell on the Northern or on the Southern side. May this be a token of the brotherly love that shall henceforth prevail between the once severed sections of our now united country. Let "peace on earth and good will toward man" be the principle that shall control the councils of the American people, and may "wisdom, justice, and moderation" guide our now peaceful States in their conduct toward each other and toward all the nations of the earth.

INDEX.

A.

Abolitionists, 69, 70, 71-74, 97, 101.
Abolition societies, 69.
Abraham, Plains of, 24.
Acknowledgment of American Independence, 35.
Adams, Charles Francis, 84.
Adams, John, President United States, 44, 50.
Adams, John, Confederate brigadier general, 378.
Adams, John Quincy, President United States, 61, 62.
Adams, Samuel, a patriot of the Revolution, 44.
African Slave Trade, 21, 104.
Aiken, S. C., 403.
Alabama, Confederate cruiser, 148, 229, 388, 389.
Alabama, State, 100.
Albemarle, Confederate ram, 300, 388.
Alexander, E. P., Confederate brigadier general, 215.
Alexandria, La., 297.
Alexandria, Va., 117.
Alien Act, 51, 52.
Allatoona, Ga., 375.
Alleghanies, 117.
Alleghany Summit, 140.
Allen, J. V. H., Confederate major, 348.
Amelia Courthouse, 412.
Amendments to the Constitution, 39, 41, 45, 428-431.
America, 19.
American Party, 86, 87, 91.
American Colonization Society, 70.
American (Know-Nothing) Party, 86, 87, 91.
Amnesty Proclamation, 426.
Anderson, Archer, Confederate colonel, quoted, 270.
Anderson, Confederate brigadier general in West Virginia, 137.
Anderson, George T., Confederate brigadier general, 310.
Anderson, Richard H., Confederate lieutenant general, 195, 198, 238, 240, 242, 252, 311, 316.
Anderson, Robert, Union major at Fort Sumter, 109.
Andersonville, Ga., 355.
Annapolis, Md., 72.
Annexation of Texas, 74-80.
Antietam Creek, Md., 198, 199.
Anti-Federalists, 49.
Appomattox Courthouse Va., 412-417.
Appomattox River, 322.
Aquia Creek, Va., 124, 188.
Archer, James G., Confederate brigadier general, 214, 249.
Archer, commander of militia at Petersburg, 330.
Arkansas Post, Ark., 229, 294.
Arkansas, ram, 168.
Arkansas, 110.

Armistead, Lewis A., Confederate brigadier general, 254.
Arms North and South, 112, 151.
Arnold, Benedict, American general in Revolution, 33.
Articles of Confederation, 35, 37, 67.
Ashby, Turner, Confederate brigadier general of cavalry, 176, 178, 180.
Atchafalaya, La., 298.
Atherton Resolutions, 72.
Atlanta, Ga., 302, 345-354, 362, 373, 374, 385.
Augusta, Ga., 22, 31, 403.
Averill, William W., Union general of cavalry, 236, 327, 338.
Averysboro', N. C., 405.

B.

Bailey, Joseph, Union colonel, 297.
Baird, Absalom, Union general, 268.
Baker, E. D., Union colonel, 136.
Baker's Creek, Miss., 261.
Baldwin, Philemon P., Union colonel, commanding brigade, 441.
Ball's Bluff, Va., 136.
Baltimore, Md., 117.
Baltimore and Ohio Railroad, 118, 151, 334, 338, 366, 372.
Banks, Nathaniel P., Union major general, 175, 178, 179, 180, 186, 188, 263, 266, 296-298.
Bankum, ——, Confederate colonel, 345.
Barksdale, William, Confederate brigadier general, 213, 214, 238, 250.
Barnes, ——, Union surgeon general, 399.
Barrett, ——, Union colonel, 420.
Barton, Wm. B., Union colonel, 292.
Bartow, Francis S., Confederate colonel, acting brigadier, 128-131.
Bate, William B., Confederate major general, 273, 343, 344, 345, 363, 405.
Bath, W. Va., 153.
Battery Gregg, S. C., 280, 282.
Battery Wagner, S. C., 278, 280, 282.
Battle, Cullen A., Confederate colonel, 330.
Beatty, Samuel, Union brigadier general, 220.
Beauregard, P. G. T., Confederate general, 109, 124, 126-134, 158-166, 229-235, 247, 264, 278, 282, 322-330, 331, 377, 387, 403, 417.
Beaver Dam Creek, Va., 182.
Bee, Barnard E., Confederate brigadier general, 126, 128-131.
Bell, John, 91.
Belmont, Mo., 146.
Benning, Henry L., Confederate brigadier general, 269, 309.
Bentonville, N. C., 405, 406.
Bermuda Hundred, 331, 332.
Beverly, W Va., 118-12., 406.
Big Bethel, Va., 117.
Big Black, Miss, 261.
Blackburn's Ford, Va., 126.
Blair, Francis P., Union major general 141, 347.

Blockade Runners, 147, 170, 232.
Bloody Angle, Va., 314-316.
Bonaparte, Napoleon, 53.
Bonaud, ———, Confederate officer, 291.
Boonsboro, Md., 197.
Boonville, Mo., 143.
Booth, John Wilkes, 419, 420.
Booth, ———, Union major, 294,
Boston, Mass., 26, 28.
Bowen, John S., Confederate brigadier general, 261.
Bradford, Mary, 382.
Bradford, ———, Union major, 294
Bragg, Braxton, Confederate general, 159, 167, 203-210, 218-221, 261, 264, 265-270, 271-275, 276, 405.
Brandywine, Pa., 30.
Brandy Station, Va., 246.
Brannan, John M., Union brigadier general, 268.
Brashear City, La., 264.
Breckinridge, John C., Confederate major general, 87, 90, 91, 159, 162, 209, 219, 268, 269, 272, 324, 325, 327-329, 335.
Brice's Cross-Roads, Miss., 354.
Bridgeport, Tenn., 271.
Brier Creek, 31.
Brooks, John M., Confederate naval officer, 171.
Brown, Isaac N., Confederate captain, Arkansas, 168.
Brown, John, 89, 90.
Brown, John C., Confederate brigadier general, 379, 380.
Brown, J. Thompson, Confederate colonel, 239.
Buchanan, Franklin, Confederate admiral, 361, 362.
Buchanan, James, President United States, 87.
Buckner, Simon B., Confederate major general, 157, 158, 268.
Buell, Don Carlos, Union major general, 154, 158, 161-166, 203-210, 302.
Buford, John, Union major general of cavalry, 248, 256.
Bull Run, 124-133, 171, 186-194.
Bummers, 386.
Bunker Hill, Mass., 28.
Bunker's Hill, Va., 202.
Burnside, Ambrose E., Union major general, 199, 200, 202, 213-216, 272, 274, 316, 331, 339.
Butler, Benjamin F., Union major general, 117, 125, 146, 168, 305, 322, 323-332, 389-395, 396.
Butler, M. C., Confederate major general of cavalry, 329, 405.

C.

Cabot, George, 54.
Cabot, John, 19.
Calhoun, John C., American statesman, 62, 71, 87, 88.
California, 82.
Camden, S. C., 32.
Campbell, John A., 107, 400.
Campbell, American officer in the Revolution, 32.
Campbell Station, Tenn., 272.
Camp Jackson, Mo., 142.
Cantey, James C., Confederate brigadier general, 343.
Carlisle, Pa., 247, 338.
Carnifax Ferry, Va., 139.
Carpet-bag governments, 432.

Carpet-baggers, 432.
Carpet-bag Troubles, 434.
Carrick's Ford, W. Va., 122, 123.
Carthage, Mo., 144.
Cassville, Ga., 344.
Casey, Silas, Union major general, 174.
Cassville, Ga., 344.
Catharine Furnace, Va., 239.
Cedar Creek, Va., 369-372.
Cedar Mountain, Va., 188, 189.
Cedar Run, Va., 188, 189-191.
Centreville, Va., 192, 284.
Chaffin's Bluff, Va., 332.
Chalmer's, James R., Confederate brigadier general, 293.
Chambersburg, Pa., 202, 247, 338.
Champion Hill, Miss., 261, 265.
Champlain, Lake, 57.
Chancellorsville, Va., 236-244.
Chantilly, Va., 193.
Charleston, S. C., 31, 109, 229, 235, 278, 282, 389, 404.
Charleston and Savannah Railroad, 230, 280.
Charlottesville, Va., 329.
Chase, Salmon P., Chief Justice United States, 422, 431.
Chatham Artillery of Savannah, 291.
Chattahoochee River, Ga., 364, 375.
Chattanooga, Tenn., 203, 204, 206, 266, 270-275, 280, 374.
Cheatham, Benj. F., Confederate major general, 207, 219, 268, 274, 348, 352, 353, 383, 405.
Cheat Mountain, W. Va., 121, 136-138.
Cheat River, W. Va., 121.
Chesapeake and Ohio Canal, 151, 334, 338, 366.
Chicago Democratic Convention of 1864, 359.
Chickahominy River, Va., 181, 182.
Chickamauga, Ga., 265, 270, 271-275, 283.
Chickasaw Bayou, Miss., 218.
Churchill, T. J., Confederate major general, 205, 229.
Cincinnati, O., 205.
City Point, Va., 391.
Civil Rights Bill, 431, 432.
Clarke, Elijah, American Colonel in Revolution, 32, 33.
Clarke, George Rogers, American general in Revolution, 30, 35, 36, 67.
Clarkesville, Tenn., 204.
Clay, Henry, American statesman, 62, 64, 70, 72, 79, 82, 87, 89.
Clayton, H. D., Confederate major general, 382.
Cleburne, Patrick, Confederate major general, 205, 207, 219, 268, 269, 274, 343, 348, 379, 380.
Clingman, Thomas L., Confederate brigadier general, 280, 331.
Clinton, Sir Henry, British general in Revolution, 30.
Clinton, George, 55.
Cobb, Howell, Confederate major general, 197, 354.
Cobb, Thomas R. R., Confederate brigadier general, 214, 215.
Coburn, ———, Union colonel, 266.
Cockrell, Francis M., Confederate brigadier general, 348, 378, 380.
Cold Harbor, Va., 182-184, 186, 319-321.
Colquitt, Alfred H., Confederate brigadier general, 280, 291-292, 322, 331.
Colquitt, Peyton, Confederate brigadier general, killed at Chickamauga, 441.
Colston, R. E., Confederate brigadier general, 239.

Columbia, S. C., 403, 404.
Columbia, Tenn., 382.
Columbus, Ga., 420.
Columbus, Ohio, 277.
Columbus, Chistopher, 19.
Comparative strength of the combatants in the civil war, 112.
Compromise, Missouri, 68, 69, 82.
Compromise of 1850, 82–84.
Concord, Mass., 28.
Confederate Commissioners. 106.
Confederate States, 104
Confiscation Laws, 431 432.
Connecti ut, 36.
Conscription Law, 170.
Constitution of Confederate States, 104.
Constitution of United States, 35–46, 67.
Controversey between Georgia and Federal Government about Indian lands, 60–61.
Cooke, J. W., Confederate captain, 201.
Cooke, Captain, of Albemarle, 300.
Corinth, Miss., 158, 166, 167, 203, 210.
Cornwallis, Lord, British general in Revolution, 34.
Corse, John M., Union major general, 375.
Couch, Darius N., Union major general, 238.
Covington, Ky., 205.
Cowpens, S. C., 32.
Cox, Jacob D., Union major general, 130–140, 379, 405.
Crampton's Gap, Md. 197–200.
Crater, Battle of, 339, 340, 341.
Crawford, Martin J., 107.
Crittenden, John J., statesman, 99.
Crittenden, T. L., Union major general, 207, 268.
Crook, George, Union major general, 305, 324, 327, 338, 368, 369, 407.
Cross Keys. Va., 180.
Cross Lanes, W. Va., 139.
Crumley, William, daring feat at Fredericksburg, 216.
Cumberland Gap, Tenn., 203, 205, 206, 210, 271.
Cumberland River, 154, 277.
Curtiss, Samuel R., Union major general, 165, 203.
Cushing, W. B., Union naval lieutenant, 388.
Custer, George A., Union major general, 301, 373, 413.
Cynthiana, Ky., 204.

D.

Dabney's Mill, Va., 407.
Dahlgren, John A., Union admiral, 278, 282. 291.
Dahlgren, Ulric, Union colonel of cavalry, 300, 301.
Dallas, Ga., 345, 375.
Dallas, George M., 79.
Dalton, Ga., 275, 342, 363, 375, 383.
Daniel, Junius, Confederate brigadier general, 318.
Davis, Jefferson, Confederate President. 82, 89, 99, 100, 104, 110, 134, 187, 247, 261, 266, 301, 373 377, 397, 399, 403, 408, 411, 417, 422, 423.
Davis, Jeff. C., Union major general, 219, 268, 269.
Davis, Joseph R., Confederate brigadier general, 310.
Dawes, E. C., Union major, quoted, 270.
Dawson, ——, Confederate officer, 138.

Dayton, William L., 86.
Dearing, James C., Confederate cavalry officer, 330.
Declaration of Independence, 28–35.
Delaware, 32-110.
Democratic Party, 49, 58, 78, 84, 86, 434.
Democrais. 58, 78, 84, 86.
Deshler, James, Confederate brigadier general. 441
Desire, slave ship, 21.
D'Wolf, James, 68—foot note.
Didwiddie Courthouse, Va., 407, 410.
District of Columbia. 71, 72.
Dodge, Gouverneur M., Union general, 347.
Doles, George, Confederate brigadier general, 242, 320.
Donelson, Andrew J., 87.
Douglas, Henry Kyd, Confederate colonel, 202.
Douglas, Stephen A., 84-90, 99.
Dowling, R. W., Confederate lieutenant of artillery, 283.
Dranesville, Va., 136.
Drayton, Percival, Union naval captain, 361.
Drewry's Bluff. Va., 174, 322, 323.
Dug Gap., Ga., 343.
Du Pont, Samuel F., Union commodore, 146, 233, 235, 278.
Durham's Station, N. C., 419–420.
Dutch, 21.

E.

Early, Jubal A., Confederate lieutenant general. 131, 199, 214, 238, 242, 246, 247, 249, 312, 334-337, 338, 339, 340, 366-373, 406, 410.
Eatonton, Ga., 354.
Eckols, John E., Confederate brigadier general, 325.
Education, 22.
Election of 1860, 90-91.
Electoral Commission, 435–437.
Elkhorn, Ark., 165.
Ellet, Charles, Union colonel. 168.
Elliott, Gilbert, builder of Albemarle, 300.
Elliott, Stephen, Confederate major, 280, 282.
Ellsworth, E. Elmer, Union colonel. 117—foot note.
Ely's Ford, Va., 305.
Elzey, Arnold, Confederate major general, 131.
Emancipation Proclamation, 225, 227.
Emancipator published at Jonesboro, Tenn., 69.
Embargo Act, 55.
Emigrant Aid Societies, 85.
Emory, William H., Union major general, 369.
England, 19, 24, 55.
Erie, Lake, 57.
Eshleman, B. F., Confederate major of artillery, 256.
Etowah River, Ga., 344, 363.
Eutaw Springs, S. C., 33.
Evans, Clement A., Confederate major general, 314, 335, 369, 407, 408, 413, 414.
Evans, Nathan G., Confederate brigadier general, 128, 134, 199.
Everett, Edward, 91.
Ewell, Richard S., Confederate lieutenant general, 176, 179, 180, 188, 244, 246, 247, 249, 251, 252, 306, 308, 310, 311, 412.
Ezra Church, Ga., 353.

F.

Fairfax, Confederate major on Longstreet's Staff, 201.
Fairfax Courthouse. 136.
Fair Oaks, Va., 174.
Falling Waters. Md., 257.
Farragut, David G., Union admiral, 167. 168, 360, 362.
Featherstone. William S., Confederate brigadier general, 348
Federal Government, 37, 60, 72.
Federalists, 49, 58.
Ferrero, Edward, Union major general, 339.
Field, Charles W., Confederate major general, 309, 312, 332.
Fillmore, Millard, 87.
Finegan, Joseph, Confederate brigadier general, 291, 334.
Finley. ——, Confederate brigadier general, 363.
Fisher, C. F., Confederate colonel, 130.
Fisher's Hill, Va., 366, 368, 372.
Five Forks, Va., 410.
Fleetwood, Va., 246.
Florence, Ala., 375.
Florida, Confederate cruiser, 389.
Florida State, 24, 76, 100, 289–293; returning board, 435.
Flournoy, Thomas S. Confederate colonel, 178.
Floyd, John B., Confederate brigadier general, 136, 138, 139, 154–157.
Foote, Andrew C., Union commodore, 154.
Forrest, Nathan B., Confederate lieutenant general, 157, 158, 204. 209, 218, 266, 268, 270, 293, 294, 354, 355, 357, 363. 377, 382, 383.
Forsyth, John, of Ala., 107.
Forsyth, Ga., 385.
Fort Alexander, Va., 411.
Fort Darling, Va., 174.
Fort Donelson Tenn.. 154–158.
Fort Fisher, N. C., 389–400,
Fort Gregg, Va., 411.
Fort Grigsby, Texas, 283.
Fort Henry, Tenn.. 154.
Fort Jackson, La., 167–168.
Fort Macon, N. C., 153.
Fort McAllister, Ga., 235, 387.
Fort Pickens, Fla., 106, 107.
Fort Pillow, Tenn., 293, 294.
Fort Pulaski, Ga., 153.
Fort St. Philip, La., 167, 168.
Fort Steadman, Va., 408–410.
Fort Stevens, near Washington, 335.
Fort Sumter, S. C.. 106, 107–110, 233–235, 280, 282.
Fort Warren, in Boston Harbor. 422.
Fortress Monroe, Va., 117, 125, 171, 422.
France, 24, 25, 55. 76.
Frankfort, Ky., 206.
Franklin, Va., 178.
Franklin, Tenn., 378, 380.
Franklin, William B., Union major general, 192, 197, 199, 214, 282, 283, 297.
Franklin, Benjamin, American statesman, 67.
Frazer's Farm, Va., 184.
Frederick, Md., 195. 335.
Fredericksburg, Va., 211, 237–242.
Free-Soil Party, 84, 97.
Freelinghuysen, Theodore, 79.
Fremont, John C., Union major general, 86, 145, 175, 178, 179, 180, 181, 186.
French, 24.
French and Indian War, 24, 25.

G.

French, Samuel G., Confederate major general, 348, 375.
Front Royal, Va., 178.
Frost, D. M., Confederate brigadier general, 141 142.
Fugitive Slave Law, 82, 89.
Fulton, Robert A., Union colonel, quoted, 348.

G.

Gadsden, Ala., 375.
Gaines's Mill. Va., 182. 184–186.
Galveston, Texas, 228, 229, 283.
Gardner, Frank, Confederate major general, 263.
Garland, Augustus H., 432.
Garnett, Richard B., Confederate brigadier general, 254.
Garnett, Robert S., Confederate brigadier general, 118–122.
Garrison, William Lloyd, 70, 71.
Gates, Horatio, American general in Revolution, 32.
Geary, John W., Union major general, 344.
Genesis Point, Ga , 235.
Georgia, 19, 22, 24, 31, 32, 60, 61, 100, 342.
Georgia, Great Seal of, 429.
Germantown, Pa., 30.
Germanna Ford, Va., 305.
Gettysburg Pa.. 244-259, 265.
Gettysburg re-union, 437–438.
Getty, George W., Union major-general, 308.
Gibbon, John, Union major-general, 411.
Gillmore, Q. A., Union major-general, 278-282, 291.
Girardeau, J. L., of Charleston, S. C., 115.
Gist, S. R , Confederate brigadier-general, 380.
Globe Tavern, Va., 389.
Godwin, A. C., Confederate brigadier-general, 367.
Gordon, G. W., Confederate brigadier-general, 365, 380.
Gordon, John B., Confederate lieutenant-general, 247, 310, 314, 316, 335, 369, 372, 407, 408 410. 412–414.
Gordonsville, Va. 188, 239, 301, 306, 329.
Govan. Daniel C., Confederate brigadier-general, 345, 365.
Gracie, Archibald, Confederate brigadier-general, 332.
Grafton W. Va., 118.
Graham, Edward, Confederate captain artillery, 280.
Graham, Wm. A., 84.
Granbury, H. B., Confederate brigadier-general, 345, 365, 380.
Grand Gulf, Miss., 260, 261.
Granger, Gordon, Union major general, 269, 360, 362.
Grant, Ulysses S., Union general, 116, 154–158, 159–166, 204, 210, 213, 218, 245, 258, 259–265, 271, 274, 302–325, 339, 340, 389–391, 395, 400, 402, 407–417, 423, 431, 434.
Great Britain, 24–25, 55, 76.
Great Lakes, 30. 54.
Greely, Horace, quoted, 102, 108, 225–227, 250, 300, 357, 358, 416, 417; signs the bond of President Davis, 422.
Greensboro, N. C., 417.
Greenbrier River, Va., 137, 139.
Greene, Nathaniel, American general in Revolution, 32.
Gregg, John C., Confederate brigadier general, 260, 269, 309.

Gregg, Maxey, Confederate brigadier general, 214.
Grierson, B. H., Union major general, 260, 261, 354.
Griffin, Ga., 385.
Griffin, Charles. Union major general, 131.
Grisby, J. Warren, Confederate brigadier general, 343.
Griswoldville, Ga., 385, 386.
Guerard, J. M., Confederate captain, 291.
Guntown, Miss., 354, 355.

H.

Hagood, Johnson, Confederate brigadier general 280, 322, 331.
Hale, John P., 84.
Halleck. Henry W., Union major general, 164, 166, 188, 203, 204, 248, 312.
Hamilton, Alexander, American statesman, 37.
Hamilton's Crossing. Va., 214.
Hamlin. Hannibal. 91.
Hampton Roads, 173, 400.
Hampton, Wade, Confederate lieutenant-general, 130, 254, 319, 328, 329, 391, 403, 405, 436.
Hancock, Md., 153.
Hancock, Winfield S., Union major-general, 238, 308, 311, 312, 314, 317, 331, 389, 390.
Hardee, William J., Confederate lieutenant-general, 159, 206, 207, 219, 272, 273, 275, 345, 351, 353, 364, 365, 387, 404, 405, 406.
Harney, William S., Union major-general, 143.
Harper's Ferry, 90, 124, 179, 180, 195, 198, 199, 200, 366.
Harris, Nathaniel H., Confederate brigadier-general, 316.
Harrisburg. Pa., 247.
Harrison. George P, Confederate brigadier-general, 280, 291, 293.
Harrison, Wm. Henry, President United States, 57.
Harrisonburg, Va., 180, 373.
Harrison's Landing, Va., 184.
Harrodsburg, Ky., 208.
Hart, ——, a West Virginia Unionist, 119.
Hartford Convention, 57, 58.
Hartsfene. H. J., Confederate captain, 233.
Harvard University, 22.
Hatch, John P., Union brigadier-general, 387.
Hatcher's Run, Va., 407.
Hatteras Inlet, N. C., 146.
Hatteras, Union war ship, 229.
Hawes, Richard, Confederate Provisional Governor of Kentucky, 206.
Hawes's Shop, 319.
Hawley, Joseph R., Union major-general, 292.
Hayes, R. B., Union brigadier-general, also President United States, 327, 435, 436, 437.
Havs, Alexander, Union major-general, 308.
Hazen, William B., Union major-general, 387.
Hegg, ——, Union brigadier-general, 441.
Helena, Ark., 294.
Helm, Benjamin H., Confederate brigadier-general, 441.
Hendricks, Thomas A., Vice-President United States, 435.
Henry, Patrick, American statesman, 40.
Heth, Henry, Confederate major-general, 205, 208, 212, 242, 248, 249, 252.

Hicksford, Va., 407.
Hickman, Ky., 293.
Hill, Ambrose P., Confederate lieutenant-general, 181, 183, 184, 188, 198, 199, 200, 202, 240, 244, 247, 248, 252, 306, 308, 310, 314, 316, 334, 389, 390, 407, 411.
Hill, C. W., Union general, 122.
Hill, Daniel H., Confederate lieutenant-general, 117, 181, 183, 197, 198, 199, 268, 270, 272.
Hindman, Thomas C., Confederate major-general, 268, 343.
Hoke, Robert F., Confederate major-general, 298, 300, 322, 331, 405.
Holland, 34.
Holly Springs, Miss., 218.
Holmes, T. H., Confederate major-general, 124.
Holt, Joseph, judge advocate, 422.
Honey Hill, S. C., 387, 388.
Hood, John B., Confederate general, 183, 198, 250, 252, 268, 343, 347, 350-358, 362-366, 373-383.
Hooker, Joseph, Union major-general, 198, 199, 214, 236-244, 246, 248, 271, 272, 274, 343, 344, 347, 348.
Hotchkiss, Jed., Confederate captain, 369.
Houston, Samuel, Governor of Texas, 76.
Houston, Texas, 283.
Howard, John, 58.
Howard, Oliver O., Union major-general, 239, 240, 244, 249, 250, 271, 345, 349, 353, 385.
Huger, Benjamin, Confederate major-general, 125.
Huguenin, T. A., Confederate Captain, 280.
Humphrey, Benjamin G., Confederate brigadier-general, 269.
Humphreys, Andrew A., Union major general, 334, 407.
Hunt, Henry J., Union major general, 250, 254, 258.
Hunter, David, Union major general, 145, 278, 325, 327, 329, 338.
Hunter's Lynchburg Expedition, 327.
Hunter, R. M. T., Confederate Peace Commissioner, 400.
Hurlbut, Stephen A., Union major general, 161, 261, 292.

I.

Illinois, 30, 68.
Imboden, John D., Confederate brigadier general, 130, 179, 181, 256, 324, 325, 326, 327, 335.
Indiana, 68, 277.
Indians, Trouble with Creeks in Georgia, 60.
Ingraham, Duncan N., Confederate commodore, 230, 232.
Irrepressible Conflict, 99.
Island Number Ten, 165.
Inka, Miss., 210.
Iverson, Alfred, Confederate brigadier general, 354, 362.

J.

Jackson, Claiborne F., Confederate governor of Missouri, 141-146.
Jackson, Andrew, President United States, 57, 61-64.
Jackson, Miss., 99, 261, 265.
Jackson, Henry R., Confederate brigadier general, 122, 137, 138, 139,

Jackson, John K., Confederate brigadier general, 345.
Jackson, J. W., 117.
Jackson, Thomas Jonathan (Stonewall), Confederate lieutenant general, 115-126, 130, 141, 151, 152, 175-186, 188-193, 195-203, 211-216, 238-244.
Jackson, Mrs. Stonewall, quoted, 244.
Jackson, Tenn., 357, 377.
Jackson, William H., Confederate general of cavalry, 363.
Jacksonville, Fla., 291.
James Island, S. C., 230, 232, 278.
James River, Va., 174, 184, 185, 188, 190, 320, 322.
Jamestown, Va., 19.
Jefferson City, Mo., 143.
Jefferson, Thomas, President United States, 53-55.
Jenkins, Charles J., Governor of Georgia, 429.
Jenkins, Albert G., Confederate brigadier general, 254.
Jenkins, Micah, Confederate brigadier general, 246.
Jenkins, Ferry, Arkansas, 297.
John's Island, near Charleston, S. C., 232.
Johnson, Andrew, President United States, 420, 426-431
Johnson, Bradley T., Confederate brigadier-general, 337.
Johnson, Bushrod, Confederate major-general, 207, 269, 331, 332.
Johnson, Edward, Confederate major-general, 140, 178, 246, 247-314.
Johnson, Herschel V., 90.
Johnson, R. W., Union major-general, 268.
Johnson, John, quoted, 282.
Johnston, Albert Sidney, Confederate general, 154, 158-165, 302.
Johnston, James D., Confederate captain, '62.
Johnston, Joseph E., Confederate general, 124, 126, 134, 171-175, 261-263, 265, 275, 342, 354, 405, 407, 417-420.
Jones, E. J., colonel Fourth Alabama, 133.
Jones, D. R., Confederate major-general, 199.
Jones, J. M., Confederate brigadier-general, 308.
Jonesboro, Ga., 364, 365.
Jonesborough, Tenn., 69.
Jones, J. Wm., quoted, 216, 422, 423.
Jones, Wm. E., Confederate brigadier-general, 254-327.
Jordan, Thomas, Confederate brigadier-general, 162.
Judah, Henry M., Union major-general, 343.
Julian, George W., 84.

K.

Kaigler, ——, Confederate captain, 413.
Kansas, 85-86.
Kansas and Nebraska Bill, 84, 85, 89.
Kanawha Valley, W. Va., 118, 136, 138.
Kautz, August V., Union major-general, 334.
Kearney, Philip, Union major-general, 193.
Kearsarge, Union vessel, 388, 389
Keitt, L. M., Confederate colonel, 280.
Kelley, B. F., Union brigadier-general, 118, 407.
Kelly, J. H., Confederate brigadier-general of cavalry, 345.

Kelley's Ford, Va., 236.
Kemper, James L., Confederate brigadier-general, 254.
Kenly, John R., Union colonel, 178, 179.
Kennesaw Mountain, Ga., 347 349.
Kentucky, 32, 68, 110, 146, 191, 203, 240, 277.
Kentucky Campaign, 203-210.
Kernstown, Va., 176, 338.
Kershaw, Joseph P., Confederate major-general, 214, 215, 216, 269, 307, 332, 334, 368, 369.
Kettle Creek, Ga., 31.
Kilmer, George, I quoted, 339, 345.
Kilpatrick, Judson, Union major-general, 256, 301, 363, 385, 403.
King, J. Floyd, Confederate officer of artillery, 335.
King, John F., Union brigadier-general, 441.
King, Rufus, 55, 58.
King, William R., 84.
King's Mountain, N. C., 32.
Kinston, N. C., 405.
Kirkland, Richard, South Carolina sergeant, heroic deed at Fredericksburg, 216.
Knoxville, Tenn., 271, 272, 274, 275.
Kulp's Farm, Ga., 347.

L.

Lake City, Fla., 291.
Lamb, William, Confederate colonel, 400.
Lane, Joseph, 91.
Lane, James H., Confederate brigadier-general, 214, 252, 314.
Latrobe, Osman, Confederate captain on Longstreet's staff, 201.
Law, E. M., Confederate major-general, 183, 214, 269, 305, 306, 309, 312,
Lawton, Alexander R., Confederate brigadier-general, 199.
Laurel Hill, W. Va., 117-123.
Lebanon, Ky., 204.
Ledlie, James H., Union major-general, 339.
Lee, Fitzhugh, Confederate major-general, 239, 254, 256, 319, 329, 410, 413, 416.
Lee, Henry (Light-Horse Harry), American general in Revolution, 32.
Lee, Robert E., Confederate general, 90, 118, 124, 136-138, 175, 181-186, 188-193, 194-203, 211-216, 236-244-258-265, 283-284, 301, 302-325, 338-340, 389-391, 404-417, 423-425, 438, 440.
Lee, Robert E., Jr., 202.
Lee, Stephen D., Confederate lieutenant-general, 218, 353, 355, 364, 365, 382.
Lee, W. H. F., Confederate major-general, 254-257.
Lee and Gordon's Mills, 266.
Leesburg, Va., 136.
Leigh, Benjamin Watkins, 64.
Letcher, John, 328.
Lewis, J. H., Confederate brigadier-general, 363, 365.
Lexington, Kentucky, 205.
Lexington, Mass., 28.
Lexington, Mo., 144, 145.
Lexington, Va., 328, 338, 423.
Liberia, 70.
Lincoln, Abraham, President United States, 91, 107, 110, 186, 211, 225-227, 387, 400, 419, 420.
Lincoln, Benjamin, American general in Revolution, 81.
Little Rock, Ark., 294, 296, 297.

Logan, John A., Union major-general, 157, 347, 348.
Long, A. L., Confederate brigadier-general, quoted, 245.
Long Island, N. Y., 29.
Longstreet, James C., Confederate lieutenant-general, 126, 184, 188, 191, 192, 198, 201, 211-216, 238, 244 247, 249, 266-270, 272, 274, 275, 283, 306. 309, 310, 311, 312, 410, 411, 413.
Lookout Mountain, Tenn., 271, 272.
Lookout Valley, Tenn., 271, 272.
Loring, Wm. W., Confederate lieutenant-general, 136, 137-140, 259, 265.
Lovejoy Station, Ga., 354, 365.
Louisa Courthouse, Va.. 328
Louisiana, 53, 68, 100; returning board, 434, 435.
Louisville, Ky. 206.
Lowrey, ——, Confederate brigadier-general, 345.
Loyalists, 29.
Lundy, Benjamin, 69, 70.
Luray Valley, 178, 180.
Lynchburg, Va., 305.
Lyon, Nathaniel, Union brigadier-general, 141, 142, 144.
Lytle, Wm. H., Union brigadier-general, 441.

M.

Macon, Ga., 354, 385, 420.
Madison, James, President United States, 37, 40, 51, 55, 102.
Magruder, J. B., Confederate major-general, 125, 174, 183, 184, 228, 229.
Mahone, Wm., Confederate major-general, 310, 312, 334. 339.
Maine, 19, 69.
Malvern Hill, Va., 184, 185.
Manassas, Va., 124, 133, 171, 186-194.
Maney, George Confederate brigadier-general, 378.
Mansfield, Joseph K., Union major-general, 198, 199.
Mansfield. La., 296.
Manson. M. D., Union brigadier general, 205.
Marblehead, Mass.. 21.
Marietta, Ga., 375
Marion, Francis, American general in Revolution, 32, 33.
Marks's Mill, Ark., 297.
Marshall, Charles, Confederate colonel, quoted, 242.
Martinsburg, Va., 246, 335.
Marye's Hill, Va., 214, 215, 216, 237, 242.
Maryland, 32, 35, 36, 72, 110, 117, 194.
Maryland Campaign, 194-203.
Massachusetts, 22.
Massanutton Mountain, Va., 369.
Mason, James M., Confederate commissioner, 148.
Meade, George G., Union major general, 213, 248-258, 283, 284, 301, 304, 334.
Meadow Bridge, Va , 181.
Meagher, Thomas F., Union brigadier general, 215.
Mechanicsville, Va., 182.
Memphis, Tenn.. 167, 168, 261, 293.
Mercer, Hugh W., Confederate brigadier general, 382, 383.
Meridian, Miss., 293.
Merrimac, or Virginia, 171.
Merritt. Wesley, Union major general, 367.

Mexico, 76, 81.
Mill Creek Gap, Ga., 343. 375.
Mill Spring, Ky., 153.
Milledgeville, Ga., 385.
Milroy, R. H., Union major general. 140. 178.
Mine Run, Va., 284.
Mississippi, 68, 99.
Mississippi River, 30.
Missionary Ridge, Tenn., 268, 270-274.
Missouri, 68, 69, 110, 141-146.
Missouri Compromise, 68, 69, 81.
Mitchell, John K., Confederate commodore, 167-168.
Mitchell John C., Confederate captain, 280.
Mobile, Ala., 360-362, 420.
Monitor, Union vessel, 171, 173.
Monocacy River, Md., 335.
Monrovia, capital of Liberia, 70.
Monterey, Va., 122, 123.
Montgomery, Ala., 102, 104, 115, 420.
Montgomery, James, Union colonel, 292.
More's Creek, N. C., 28.
Morgan, Daniel, American general in Revolution, 32.
Morgan, George W., Union brigadier general, 203, 205, 206.
Morgan, John H., Confederate major general, 204; Ohio Raid, 276-278.
Mormons, 86.
Morris, Thomas A., Union major general, 118-123.
Morris Island, S. C., 278 280.
Mount Jackson, Va., 368, 372.
Mosby, John S., Confederate brigadier general, 389, 406, 407.
Mulligan, James A., Union brigadier-general, 145.
Mumfordsville, Ky., 206.
Murfreesboro, Tenn., 204, 209, 211, 218, 221, 265.
McCausland, John, Confederate brigadier-general, 335, 338.
McClanahan, Confederate captain artillery, 325.
McClellan, George B., Union major-general, 117, 123, 124, 125, 134, 171-175, 181-186, 188, 190, 192, 195-203, 211.
McClernand, John A., Union major-general, 161, 229, 262.
McCook, Alexander, Union major-general, 219, 266, 268.
McCook, Edward M., Union cavalry brigadier-general, 353, 354.
McCormick, ——, Confederate colonel, 291.
McCown John P., Confederate major-general, 203, 219.
McCulloch, Benjamin, Confederate brigadier-general, 144.
McDonough. American commodore, 57.
McDowell, Irvin, Union major-gener l, 125, 133, 175, 180.
McDowell, Va., 178.
McGowan, Samuel, Confederate brigadier-general, 316.
McIntosh, a Creek chief, 60.
McLaws, Lafayette, Confederate major-general, 195, 198, 199, 216, 238, 240, 242, 250, 252.
McLaughlin, Wm., Confederate major artillery, 325.
McLean, Wilmer, 414.
McMahon, Martin T., Union major-general, quoted, 301, 319.
McMinnville, Tenn., 207.
McNair, Evander, Confederate brigadier, 269.

McNeill, John H., Confederate captain of cavalry, 406, 407.
McPherson, James B., Union major-general, 261, 262, 292, 343, 345, 349, 351-353.

N.

Nashville, Confederate cruiser, 148.
Nashville, Tenn., 154, 156, 158, 209, 218, 374, 377, 380-383.
Nebraska, 84, 85, 89.
Negley, James S., Union major-general, 219, 268.
Negro churches and Sunday schools, 114, 115.
Nelson, William, Union major-general, 164, 205.
Nelson, William, Confederate colonel of artillery, 335.
Neasho, Mo., 145.
New England, 21, 24, 30, 31, 55.
New Hampshire, 72.
New Hope Church, Ga., 344, 345.
New Jersey, 29.
New Market, Va., 178, 324, 325, 327, 368, 372.
New Mexico, 82.
New Orleans, La., 24, 57, 167, 168, 263, 423.
Newman, Ga., 354.
Newport News, Va., 173.
Newton, John, Union major-general, 343.
Newtown, Va., 179.
New York, 29, 30.
New York Tribune on secession (1860), 102.
Non-Intercourse Act, 56.
Norfolk. Va., 124, 125, 171, 174.
North Anna, Va., 317.
North Carolina, 32, 44, 45, 70, 71, 110.
Northwest Territory, 30, 35, 36, 67.
Nueces River, 81.
Nullification, 61-64, 89.

O.

Oakey, Daniel, Union captain, quoted, 385.
Oak Hill, Mo., 144.
Odlum, F. H., Confederate captain, 283.
Ogeechee River, Ga., 235.
Oglesby, Richard J., Union major-general, 157.
Ohio, 68, 71, 277.
Ohio River, 30.
Okalona, Miss., 293.
Olmstead, Chas. H., Confederate colonel, defender of For Pulaski, 153.
Olustee, Fla., 292.
Ostenaula River, Ga., 344.
Opdyeke, Emerson, Union brigadier-general, 379.
Opequon, Va., 367, 368.
Ord. Edward O., Union major-general, 136.
Oregon, 76, 79, 435.
Ould, Robert, Confederate commissioner of exchange, 396, 397, 399.
Overland Campaign, 304-323.
Ox Hill, Va., 193.

P.

Paducah, Ky., 293.
Page, R. L., Confederate brigadier-general, 362.
Palmer, John M., Union major-general, 268, 348.
Palmer, I. N., Union brigadier-general, Washington, D. C., 300.

Palmetto, Ga., 373.
Palmetto Ranch, Texas, 420-422.
Pamlico Sound, N. C., 300.
Parliament, 25, 26.
Parsons, Virginia mountaineer, 123
Patterson, Robert, Union majo.-general, 125-126.
Peace Congress, 104, 105.
Peace negotiations, 400.
Peach Tree Creek, Ga., 353.
Pea Ridge, or Elkhorn, Ark., 165.
Pegram, John, lieutenant-colonel, 119, 120, 314, 369.
Pegram, Robert B., Confederate officer, 148.
Pelham, Confederate major of artillery, 214-236.
Pemberton, John C., Confederate lieutenant-general. 216. 218, 260-265.
Pender, Wm. D.. Confederate major-general, 182, 214, 240, 242, 248, 250.
Pendleton, Wm. N., Confederate brigadier-general, 130, 238.
Peninsula, Va., 171.
Pennsylvania, 244, 259, 337, 338.
Pensacola, Fla., 106, 107.
Perrin, Abner, Confederate brigadier-general, 316.
Perry, E. A., Confederate brigadier-general, 250.
Perry, Oliver Hazard, American commodore, 57.
Perryville, Ky., 207, 208.
Petersburg, Va., 305, 322, 329, 330-339, 389, 407, 411, 412.
Petersburg Mine, 339.
Pettigrew, John J., Confederate brigadier-general, 252, 257.
Pettus, John J., Confederate Governor Mississippi, 99.
Philadelphia, Pa., 30, 245.
Philadelphia Station, Tenn., 271.
Philippi, W. Va., 118.
Pickens, Andrew, American general in Revolution, 32, 33.
Pickens. F. W., Governor of South Carolina, 105.
Pickering, Timothy, 101.
Pickett, George E., Confederate major-general, 251, 252, 254, 332,
Pickett's Mill, Ga., 345.
Piedmont Virginia, 327.
Pierce, Franklin, President United States, 84.
Pillow, Gideon J., Confederate brigadier-general, 146, 154-157.
Pinckney, Charles Cotesworth, 55.
Pine Mountain, Ga., 347.
Pittsburg Landing, Tenn, 158, 166.
Pleasant Hill, La., 297.
Pleasanton, Alfred. Union major general, 289, 246.
Plymouth, N. C., 300, 388.
Po River, Va., 312.
Poague, W. T., Confederate artillery officer, 308.
Pocotaligo, S. C., 230.
Polk, James K., President of the United States, 79.
Polk, Leonidas, Confederate lieutenant general, 159, 206, 219, 220, 268, 272, 343, 347.
Pope, John, Union major general, 165, 186, 188-193, 195.
Porter, David D., Union admiral, 229, 259, 296-298 389, 400.
Porter, Fitz-John, Union major general, 182, 184, 192, 199, 200.

Porter, John L., chief constructor of Confederate ram Albemarle, 300.
Porterfield, G. A., Confederate colonel, 118.
Port Gibson, Miss., 261.
Port Hudson, La., 26 -265.
Port Republic, Va., 180 181, 368.
Port Royal, S. C., 146.
Portsmouth, Va., 124.
Potomac River, 195, 199, 200, 246.
Powhite Creek, Va., 162.
Prentiss, Benjamin M , Union major general, 161.
Presstman, S. W., Confederate colonel, 378.
Price, Sterling, Confederate major general, 143-145, 65, 203, 204, 210, 388.
Princeton College, 22.
Princeton, N. J., 29
Prisoners of War, 395-399.
Privateers, 148

Q.

Quarles, William A., Confederate brigadier general, 386.
Quebec, 24.
Quincy, Josiah, 101.

R.

Rains, James E., Confederate brigadier-general, 144, 45.
Raleigh, N. C., 69, 405.
Ramseur, Stephen D., Confederate major-general, 316, 335, 369, 371 372.
Ramsey, James, Confederate colonel, 122-123.
Randall, James R., author of " Maryland. My Maryland," 195.
Ransom, Matthew W., Confederate brigadier-general, 300.
Ransom, Robert, Confederate major-general, 214, 215, 322.
Rapidan River, Va., 190, 284, 304.
Rappahannock River, Va., 190, 236, 242, 284, 320.
Rappahannock Station, 284.
Raymond, Miss., 261, 265.
Ream's Station, Va., 389, 390.
Reconstruction, 426-431.
Red House, 122.
Red River expedition, 294.
Renshaw, W. B., Union naval officer, 228.
Republican Party, 86-91, 97.
Resaca, Ga., 343, 344, 363, 375.
Returning boards, 435-437.
Re nolds, D. H., Confederate brigadier-general, 343.
Reynolds, Joseph J., Union major-general, 139, 268.
Reynolds, John F., Union major general, 249.
Rhett, Alfred C., Confederate colonel, 280.
Rhode Island, 36, 37, 44, 45.
Rice, James C. Union brigadier-general, 312.
Richmond, Va., 115, 124, 181-187, 278, 302-322, 389, 407, 411, 412.
Richmond, Ky., 194, 205.
Rich Mountain, W. Va., 118-120.
Ricketts, James B., Union major-general, 131, 335.
Ringgold, Ga., 274.
Rio Grande River, 81.
Ripley, Roswell S., Confederate brigadier-general, 182, 232.

Roanoke Island, N. C., 152.
Roaring Creek, W. Va., 119.
Robertson, Beverly H., Confederate brigadier-general, 254, 269.
Robinson, P., Confederate captain, 259.
Rockbridge Artillery, 202.
Rocky Fare Ridge, Ga., 343.
Roddey, Philip D., Confederate brigadier general, 266, 355.
Rodes, Robert E., Confederate major general, 239, 240, 242, 247, 49, 316, 335, 367.
Roman, Andrew B., 107.
Rome, a., 266.
Romney, W. Va., 151, 152.
Rosecrans, William S., Union major general, 119, 120, 136, 138-140, 210, 218-221, 265-270, 271, 283, 388.
Rosser, Thomas L., Confederate major general, 372, 406.
Rossville, Tenn., 268, 269.
Rudersill, Frank, Confederate surgeon, 440. Note 11.
Rush, Richard, 62.
Russell, David A., Union major general, 284, 367.
Rust, Albert C., Confederate colonel, 137.
Rutledge, John, Confederate naval officer, 230.

S.

Sabine River, 81, 282.
Sabine Cross Roads, La., 296.
Sabine Pass, Texas, 229, 283.
Sailor's Creek, Va., 412.
Saint Louis, Mo., 141.
Salem Church, Va., 242.
Santa Anna, Mexican general, 76.
Saratoga, N. Y., 30.
Sargent, John, 62.
Savage's Station, Va., 184.
Savannah, Ga., 22, 28, 31, 153, 235, 386
Saxton, Rufus, Union major general, 179.
Scalawags, 432.
Scales, Alfred M., Confederate brigadier general, 252.
Schenck, Robert C., Union major general, 178.
Schofield, John M., Union major general, 347, 349, 363, 37, 79, 380.
Scott, John S. Confederate colonel, 205.
Scott, Winfield, Union major general, 84, 126.
Secession, 97-100; threatened by New England, 101.
Secessionville, S. C., 230.
Sedgwick, John, Union major-general, 237, 238, 242, 308, 311, 312.
Sedition Act, 51.
Seizure of forts and arsenals, 106.
Selma, Ala., 429.
Semmes, Paul J., Confederate brigadier-general, 250.
Semmes, Raphael Confederate admiral, 148, 229.
Seven Days' Battles (Virginia), 181-187.
Seven Pines, Va., 174, 175.
Sevier, Colonel, 32—foot note.
Seward, Wm. H., American statesman, 99, 107, 108, 400.
Sewell Mountain, 139.
Sewell's Point, Va., 173.
Seymour, Truman, Union major-general, 291 293, 310.
Sharpsburg, Md., 198, 200.
Shaler, Alexander, Union major-general, 810.
Sheetz, G. F., Confederate captain, 178.

Shelby, —— colonel, 32—foot note.
Shepherdstown. Md., 200, 338.
Shenandoah Valley, Va., 124, 175, 181, 246, 325, 367, 410.
Sheridan, Philip, Union major-general, 219, 268, 269, 273, 311, 317, 328, 329, 366-373, 410-413.
Sherman, T. W., Union major-general, 146.
Sherman, Wm. T., Union general, 131, 159-161, 218, 259, 261, 262, 271, 274, 275, 292, 293, 294, 296, 304, 342, 354, 362-366, 373-385, 402-406, 417-420.
Shields, James, Union major-general, 176, 179, 180, 181, 186.
Shiloh, Tenn., 158-166, 302.
Ship, Scott. Confederate colonel of cadets, 324.
Shreveport, La., 296.
Sickles, Daniel, Union major-general, 239, 249, 250.
Sigel, Franz, Union major-general, 143, 144, 305, 323-325, 327, 335.
Slaughter, J. E., Confederate brigadier-general, 422.
Slaughter Mountain, Va., 189-191.
Slaveholders' Convention, 72, 73.
Slavery, 21, 66, 71, 72-91.
Slavery quarrel, 66-91.
Slave Trade, 21, 66, 67.
Slaves during the war, 114.
Slidell, John, 148.
Slocum, Henry W., Union major-general, 364, 385, 387.
Smith, A. J., Union general, 298, 355.
Smith, C. F., Union major-general, 157.
Smith Caraway, Confederate Colonel, 291.
Smith, Edmund Kirby, Confederate general, 131, 194, 203-210, 296-298, 420.
Smith, George H., colonel 62d Virginia, 325.
Smith, George W., Confederate major-general, 175, 351, 352, 385, 387.
Smith, Gerritt, signs the bond of President Davis, 422.
Smith, Jas. M., Governor of Georgia, 429.
Smith, James P., referred to, 240.
Smith, Leon, captain Confederate navy, 228, 229.
Smith, Preston, Confederate major-general, 441.
Smith, Wm. Farrar, Union major-general, 330, 331.
Smith, Wm. Sooy, Union brigadier-general, 293.
Snake Creek Gap, Ga., 343.
Sorrel, G. M., Confederate major, afterwards brigadier-general on Longstreet's staff, 201.
Southampton, Va., 71.
South Carolina, 24, 31, 61, 97, 98, 435.
South Mountain, Md., 197, 198, 200.
Southside Road, Va., 407, 411.
Spain, 19, 24, 25, 76.
Spaniards, 24.
Spotsylvania Courthouse, Va., 311-317.
Springfield, Mo., 144, 145.
Spring Hill, Tenn., 266, 378, 379, 380.
Squatter Sovereignty, 35.
Staunton, Va., 118, 176, 305, 327, 334, 368, 372.
Stamp Act, 26.
Stanley, David, Union major-general, 379.
Stanton, Edwin M., Union Secretary of War, 399, 422, 423, 431.
Starke, Wm. E., Confederate brigadier-general, 199.
State Sovereignty, 35.
Steele, Frederick, Union major-general, 296-298.

Stephens, Alexander H., Confederate Vice-President, 100-102, 400, 422.
Stevens, Isaac, Union major-general, 198.
Stevenson, Carter L., Confederate major-general, 205, 206, 343, 382, 405.
Stevenson, T. G., Union major-general, 312.
Stewart, Alexander P., Confederate lieutenant-general, 343, 344, 351, 352.
Stone, Henry, Union colonel, quoted, 378, 379.
Stoneman, George, Union major-general, 236-238, 354.
Stone River, Tenn., 218-221.
Stono River, near Charleston, S. C., 236.
Strahl, O. T., Confederate brigadier general, 380.
Strasburg, Va., 369.
Stringham, Silas H., Union commodore, 146.
Streight, Albert D., Union brigadier general, 266.
Strong, C. C., Union major general, 278.
Stuart, J. E. B., Confederate lieutenant general, 132, 136, 181, 190, 202, 203, 214, 238, 239-241, 247, 254, 256, 311, 317, 318.
Sturdivant, N. A., Confederate artillery captain, 330.
Sturgis, Samuel D., Union major general, 354.
Sumner, Edwin V., Union major general, 192, 199, 213.
Sumter, Thomas, American general in the Revolution, 32.
Supreme Court of the United States, 38, 432.
Swamp Angel, S. C., 382.
Sweeny, Thomas W., Union brigadier general, 143, 345.
Swinton, quoted, 357, 417.
Sykes, George, Union major general, 131, 238.
Susquehanna River, Penn., 247.

T.

Taliaferro, W. B., Confederate major general, 122-123, 214, 278, 280.
Tariff, 61.
Taylor, Richard (son of Zachary Taylor, President of the United States), Confederate general, 264, 296.
Taylor's Ridge, Ga., 274.
Taylor, Walter H., quoted, 323.
Tennessee, 32, 68.
Tennessee, ram, 360, 362.
Tennessee River, 266, 271.
Terry, A. H., Union major general, 400.
Test Oaths, 431, 432.
Texas, 71, 100, 228, 229.
Tilden, Samuel J., 435.
Tishamingo Creek, Miss., 354.
Thomas, George H., Union major general, 153, 266-270, 271, 272, 273, 274, 351, 353, 377, 382, 383.
Thoroughfare Gap, Va., 191.
Tompkins, Daniel D., 58.
Toombs, Robert, Confederate brigadier general, 79, 99, 199.
Torbert, Albert T., Union major general, 367, 368, 369, 371, 373.
Tories, 29.
Totopotomy River, Va., 319.
Trans-Mississippi Department, 296.
Trent seizure, 148.
Trenton, 29.
Trevilian Station, 328, 329.

Trimble, Isaac R., Confederate major-general, 199 252.
Troup, George M., 61.
Tucker. Johh R., Confederate naval officer, 230.
Tullahoma. Tenn., 221, 261, 265, 266.
Tuni.el Hill, Ga., 375.
Tupelo, Miss., 166, 203, 355, 383.
Turner, Nat., 71.
Tygart River, 118.
Tyler, Daniel, Union brigadier-general, 126.
Tyler, Erastus B., Union major-general, 139, 180.
Tyler, John, President United States, 78, 105.
Tyler, R. C., Confederate brigadier-general, 363.

U.

Union and Confederate armies, note, 423.
United States, 28, 35, 54-57, 76.
Utah, 82.
Utoy Creek, Ga., 363.

V.

Valley campaign of Jackson. 175-181.
Van Buren, Martin, President United States, 62, 84.
Van Cleve. Horatio P., Union major-general, 268, 269.
Vanderbilt, Cornelius, signs the bond of President Davis, 422.
Van Dorn. Earl, Confederate major-general, 165. 168. 203, 204, 210, 216. 218.
Vaughn, John C., Confederate brigadier-general, 327.
Venable. Charles C., Confederate colonel, 399, quoted, 332.
Vermont, 68.
Varplank, 64.
Vicksburg, Miss., 167, 168, 211, 216, 218, 245, 258. 259-265.
Virginia and Kentucky resolutions, 51,52.
Virginia, Confederate ram, 171-174.
Virginia Military Institute, 324, 325, 328.
Virginia, 19, 21, 30, 32. 35, 36, 70, 104, 105, 110, 117, 124.
Vote by States on annexation of Texas, 80.

W.

Wadsworth, James S., Union major-general, 309.
Wagoner's Fight, 256.
Walker, John G., Confederate major-general, 197, 198, 199.
Walker, Lindsay, Confederate captain, 131.
Walker, Wm. H. T., Confederate major-general, 268, 343. 344, 348, 353.
Wallace, Lew. Union major-general, 154, 161, 164, 335, 336.
Wallace, W. H. L., Union major-general, 157, 161.
Walthall, E. C., Confederate major-general, 382.
Warren. Gouverneur K., Union major-general, 238, 308, 311, 312, 331, 389, 407.
Washington Artillery Battalion of New Orleans, 215, 256.
Washington City, 105, 125, 179, 284; Early's march against, 334-337.
Washington College, Lexington, Va., 328, 423; name changed to Washington-Lee University, 423.

Washington, George, first President United States, 29, 33, 34, 37. 44, 49, 51.
Washington, J. A., Confederate colonel, 138.
Washington N, C., 300.
Watkins. O. M., Confederate major, 229.
Watts, James W., Confederate colonel, 178.
Waynesboro, Va., 410.
Webb, A. S., Union major-general, quoted, 305, 311.
Webster, Daniel, American statesman, 82, 87, 89.
Weldon Road, Va., 334, 389-391, 407.
Wessels. Henry W., Union brigadier-general, 300.
West Virginia, 117-123, 125, 137-139, 227, 228.
Wharton, Gabrie. C., Confederate brigadier-general, 325. 369, 372.
Wheeler, Joseph, Confederate lieutenant-general, 204, 209, 218, 268, 352, 354, 362, 363, 377, 385, 386, 403.
Wheeler, W. A., Vice-President United States. 434. 436.
Whigs, 62, 78, 84-87; Old Line 87.
White Oak Road, 410.
White Oak Swamp, Va., 184.
Whiting, W. H. C., Confederate major-general, 181 183, 322, 400.
Wigfall, Louis T., Confederate colonel, 109.
Wilcox, Cadmus M.. Confederate major-general, 250, 252, 308.
Wilderness, Va., 306-311.
Wilkes, Charles, captain United States Navy, 148.
William and Mary College, Va., 22.
Williams, colonel. 32—foot note.
Williamsburg, Va., 174.
Williamsport, Md., 125, 202, 256, 257, 338.
Wilmington. N. C, 322, 400.
Wilmot, Proviso, 81, 82.
Wilson, James H., Union major-general, 334, 383, 420.
Wilson's Creek, Mo., 144.
Winchester, Va., 126, 179, 202, 211, 246, 258, 335, 366-368, 371.
Wise, Henry A.. Confederate brigadier-general, 118, 136, 138, 139, 322, 330.
Withers, Jones M., Confederate major-general, 130, 219.
Wofford, Wm. T., Confederate brigadier-general, 310.
Wolford. Frank, Union colonel, 277.
Wolseley, Garnett. British general, 202.
Wood, ———, Confederate colonel at Petersburg, 330.
Wood, Thomas J., Union major-general, 268, 273.
Worden, John L., Union commodore, 235.
Wright, A, R., Confederate major-general, 250.
Wright, Horatio, Union major-general, 316, 317, 337, 369, 371.
Wyatt, Henry. 117.
Wrightsville, Pa., 247.

Y.

Yates, Joseph A., Confederate colonel, 282.
Yazoo River, Miss., 168.
Yellow Tavern, Va., 317.
York River, Va., 320.
Yorktown, Va., 125,

Z.

Zollicoffer, Felix K., Confederate brigadier-general, 153.